Ceremony
and
Civility
in
English
Renaissance
Prose

Ceremony and Civility in English Renaissance Prose

Anne Drury Hall

The Pennsylvania State University Press
University Park, Pennsylvania

992083

Library of Congress Cataloging-in-Publication Data

Hall, Anne Drury.
    Ceremony and civility in English Renaissance prose / Anne Drury
Hall.
        p.   cm.
    Includes bibliographical references and index.
    ISBN 0-271-00770-2
    1. English prose literature—Early modern, 1500–1700—History and
criticism.   2. Great Britain—Civilization—16th century.   3. Great
Britain—Civilization—17th century.   4. Rites and ceremonies in
literature.   5. Authority in literature.   6. Praise in literature.
7. Renaissance—England.   8. Rhetoric—1500–1800.   I. Title.
PR769.H35   1991
828'.30809—dc20   91–10227
                                                                CIP

It is the policy of The Pennsylvania State University Press to use acid-free
paper for the first printing of all clothbound books. Publications on uncoated
stock satisfy the minimum requirements of American National Standard for
Information Sciences—Permanence of Paper for Printed Library Materials,
ANSI Z39.48–1984.

Contents

Acknowledgments

I wish to thank colleagues at the University of North Carolina and elsewhere who read sections of this book at various stages of its composition: Reid Barbour, Jane Burns, Donald Kennedy, Jerry Mills, Deborah Shuger, James Thompson, Joseph Wittig, and especially John Headley and Peter Kaufman. For the patience and good humor of my secretary, Frances Coombs, I am very grateful.

To John Auchard, Larry and Raquel Goldberg, Nanette Mengel, and Emily Stockard goes a different kind of thanks, to people whose affection and intelligence have enlivened many evenings of conversation and who have influenced this book in profound ways. To my children, Caedmon and Heron Haas, I owe lessons that they are still too young to understand. And finally, I thank my husband, Ted Haas, for his grace and good spirits and also for the *lumen siccum* (in the manner of Bacon) of his prosaic wit.

Introduction

This book has two goals. The first is to describe the ceremonial discourse that underlies much medieval and Renaissance literature and its transformations with the rise of "prosaicism," that is, the characteristically modern resistance to enchantment. I shall focus on four English works of the sixteenth and early seventeenth centuries: Thomas More's *History of King Richard III*, Philip Sidney's *Defense of Poetry*, Richard Hooker's *Of the Laws of Ecclesiastical Polity*, and Thomas Browne's *Religio Medici*. In each, the pathos and exaltation of an erotic-pastoral-spiritual discourse are reinflected with the circumspections, hesitations, and ironic deflections of modern civil prose.

But along with the historical study is a philosophical consideration of this ceremonial discourse. Since the mid-1970s, there have been two chief arguments about Renaissance literature. The first is that most Renaissance writers used traditional forms to bolster authority and that therefore these writers should be regarded with suspicion.

The second is that some Renaissance writers altered traditional forms to subvert authority and that therefore they should be admired. But an alternative position has yet to be voiced: that many Renaissance writers used tradition to bolster authority *and* that their versions of tradition and authority deserve a hearing beyond the by now standard attacks on their racism (as in *Merchant of Venice*), coercive violence (as with Spenser's Talus), and colonialist repression (as in *The Tempest*). Not that the racism, violence and repression should not be remarked. To point out their existence, however, in texts that were once thought to be about love and education loses in shock value when one realizes that racism, violence, and repression are not the issue. The issue is rather a normative definition of human nature and, in the Renaissance, the right of institutional authority to make that definition a standard for human behavior. For modern liberal democrats, the issue is inflected slightly differently; it is the right of institutional authority to encourage the acceptance of that definition as a standard for human behavior. As heirs of the Enlightenment, we are still caught in the Enlightenment dilemma: everyone has a right to his or her version of truth, but no one has the grounds to persuade someone of a "better" truth. The second aim of this book, then, is to give Renaissance authors the opportunity they never had to argue with us as heirs of the Enlightenment. In this study, I admit frankly that history affords an occasion to reflect on our own values, here in particular the value of the old narrative of wandering-and-coming-home and its assumption of "home's" authority, in an intellectual climate of philosophical skepticism and scientific rejection of the past.

The place of this narrative in modern thinking is no small problem. The central plot of a ceremonial discourse (the spiritual quest) and its central impulse (devotion) are involved in institutions the Enlightenment emphatically rejected: religion, absolute monarchy, and tradition. Our ability to recapture the narrative without commitment to the institutions depends on an Enlightenment category that the post-Enlightenment has rejected: the quasi-religious category of "the aesthetic" and its imaginative "paradise within." How then are modern democrats to regard, think about, take in, a story that is (or, in the view of some, ought to be) so foreign to us? Is Auden's solution in "In Praise of Limestone" the only one possible, to ally oneself with modern secularity and then admit, with no attempt at logical coherence, that the pre-Enlightenment world still has its charm?

1

A medieval ceremonial discourse has been called by other names; for Bakhtin, it is "monologism"; for Foucault, it is the "language of resemblance," which resonates with "being." In this book I call it "ceremonial," a term that captures its stylization and its assumption of commonly held truths. A ceremonial discourse can afford the monologism of stylization precisely because what it praises is the incontrovertible truth of "being" that is both attainable and unattainable. The stylization puts the truth just beyond human speech; one can never quite get to "being," which is perfect because it is everything that is better-than-human. On the other hand, the fullness of truth still comes vividly to the human imagination, with its promises of security and stability. Lear is still seeking Cordelia at the end of the play; but he was able to see her, comprehend her, fully before he died. A ceremonial discourse combines both yearning and assurance, labor and fulfillment.

When during the early modern period in England, 1485–1600, a stylized discourse of praise gave way to civil prose, a fundamental tension was created between a traditional story and sharper rhetorical self-consciousness about that story. This tension is captured in the peculiarly unfocused composition of Ghirlandaio's *Adoration of the Magi* (1487) that hangs in the Uffizi. In the center of the tondo sits a girlish Madonna. The child is on her lap. He is worshiped by a kneeling Magus. In the rear is a classical, porticolike stable. At the left and right is the retinue of the Magi, the soldiers' spears silhouetted against a white horse, the pale portico, and the sky. Between these retainers and the Virgin is an area of flat stones that sets off the mother and child. In the left foreground, a second Magus kneels, waiting his turn to present gifts. Among these figures, all eyes are turned toward the center of the painting. The third Magus in the right foreground, however, is not adoring the Christ child but looking over his left shoulder out of the painting.[1] His expression is sober; he lifts

1. The sagacity and innocence that Ghirlandaio combines in this painting are kept quite separate in his other portrayals of the Virgin. The Virgin in his *Adoration of the Shepherds* is also a girlish Madonna. But the innocence of the mother-and-child scene is emphasized by the Christ child's sucking his thumb, by a prominent cow and donkey, and by the flowers and grass of the foreground. Unlike the *Adoration of the Magi* for the Hospital of the Innocents, in which the Magi are beautiful young men, the Magi of the Uffizi *Adoration* are old. The "wise man looking over his left shoulder" appears in the figure of St. Clement in the *Madonna Enthroned* of the Accademia, but the Madonna is not an innocent. In *Della Pittura*, Alberti had recommended such a figure to establish

his chin in a confident and worldly-wise manner. He mediates between the beholders outside of the frame of the painting and the Virgin and child. His aloof calm keeps the beholders at a distance, for his experience with human nature has taught him that there are always some people disinclined to worship. In the same way that the soldiers' spears at middle, left, and right physically protect the central event, he protects its innocence from those who do not come to revere. For all of these reasons, he disturbs the centripetal pull of the painting toward the mother and child.[2] "Compositional" skill, in both the visual arts and in literature, refurbished a very old story of grief, hope, loss, and happiness. But the skill eventually split the audience into traditional worshipers and their protectors, who know that the story does not command the instinctive adoration it once used to and see themselves as its political guardians. Mary has to be shielded from a danger she cannot imagine, and which, her virtue being innocence itself, she should not be required to imagine.

The various incursions of modern prose on a discourse of praise are familiar. For Bakhtin, they are related to the carnivalesque and the emergence of novelistic prose.[3] For Morris Croll, they are the result of the aristocracy's new preference for Cicero over Seneca as the model for literary imitation.[4] For Janel Mueller, they are related to English Protestant translations of the Bible.[5] But because Bakhtin, Croll, and

a link between beholder and scene of the painting. It is highly likely that Ghirlandaio's worldly Magus is a portrait of an important Florentine figure; Ghirlandaio had included portraits in the Sassetti Chapel of Santa Trinità in Florence in 1485 and in frescoes in the Sistine Chapel and in Santa Maria Novella; see L. M. Sleptzoff, *Men or Supermen? The Italian Portrait in the Fifteenth Century* (Jerusalem: Magnes Press, Hebrew University, 1978), 63 and 69.

2. Judging the painting by compositional unity, some have found it a failure. See, for example, Gerald S. Davies, *Ghirlandaio* (London: Methuen, 1908), 90.

3. M. M. Bakhtin, "Discourse in the Novel," in *The Dialogic Imagination: Four Essays by M. M. Bakhtin*, trans. and ed. Michael Holquist and Caryl Emerson (Austin: University of Texas Press, 1981), 418–21.

4. "Attic Prose in the Seventeenth Century," in *Style, Rhetoric, and Rhythm: Essays by Morris W. Croll*, ed. J. Max Patrick et al. (Princeton: Princeton University Press, 1966), 167–202.

5. *The Native Tongue and the Word: Developments in English Prose Style 1380–1580* (Chicago: University of Chicago Press, 1984). At what point modernity in English prose begins is a matter of scholarly debate. If "modernity" is characterized by a straightforward, simple syntax, then, according to Mueller, modern English prose begins in the late fourteenth century. Mueller thus challenges the position that modernity in prose is a matter of the assimilation of classical values, a view advanced most persuasively by Croll, for whom modern English prose does not appear until the late sixteenth century. Others place modernity in English prose later in the seventeenth century, with the rise

Mueller are sure that modern prose is better prose, they fail to describe a ceremonial discourse with the amount of care they lavish on a prose that throws the experiences of different classes into a linguistic carnival (Bakhtin) or refines the subtle perceptions of the urbane and witty man (Croll) or declares the individual's simple and direct response to God (Mueller). Bakhtin's insight, however, that prosaic-prose is itself a sign of the emergence of modernity has the great virtue of extending an account of prose from the details of syntax to broad cultural changes. Prose is not just a block of writing that runs to the right hand margin. It is "prosaicism." Its pleasure lies in demystifying authority. Its satisfaction is the promise of independence.

The epistemological, philosophical, and ethical foundation of civil prose are described by Bacon in *The Advancement of Learning*. For Bacon, prose is a discourse inflected against eager credulity. Prose does not give the immediate assent of reverence; it does not indulge in supernatural visions and ornamented rhetoric; it does not believe the stage stories of love. Methodologically, prose does not jump too swiftly from the historical to the ideal, introduce the divine as a solution to all intellectual problems, and confuse inquiry with undifferentiated intellectual categories. Further, Bacon's prosaicism is inflected not only against credulity but against the credulity of an earlier age. *The Advancement*'s famous history of Renaissance prose is noteworthy not just for the remarks about *copia* but for the magisterial survey of an era regarded as the childish past that adult modernity has shed, a historical self-awareness that eventually comes to a head in the battle between the ancients and moderns. The emergence of prose divides intellects into the mature and childish, a division theorized by Kant in his essay "What is Enlightenment?" The responsible (adult) intelligence is wary of the past and confident that judgments can be made independent of tradition. These assumptions are still with us, systematized as "Enlightenment thinking." They are the source of modernity and of the various attacks on modernity.

---

of scientific rationalism: see R. F. Jones, "Science and English Prose Style in the Third Quarter of the Seventeenth Century," *PMLA* 45 (1930): 977–1009; and Robert Adolph, *The Rise of Modern Prose Style* (Cambridge: MIT Press, 1968). See also John M. Steadman, *The Hill and the Labyrinth: Discourse and Certitude in Milton and His Near-Contemporaries* (Berkeley and Los Angeles: University of California Press, 1984). For the complex relationship between poety and prose in Renaissance generic definitions, see Ann E. Imbrie, "Defining Nonfiction Genres," in *Renaissance Genres: Essays on Theory, History, and Interpretation*, ed. Barbara Kiefer Lewalski (Cambridge: Harvard University Press, 1986), 45–69.

The first chapter of this study describes "civil" prose as it is realized in classical rhetorical debate, a discourse that the ancients define by distinguishing it from philosophy and poetry. This discourse is closely associated with the political institutions that encourage debate about the polity. Classical civil prose assumes the reality of the natural world in which human beings construct their governments. It assumes also that the truth can be only probably known and is arrived at partly from experience, partly from the authority of past opinion, and partly by the examination of those opinions by rational human beings. In representing the political dimension of human life, classical civil prose does more than register aesthetically the varieties of experience at a particular moment in the cunning plot of history, as Bakhtin would have it. Rather, it negotiates between an emotional appeal to tradition (by means of rhythm and commonplaces) and a new analysis, in which the speaker has an interested stake. Ethically, it assumes the hierarchy of reason over passion; politically, the government of the passionate by the rational. At the heart of classical rhetoric, however, is an assumption that the ancients took for granted: that a polity in which human beings rule and are ruled equally is superior because it encourages the highest human faculties and that such a polity depends upon rational debate.

It is a commonplace that in the effort to overcome the barbarism of vernacular literature, Renaissance humanists took their model for good rhetoric from the classics. But what resulted was not classical civil prose. Instead of adopting both the *ratio et oratio* of the ancients— debate and ornament—early humanists took chiefly the ornament, dressing up medieval enchantment a little more elegantly. Debate as it was understood by classical rhetoricians was short-circuited by the centrality of God to practically all Renaissance arguments and by the erotic-pastoral-spiritual discourse that the Renaissance inherited from the Middle Ages.

In the Middle Ages, this discourse underlies many genres in both prose and poetry: romances, romance-epics, histories, elegies, erotic lyrics, religious lyrics, saints' lives, *artes moriendi*. Its heart is a spiritual quest and praise of the truth. I might have called this discourse of quest-and-praise "epideictic" rather than "ceremonial." But epideixis depends on the epistemological, ethical, and political assumptions of classical rhetoric, which are wholly different from those of ceremony. Boethius's *Consolation of Philosophy* serves as an excellent example of these different assumptions, for in it, classical dialogue and classical-sounding arguments are swallowed up in a narrative that is far from classical: the visionary gaze into the supernatural. The highest human life is submission to that vision. Reason still governs the passions, but in being aided by "grace," it has a considerable infusion of passion of another sort.[6] Earthly political life is either wholly unimportant compared to the "city" outside of this world or happily coincident with God's toleration of the variety of custom. In a ceremonial mode, human speech does not order the world; it enacts an order established in a divinely governed nature.

In its ability to exhort, enchant, and enfold the individual in the political unit of God's nature, a ceremonial discourse has powerful socializing effects, reinforcing a communal society and deterring criticism. Because in the vernaculars, it is confined almost exclusively to concrete description and storytelling, it is virtually mute, unable to explain itself as one way of organizing the world as opposed to another. Indeed, its very muteness contributes to its powers of socialization; an opposition is not even imagined. With the coincidence of various intellectual, social, and political pressures—the divorce of reason from religion, the conflicts of the Reformation, the centralization of power at the Tudor court—this once "innocent" discourse needed an articulate defense. In early sixteenth-century England, Protestants like Tyndale see a better religion in another camp; humanists like More see a better polity in another world. At the end of the sixteenth century, recusant Puritans force Anglicans to justify traditional ritual, custom, and a Thomistic understanding of human reason. In the seventeenth century, increasing Puritan criticism of the Stuart court, constitutional struggles, and religious sectarianism all motivate discussion, to put it mildly. When Charles I was beheaded, the quest for the truth could no longer end in the king; people who continued to think it did were regarded by others as naive.

Not all thinkers of the English Renaissance are confident that modern prose is better prose. For Thomas More, it is a mixed blessing at best. It has the benefit of irony's silent quotation marks, which "reaccent" (Bakhtin's word[7]) a ceremonial mode. Instead of the upward gaze to a superior being, irony refocuses the attention horizontally: one does not look to one's betters for guidance; one looks to one's colleagues for consultation. On the other hand, More's *History of King Richard III* demonstrates the liabilities of irony. Al-

6. Marcia L. Colish, *The Mirror of Language: A Study in the Medieval Theory of Knowledge*, rev. ed. (Lincoln: University of Nebraska Press, 1983), ix.
7. Bakhtin, "Discourse in the Novel," in *The Dialogic Imagination*, ed. Holquist and Emerson, 418–21.

though it successfully scrutinizes the legitimizing power of the ceremonial chronicle, the linguistic and political sophistication it elicits from one audience dismisses another audience as irrelevant and so fractures any putative "community." More's intellectual preference for sophistication (because it understands the ways of kings) but his belief in simplicity (because it is allied with God) causes his text to wobble uncertainly between an analysis of self-aggrandizing rhetoric and allegiance to unquestioned truth.

In a historical narrative, More can obscure the contradiction between tradition and mockery of tradition fairly easily. In the end of his history, the rhetorically sophisticated bad king fortunately loses. Sidney and Hooker have more difficulties. In describing poetry's power to civilize stony and beastly human beings, Sidney spells out the socializing purpose of ceremony: to charm an audience into obedience by means of wonderful stories. When the stories fail to charm, however, there is no recourse except to coercive authority. This is a stumbling point, needless to say, for modern democrats with constitutionalism in their blood; social management should be a little more aboveboard. But Sidney does not want to discuss explicitly "social management." Prosaic disquisitions would only diffuse the affect of personal leadership that is his central concern in the *Defense*. Moreover, Sidney's poetry has a religious justification, and, if religion is to remain "true," it has to be the truth for the whole society. From this premise, coercion is likely to follow. The best society is held together by love of God; leaders should be beautiful and cultivated visual emblems of that love; in following those leaders, others will learn devotion themselves. But insofar as some people are incapable of devotion, the wise leader must sometimes exercise force for the sake of the whole. Some people do destructive things; in certain situations they must be disciplined. That this position sometimes led to terror and violence is no doubt true. But to hold that all discipline is terror and violence is surely an exaggeration.

In *Of the Laws of Ecclesiastical Polity*, Richard Hooker explicitly justifies coercion. The result is even more difficult for a twentieth-century democrat, for while Sidney is at least affable, Hooker is severe. Some people are wiser than others. It is the responsibility of the wise to hold the community together by refusing to countenance thoughtless tinkering with custom. For Hooker the loss of a ceremonial ritual is a great danger; it entices clever but shallow minds to think they can separate religious ritual from traditional customs and not fracture a deep social bond. Hooker is clear about the dangers of linguistic sophistication. When there were righteous men in the world, "they reverentlie harkned to the readinges of the law of God, they kept in minde the oracles and aphorismes of wisdom which tended unto vertuous life," and before they took any action, they sought "counsell and advise . . . for feare least rashlie they might offende." By contrast, we in the present age "are now more confident . . . because our desires are an other waie. Theire scope was obedience, ours is skill . . . they in practise of theire religion wearied chieflie theire knees and handes, wee especiallie our eares and tungues."[8] The new age is characterized by "skill" with "tungues," and, as Hooker argues when he associates skill with disobedience, linguistic facility in debate can easily change language from the means a wise God gave to his creature for understanding creation to (in his view) a much lesser thing: a humanly constructed tool.

Hooker's rhetorical problem throughout the *Laws* is to balance a paradox that can easily become a fatal contradiction. He must defend familiar ritual articulately and self-consciously and at the same time call on its evocative power. In the very act of carrying on a defense, however, Hooker tacitly admits that a story of the communal spiritual quest does not persuade all members of society. He thus undermines its power as a political myth; believers most powerfully believe when they are not aware that others do not. He also tacitly admits that rational debate is superior to unexamined belief. With this admission, he immensely complicates the relationship between intelligent human action and the social cohesion of a traditional society. Rational debate carried on in the vernacular languages and in printed books inevitably weakens the old web of mutual obligations that Hooker wishes to defend. Hence, Hooker's rhetoric raises questions about the way different members of the community believe. If some people "choose" their belief from known alternatives, while others drink it in as part of their cultural milk, both cannot be said to believe in the same way. The charge is easily made that the "choosing" believers use their sophisticated version of belief to justify their authority over the "simple minded". Still, it is possible that they are the benevolent protectors they imagine themselves. Paternalism is not always an ugly thing.

8. Richard Hooker, *Of the Laws of Ecclesiastical Polity*, in *The Folger Library Edition of the Works of Richard Hooker*, gen. ed. W. Speed Hill, 4 vols. (Cambridge: Belknap Press of Harvard University Press, 1977–82), 5. 81. 10. All further references to the *Laws* will be to this edition. In citing Hooker's *Laws*, I have followed the policy of the editors in using the references by book, chapter, and paragraph established by John Kebel in his nineteenth-century edition.

The seventeenth century brings other contradictions. For classical rhetoricians, an individual moral ideal coincides with a political ideal; the emotional spirit behind courage contributes to a flourishing polity. But because the sectarianism of the seventeenth century turns "courage" from a political to a religious virtue (a mixture of conscience and enthusiasm), the only way for a civil polity to work in the manner Hobbes and Locke think it should is to separate politics from private religious commitments. The consequent separation of public procedures from private belief—a separation more rigid than the classical world knew—is reinforced by a growing opposition between the discourses of the private and public worlds, one expressive and emotional and the other dispassionate, linguistically precise, and methodologically self-conscious.

Another contradiction of the early seventeenth century lies in the argument that legitimizes the polity. Contractual theories of government remove the polity from nature, yet at the same time nature is revived in a "natural human spirit." Nature is to be combatted, and yet it is the telos for combatting it in the first place. The contradictions in this narrative mirror the post-Enlightenment dilemma. On the one hand, we are committed to intellectual argument that strips nature of its legitimizing status, especially nature as used in an analogy between "natural rulers" (the hierarchies of the universe) and kings. But then nature comes back in a new form. The "rights of man" derive from "nature," that which cannot be contradicted, a truth that is self-evident.

These contradictions in the Enlightenment version of "civil prose" sharpen the contrast with classical rhetoric. Classical civil prose is rationalism inflected with ceremonial truths; how else could Cicero have claimed that rhetoric could gather scattered humanity into a whole? Modern civility, by contrast, sets the prosaic *against* the ceremonial. Modern is better; modern means an objective reexamination of the "natural truths" that might encourage rhythmic celebration; modern means an energetic assault on the innocent naivetés of the past. The modern thinks critically. For minds predisposed to criticism, Cicero's rhythmic celebrations of self-evident truths serve only for occasions of state, in which there is little to be enjoyed and much to be endured. "Rhythm" is restricted to private reflections and refined into "lyricism."

For Foucault, modern subjectivity begins with the rise of the disciplinary society.[9] Recent arguments over the rise of the novel have extended Foucault's argument to the social arena. The novel has its source in an epistemological shift from idealism to empiricism-skepticism and a redefinition of virtue from aristocratic station to inner worth; or from a bourgeois reinflection of gender and its deployment in an ideology of the household and the domestic female.[10] But on one thing historians agree: the burden of modern individualism—the lyric inner world that may be freedom or may be prison—is to be laid at the door of the seventeenth century.

Browne's *Religio Medici* stands at the beginning of modern subjectivity. In Browne's version of subjectivity, the most important element is the separation of public procedures from private belief: rational consent to public procedures establishes order by defining passion as disorderly and removing it from social intercourse.[11] The gain is an individualized sensitivity that constructs its own version of a ceremonial discourse. The price is the loss of ceremony as a public expression. Exaltations that were once communal now retreat to private conversation with friends or with oneself; in each case, the emotional connection of the individual to a God-filled universe is short-circuited. Paradoxically, Browne recovered Christianity by doubting he had to believe in it, or at least by doubting that he had to believe in it the way he knew other people did. The past can be recovered but only by declaring it a personal version of the past, never presumed to be doctrine for anyone else.

2

Browne has raised a surprising number of hackles for a relatively minor writer. His admirers say he offers a persuasive imaginative

9. For Foucault, this subjectivity was created in the disappearance of the spectacle of punishment from the public space and its hidden subjection to the "cures" of science (*Discipline and Punish: The Birth of the Prison*, trans. Alan Sheridan [New York: Random House, 1979]). Francis Barker dovetails the Foucault of *Discipline and Punish* with the Foucault of *The Order of Things* (New York: Random House, 1970): the changes in forms of punishment, signaling a new separation between public and private, is reinforced by a rationalism that checks the individual soul's "wanderings" from rational common sense (*The Tremulous Private Body: Essays on Subjection* [London: Methuen, 1984]).

10. Michael McKeon, *The Origins of the English Novel 1600–1740* (Baltimore: Johns Hopkins University Press, 1987); Nancy Armstrong, *Desire and Domestic Fiction: A Political History of the Novel* (London: Oxford University Press, 1987).

11. Peter Stallybrass and Allon White, *The Politics and Poetics of Transgression* (Ithaca: Cornell University Press, 1986).

outline of what toleration feels like; others say he ought to have been more of a believer. But the old problem with literature—whether it is a harmless world of play or a groping for the truth—lies at the heart of whatever attitude we take. The conflict between "worlds of play" (toleration) and "the truth" (belief) are now found in other genres as well: history, philosophy, or theory. Is history a discourse with serious practical consequences because it can show that social institutions we thought were universal came into being at a specific time, or is it a discourse of rich play, a narrative with all the moves of "belief" and "engagement" without any of their practical commitments?

This question is pertinent to the consideration of what exactly is "literary history." This genre, so some people argue, needs to be improved with the same generic consistency that Bacon argued leads to intellectual clarity. In the seventeenth century, intellectual clarity came from generic differentiation, restricting the "God category" to certain areas of inquiry and allowing secondary causes their own realm.[12] Now, it seems, the pendulum has swung the other way. Having discovered what is right and true, moderns do not need to save a false category for God-talk. In fact, they have to root out the God-talk that is still lurking in areas once considered parts of "secular humanism": man, nature, art, the autonomous self, and related transcendentals. While the Enlightenment program held that the differentiation of discourses could lead to intellectual clarity, it now seems that the differentiation is breaking down in favor of a fully realized prosaic. "Literary history" has been exposed as an intellectually sloppy effort to have it both ways, "constructing historical man" and "identifying with great minds," or "getting at the real past" and "making the past speak to us now." The enterprise can only gain respectability, some say, by relegating the "literary" part to the genre of liberal humanism, a category that, itself being a vestigial superstition, can be allowed to die. Oddly, however, the resistance to full prosaicism is hard to suppress. One acquiesces to discourses of containment (historicized history), but somehow there are still pockets of subversion, especially in the form of "play." Foucault-and-Bakhtin write the bad cop–good cop script of many recent literary histories of the Renaissance.

Many critics do not seem to know that the attacks on liberal

12. See the suggestive article of John D. Schaefer, "The Use and Misuse of Giambattista Vico: Rhetoric, Orality, and Theories of Discourse," in *The New Historicism*, ed. H. Aram Veeser (New York: Routledge, Chapman and Hall, 1989), 89–101.

humanism that have been coming out since the mid-1970s require a justification of their "readings" of Renaissance literature (or for that matter, their "readings" of Renaissance history). We tend to talk as if we choose our academic "fields" for no more compelling reason than the necessity for specialization and a vague "interest" in the period. (It might indeed be interesting if professors were called upon to articulate those choices.) But the Renaissance is not just one field among many. As the pre-Enlightenment era, it stands in a particular relationship to us, a relationship that is defensive on two counts. First, modern democrats do not believe in the regime in which English Renaissance literature was implicated; history has put monarchy to rest. We do not believe in worshipful loyalty as the proper (i.e., dignified, in the sense of "worthy of a human being") foundation for political cohesion. A polity of contractual agreements among intelligent human beings does not need a discourse that promotes the "natural" love of an inferior being for a superior. It needs instead one that reinforces reason as "the reckoning of consequences," in Hobbes's phrase; reason can keep demystifying assaults on ignorance and superstition steady, sharp, and eager. There are chronic denunciations of modern alienation. But we tacitly acknowledge that there is no putting the genie of rational analysis back in the bottle. Even attacks on the repressiveness of Enlightenment reason are offered in more or less rational arguments, or at least more rational than reciting pre-Enlightenment texts as "arguments against the Enlightenment." On the other side, arguments in favor of the irrational have a slightly desperate air about them because their authors know the genie is out for good, or at least for a long while.

The second reason why Renaissance literature is on the defensive is the suspect category of "literature." This category, so it is argued, has been all too successful as the modern, bourgeois version of "saving the appearances." It has given the objects of the past a transcendental glow but only by extracting them from the reality of their historical circumstances. The Kantian category of the "aesthetic," once held to be a discourse without claims to truth or moral suasion, has been discovered to have a hidden program. It is a priestly holdover of a "language of being," that, in the social arena, gives a false afterlife to aristocratic values. All this is worth listening to. But with Renaissance studies, the question that logically follows is serious: of what use is it to retell the story of a period whose religious and political superstitions history has done well to reject, whose superstitious poetics recent criticism has done well to reject, and which can only be recuperated through the illusory category of "literature"?

To find an answer leads to the difficulties of sorting out values. Historians like to justify talking about "the period of the Renaissance" because it is the beginning of modernity. In the view of William Kerrigan and Gordon Braden, the Renaissance is worth talking about because, as Burckhardt argued, it is the historical period when individualism was rediscovered.[13] Thomas M. Greene, on the other hand, finds the Renaissance admirable because of its pluralism: "What is extraordinary . . . is the fecundity of the culture, or rather a series of vaguely kindred cultures strung across several centuries in several countries, each superbly pluralistic, each witnessing the creation of radically various currents, schools, genres, and individual geniuses."[14] Here again, the Renaissance is worth thinking about because of its modernity; in Greene's construction, it is a model of literary liberalism. Both approaches attribute to an historical period (and perhaps to the text that constructs it) the dynamism, tension, energy that New Critics used to attribute to poems.

It may be, however, that those who see themselves as "doing history" and who find energy, dynamism, and challenges to authority in Renaissance Italy, see only as much of the historicized Other as their contemplative pleasures allow them. They find it interesting to talk about energy and dynamism (or about power and containment, as the case may be[15]); they also find it good to talk about energy and

13. William Kerrigan and Gordon Braden, *The Idea of the Renaissance* (Baltimore: Johns Hopkins University Press, 1989), xi.

14. Thomas M. Greene, *The Vulnerable Text: Essays on Renaissance Literature* (New York: Columbia University Press, 1986), xii. See also the interesting introduction of A. Leigh DeNeef to his *Traherne in Dialogue: Heidegger, Lacan, and Derrida* (Durham: Duke University Press, 1988), which ably confronts some of the simplifications of New Historicism. But once again the appearances are saved by turning Traherne into a proto-modern. DeNeef sidesteps the obvious stumbling block that Traherne was a believer.

15. The argument that Renaissance orthodoxy produced and contained its own subversion is the theme of Stephen Greenblatt's *Renaissance Self-Fashioning from More to Shakespeare* (Chicago: University of Chicago Press, 1980) and *Shakespearean Negotiations: The Circulation of Social Energy in Renaissance England* (Berkeley and Los Angeles: University of California Press, 1988). On the New Historicist (especially Stephen Greenblatt) as practicing an aesthetics of power and of the alienated self, see Frank Lentricchia, *Ariel and the Police: Michel Foucault, William James, Wallace Stevens* (Madison: University of Wisconsin Press, 1988), 86–102; and David Norbrook in "The Death of Renaissance Man," *Raritan* 8 (1989): 89–110, esp. 90. On Greenblatt's analysis of the historical event as synecdoche for an entire culture and even for human universals, see Carolyn Porter, "Are We Being Historical Yet?" *South Atlantic Quarterly* 87 (1988): 743–85; and Vincent Pecora, "The Limits of Local Knowledge," in *The New Historicism*, ed. H. Aram Veeser, 243–76. But then, shying away from universals, the preferred kind

dynamism because we in the modern age need to be encouraged to be energetic and dynamic ourselves. This argument admits that vitality is a good thing and that we take our vitality where we find it. It does not admit that history is still similar to what it was before the nineteenth century: a text that encourages certain values, a text that gives us a mirror of our own commitments.

In many historical studies, we might do well to admit that the argument is really about values and that history is a means (or "medicine of cherries," in Sidney's phrase) for discussing them—and a very attractive means at that, for it permits us to inflect ceremony and civility in ways that sidestep the modern opposition between them.[16] The new narratives-of-literary-history-by-writers-who-do-not-believe-in-literature can offer the pleasure of an anti-pathetic rhetoric, already well established in several existentialist varieties, in a genre that carries the authority of empiricism (hard-nosed historical fact) and yet stands in the domains of traditional wisdom (the canonical texts). What results is a talky, discursive "analysis" of the great arachnid of a power, a "dispassionate" (tonally minimalist) theater of menace. These narratives teach their lessons well. Challenges to orthodoxy are to be congratulated, no matter what their philosophical base; the truth for life is better discovered by analyzing institutions than by considering the motivations of an individual life; self-serving rhetoric must be vigilantly guarded against, for everyone has his own class interest at heart. These positions may have some truth. But just as the liberal humanism they are meant to combat is an argument with an opposition, so also are these positions arguments with oppositions. And, after all, the new histories that have little use

---

of historicization has its own difficulties. The analysis of a configuration of events as unique drives to a dead end because the uniqueness disqualifies any claim that understanding of the event can be instructive. Certainly the calls for histories of "marginalized voices" imply that sympathy for the oppressed, if it is not a universal, ought to be one. It is also hard to imagine how the most serious and toughest historicization, one that vigilantly detects the tried-and-true "Western narratives" behind all attempts to theorize the "other," can do without at least one Western story that is treated as a universal. Surely the goal of empowerment for all will depend on the old Western narrative of "natural rights."

16. Whether or not subversion was possible at all during the Renaissance is a matter of dispute among recent literary historians. Annabel Patterson maintains that subversion of a dominant and dominating discourse was possible: literature has a "utopian prerogative, and one of the tasks of literary theory is to see it maintained" ("The Very Name of the Game: Theories of Order and Disorder," *South Atlantic Quarterly* 86 [1987]: 541). Is "utopian prerogative" a political "truth" by which current regimes are measured?

for the old hope-and-fortitude stories of Shakespeare and Spenser are still reciting such a story when they ask us to rejoice with earlier challenges to authority. To my ear, the hope-and-fortitude sounds a lot better coming from "literature" as the liberal humanist constitutes it than from a kind of "politic-history" that aestheticizes power into a prosaic thrill.

Tudor England does not lend itself nearly so well to a story of challenges to orthodoxy as does Renaissance Italy. The tale it tells has little to do with modern individualism or modern liberalism. The erotic-pastoral-spiritual literature of the English Renaissance assumes that human life is a quest for wisdom, that the quest is for Everyman, and that, in the midst of the quest, the natural sociability of human beings is a comradeship both consoling and inspiring. The tale is a story of dedication that does not giddily think life can be mastered: "The world is full of snares and traps. We practice and deceive others. And we are practiced and deceived upon. In the journey to the truth, we are lazy and cowardly. But besides what is hoped for in the far future, in the near future we can hope for the succor of our fellows. Hope is not overcome by despair, but neither is despair a weak foe. Once in a while a great leader may appear, inspiring us to love the truth as devotedly as he or she does. At the end of the journey, there will be rejoicing among those who have taken it before and who will admire us for having endured." This little narrative tells of struggle, devotion, and gratitude. Its truth is simple enough to be expressed in the proverbs of an oral culture or in visual emblems. Its politics is the family. Its great leaders do not have superior faculties of analysis; rather, they have superior powers of vision, which can come even to simple people.

For heirs of the Enlightenment practiced in holding the pathos of such a story at bay, this narrative would have to be rewritten considerably. The additions would best be described as Horatian hesitations: "All human beings seek to understand their lives. Life is not without difficulties and often baffling. Because we practice and deceive ourselves, it should come as no surprise that others will practice on us and deceive us. History makes us wonder what we can hope for in the far future. Perhaps the most we can expect of 'heaven' is the conversation of people whose intelligence we trust and whose company we enjoy. The most we can hope for from love is a quiet but full attention. At moments, perhaps, we can stop restlessly seeking to understand something that may after all elude understanding."

The hesitations are a commitment to Enlightenment doubt—

rational, systematic, scientific—which cuts short the old passionate story of Everyman's despair and coming home; in the age of irony, pathos had better be prepared for the raised eyebrows. But the hesitations are also prompted by two other important changes. The first is that the truth is no longer simple and cannot be embodied in the proverbs of an oral culture. It now requires the analysis of society as a system, whether the metaphor be organic or mechanical, and the analysis of a system requires the disengagement of science and skill in articulateness, of which hypotaxis, precise terminology, and books are parts. The second change follows from this; the Enlightenment leader is justified by superior analytical intelligence, not by superior vision. The communal myth of the Renaissance required those with power to love and care for the weak and helpless. The political myth of the moderns requires the powerful to *think* about the weak and uneducated, knowing full well that the weak and uneducated will never understand the institutional analysis from which presumably they will benefit, a difficulty that much current criticism fails to confront.

The anti–liberal-humanist complains that the modern Horatian version borrows the distancing moves of scientific exposition without commitment to a scientific system, thereby evading refutation. Created in the nineteenth century, it is the rhetoric of the cultivated humanist persuading by his urbanity, not by argument. In the next century, it was refined by the New Critic, whose responses were both fine and tough, but tough in a lyric sort of way (a subdued form of romantic irony). There is much to this charge. The New Critic at his worst was a shaman, sentimentalizing art and pulling worshipful beauty out of words on a page, often from the words of "every drawling versifier," as Milton put it in his characteristically un-understated way.[17] But not all New Critics were shamans, litterateurs offering their judgments on taste, sometimes with the deftness of the great man's easy authority, sometimes with the sentimentality of his weak epigone. At their best, they could tell the other side of the story: that although politics has deep effects on our lives, those with systems and methods and theories of social process are still people making moral decisions, and that they become more trustworthy

17. John Milton, "An Apology against a Pamphlet Call'd A Modest Confutation of the Animadversions upon the Remonstrant against Smectymnuus," in *The Complete Prose Works of John Milton*, ed. Don M. Wolfe, 8 vols. (New Haven: Yale University Press, 1953–82), 1:914. All further references to the prose works of Milton will be to this edition.

when they acknowledge that the truth for life lies in politics and in something else besides politics.[18] Surely the narratives of hope, fortitude, and a common journey cannot be valid only for those outside of Western domination and hence guaranteed to be innocent of its duplicities. Surely for those inside Western domination and enjoying its fruits, such narratives are not merely the bourgeoisie's way of being easy on itself.

Despite our practice in skepticism, the old Everyman story is not absolutely tuneless. Many people still hear it. Some are not abashed by the thought that it is good for them to hear it. The myth of simple comradeship that flourished during the Middle Ages and Renaissance is valuable to the community that thrives on intellectual excitement because it calls into question the delight in sheer technique, rhetorical or methodological. That human beings are by nature joined together in a story of common suffering and common triumph is rarely articulated in Elizabethan literature, or at least rarely articulated as the kind of argued position that heirs of the Enlightenment would prefer. The closest to a full-scale defense is Richard Hooker's *Laws of Ecclesiastical Polity*. That this defense is not offered by Sidney, Spenser, and Shakespeare should hardly be held against them, first, because the courtly literature of the Renaissance is based on the concrete, romance storytelling of the Middle Ages; second, because the Renaissance did not know it would be arguing with professional heirs of the Enlightenment (or, in some cases, professional heirs of the Enlightenment meditating in a post-Enlightenment fashion on their own Enlightenment assumptions); and third, because a theory of a mysterious nature to which we are all bound cannot bear too much articulation without violating the motivating principle of the story: "behold: here is something you cannot understand fully, but you should not lend a deaf ear to your inclinations to respond to it." Too much articulation, too much systematic analysis spoil the simplicity of the story and create the illusion that it is possible to analyze the myth without destroying its social bond. Even Hooker, who recognized more clearly than any of his contemporaries the need for an articulate defense of "the natural," is always working his philosophical "definitions, divisions, and distinctions" (as Sidney calls them in the *Defense*) around to a "behold." The religious resonances of "behold" make some people nervous. The problem is to find a way to accommodate it in the way we speak and write.

18. For example, see Frank Kermode, *History and Value: The Clarendon Lectures and the Northcliffe Lectures, 1987* (Oxford: Clarendon Press, 1988).

Detachment in historical studies requires something besides the refusal to take the stories of the past at face value. It is true that literary criticism has for too long been a refined sort of ventriloquizing. We used writers of the past to make our arguments for us, and, insofar as most of us wrote about authors we liked for one reason or another, our prose gradually took on the exaltations of agreement and then finally belief. Although the bluff has been called on this procedure, I do not, in this study, wish to be false on the other side, to refuse assent of any kind. The old ventriloquism meant we listened to writers without raising objections. But analysis that amounts to systematic *dis*belief, dissolving individuals and their statements into social institutions and historical processes, has its limitations too; we turn a possible dialogue into a parody. Rather than swinging between the two poles of awe before a ceremonial discourse's "beautiful ideas" and its dissolution into a cultural function, we might do better to adopt the habits of mind suggested by Aristotle's continual recourse in the *Nicomachean Ethics* to "measuring" (*metrein*), "judging" (*krinein*), and "estimating" (*axioun*).[19] "Esteeming" the works of the past negotiates between criticizing them and submitting ourselves to criticism. In relationship to the courtly culture of the Renaissance, we are the heirs of Malvolio; we do not agree that leaders are justified by being "generous, guiltless, and of free disposition," in Olivia's words.[20] Perhaps this ancestry should be characterized differently: in certain ways we are already the heirs of Malvolio and in other ways we risk becoming his heirs. Rather than wishing to revenge ourselves on the past as Malvolio wished to revenge himself on the whole pack of Olivia's great house, we might rather deliberate with it.

This deliberation, admittedly, will be unequal; few of us are about to argue that we should reinstitute monarchy. Still, if it is silly even to imagine renouncing our Enlightenment commitments, we can understand our own excesses by listening to the charges that might be brought against them. The contradiction in the Enlightenment conviction that maturity for all is signaled by making judgments independent of "the all"—the larger community—harks back to an old rhetorical problem: How do we use reason to lead an audience out of stultifying habits and at the same time bind a community together by

---

19. For the value of "esteeming" in this sense, I am indebted to Larry Goldberg's "Compassion in Politics," unpublished ms.

20. *Twelfth Night*, 1. 5. 86–87, in *William Shakespeare: The Complete Works*, gen. ed. Alfred Harbage, rev. ed. (Baltimore: Penguin, 1969). All references to Shakespeare will be to this edition.

appealing to accepted truths? The Renaissance defense of a ceremonial discourse presents a version of this problem. We understand
the problem more fully by reflecting on its configuration in a period
when tradition was, on a variety of fronts, being attacked, reformed,
improved—or simply set aside.

1

Classical Civility
and Medieval Ceremony

The Civil Mode
of Classical Rhetoric

Renaissance rhetoric is traditionally said to be based on classical sources. For the Middle Ages, these texts were the *Ad Herennium* and the youthful Cicero's *De Inventione*.[1] For the Renaissance, they were Cicero's *De Oratore*, the complete text of Quintilian's *Institutes*, and Aristotle's *Rhetoric* used as a rhetorical treatise, not as a treatise in moral philosophy. What Renaissance rhetoricians borrowed from the ancients is readily apparent: the five parts of rhetoric (invention, disposition, style, delivery, and memory), the divisions of a speech, and the technical terms for the figures of speech. Less apparent are the profound differences between classical rhetoric and the form it took when a religious and courtly culture changed it into something

1. James J. Murphy, *Rhetoric in the Middle Ages: A History of Rhetorical Theory from Saint Augustine to the Renaissance* (Berkeley and Los Angeles: University of California Press, 1974), 109.

rich and strange. We can only derive these differences from the implications of the ancient treatises; classical rhetoricians do not straightforwardly confront them. This omission is hardly surprising. Cicero did not know he would become the beloved *auctor* of a courtly and religious culture. If he had, he would have made much more explicit the assumptions on which classical rhetoric is based.

When Renaissance rhetoricians read classical treatises, what attracted them most were the devices for eloquence, for these could be used to elaborate and refine the oral fluency of the Middle Ages.[2] These authors did not see rhetoric as the linguistic analogue of a republic, the dynamic tension among institutions that Machiavelli, in *The Discourses on the First Ten Books of Titus Livy*, saw in ancient Rome. Observing around him short-lived regimes collapsing under invasion from without or upheaval from within, Machiavelli admired the Roman "system" of constitution, customs, traditions, and good leadership, the flexibility of which allowed the republic to turn to its advantage a constant conflict between a rational governing class and an irrational plebeian class. In Machiavelli's view, Rome's constitution mitigated the potential for radical change, yet its flexibility encouraged leaders to meet moments of crisis with vigor and daring— Machiavelli's version of "virtue." A rhetorician with Machiavelli's intellectual appreciation for the tension between laws and the vitality of individual leadership might have seen in classical rhetoric a similar tension between the rules that ensure linguistic stability and the innovations of great fabricators of the language. Convinced that his education gave him a right to power, this imagined rhetorician might have criticized the vernaculars for diffusing political challenge in questing adventures, erotic praises of mistresses, and pastoral fantasies. He would have urged writers to work out a system that could negotiate the intellectual clarity and boldness necessary for a healthy political culture as Machiavelli conceives of it in the *Discourses*.

2. Hanna H. Gray, "Renaissance Humanism: The Pursuit of Eloquence," *Journal of the History of Ideas* 24 (1963): 497–514. Paul Oskar Kristeller emphasized the centrality of eloquence to Renaissance humanism ("Humanism and Scholasticism," in his *Renaissance Thought: The Classic, Scholastic, and Humanist Strains* [New York: Harper Torchbooks, 1961], 92–120, esp. 100). That humanists were first and foremost professional rhetoricians has been reemphasized by Michael Baxandall in *Giotto and the Orators: Humanist Observers of Painting in Italy and the Discovery of Pictorial Composition 1350–1450* (Oxford: Clarendon Press, 1971), 1–50, and by Anthony Grafton and Lisa Jardine in *From Humanism to the Humanities: Education and the Liberal Arts in Fifteenth- and Sixteenth-Century Europe* (London: Duckworth, 1986). On the understanding of rhetoric as linguistic plenitude, see Terence Cave, *The Cornucopian Text: Problems of Writing in the French Renaissance* (Oxford: Clarendon Press, 1979).

Our rhetorician's effort might have prompted a stronger defense of rhetoric than the ancients had been able to provide and one especially necessary to the Renaissance. For the ancients, rhetoric, when compared with philosophy, did not fare well; while philosophy discovers an exact truth, rhetoric discovers only the probable truths of the future or the general truths of human opinion.[3] But a Machiavellian rhetorician might have argued that rhetoric need not be philosophy's weak sibling. Its great advantage is its capacity for negotiating with contingency. It faces up to the limitations of life. As Machiavelli remarked, "[M]en work either of necessity or by choice," and "there is found to be greater virtue where choice has less to say to it."[4] Indeed, in *The History of Rome*, Livy implicitly argues that the narrative of a nation's negotiation with particulars *is* its identity as a people. With the historical self-consciousness of hindsight, a Renaissance rhetorician might have urged his compeers to face the realities of the age: "If the intelligent are to govern and not those who happen to have the right lineage, then we have to explode the communal myths by which these people consolidate their power. We have to create a discourse that will keep the intelligent members of the state focused on their interest in self-governing, teach them first political realities, and then how to negotiate with each other—so we may all enjoy the fruits of leadership." Machiavelli was shocking, but his pragmatic advice hardly bothered rulers; they could *use* it. But a rhetorician's explicitness about the mutuality of a healthy political culture would have been dangerous, especially in England. It might, in the long run, also have been pernicious; after all, in defining the benefits of leadership, Machiavelli gave much more weight to mutually exercised power and to patriotism than any other public goal.

In the dynamic system of classical rhetoric, it is assumed that at a particular moment in the history of a polity there are questions about which intelligent citizens may reasonably disagree. Rhetorical knowledge is derived from tradition and the thoughtful reexamination of tradition. Because conclusions will always be subject to revision, differences of opinion cannot be settled by the demonstrative logic of

---

3. Isocrates, *Antidosis*, in *Isocrates*, trans. George Norlin (Loeb Classical Library; London: Heinemann, 1928), 271, and *Against the Sophists* 8. All further references to Isocrates will be to this edition. On Isocrates' quarrel with Plato and the philosophers generally, see Wesley Trimpi, *Muses of One Mind: The Literary Analysis of Experience and Its Continuity* (Princeton: Princeton University Press, 1983), 11–17.

4. *The Discourses of Niccolò Machiavelli*, 1.1.7, trans. Leslie J. Walker, S.J. (London: Routledge and Kegan Paul, 1950), 1:209.

science or of philosophy. Even in epideictic oratory, in which a speaker does not have the opposition of another advocate (as in forensic oratory) or a political rival (as in deliberative oratory), he still assumes that some members of the audience will regard his subject as perfectly ordinary (and hence not worthy of special praise) or as praiseworthy on other grounds.[5] In a rhetorical text, a writer is always parrying with anticipated disagreement.

At its best, the competition of rhetorical debate inspires creative leadership among peers. It is not just debate for its own sake. For Aristotle, the highest form of oratory is political deliberation (*Rhetoric* 1354b). If the polity is to survive, it must constantly find solutions to the difficulties that are inevitably going to emerge, and the more minds working on a problem, the better. Because the good faith of citizens cannot always be trusted, however, fruitful disagreement depends upon the protection of debate by legal procedures. In the *Rhetoric*, Aristotle's definition of the virtues is significantly related to a society of law:

> Justice is the virtue through which everybody enjoys his own possessions in accordance with the law; its opposite is injustice, through which men enjoy the possessions of others in defiance of the law. Courage is the virtue that disposes men to do noble deeds in situations of danger, in accordance with the law and in obedience to its commands; cowardice is the opposite. Temperance is the virtue that disposes us to obey the law where physical pleasure is concerned.[6]

Aristotle's inclusion of temperance as a virtue that encourages obedience to the law is especially noteworthy. Classical rhetoric both depends upon and reinforces the restraint that disposes citizens to limit their own personal self-interest in the interest of the wider political group. It mediates between the orator's desire for political power and dedication to public good. Nowhere does this mediation appear more fragile than in Thucydides' account of the Peloponnesian War, where the pursuit of individual glory prevails over concern

5. Isocrates' epideictic speech in praise of Helen begins with a criticism of those who have praised her with outlandish novelty. His speech in praise of Busiris opens with an address to Polycrates in which Isocrates criticizes Polycrates' speech on a similar subject.

6. Aristotle, *Rhetoric*, in *The Rhetoric and Poetics of Aristotle*, trans. W. Rhys Roberts and Ingram Bywater (New York: Random House, 1954), 1366b. All further references will be to this translation of the *Rhetoric* unless otherwise noted.

for the welfare of Athens. When the legal protections for political debate disappear, then rhetoric becomes something less. In the *Dialogus,* Tacitus urges the fundamental connection between the structure of government and the vigor of public oratory. In the empire, the kind of rhetoric that Cicero practiced has disappeared.

When the orator does trust his hearers' good faith, he anticipates a mutual enterprise, *collaboration* in debate. At its narrowest, this collaboration is expressed in the mutuality of a linguistic, social, and rhetorical standard.[7] In book 3 of the *Rhetoric,* Aristotle says that the rhetorician must first know how to speak good Greek (*hellenizein,* 1413b).[8] A linguistic bond is also a social bond, solidifying speaker and audience as members of an urban culture. For Cicero, proper diction should be neither rustic nor antique; idioms should belong to the capital, not to the provinces.[9]

Most important, a standard functions as an educational bond. A rhetorical standard solidifies the intellectual heritage of an articulate class.[10] A philosophical heritage urges reason and clarity. For Aristotle, a standard gives an argument sufficient determinacy of meaning to allow it to be refuted; diviners like to use oracular speech because "their predictions are thus, as a rule, less likely to be falsified" (1407b). A philosophical heritage also urges the abstractions that enable a human "making" of a text by stipulating degrees of relevance; some things belong in the one category and are therefore directly pertinent; others, belonging in another, are "moreover," or "by analogy." When philosophical abstractions become rhetorical generalizations, they can "measure" experience. A person or event is assessed in comparison to other persons or events as more or less amazing, disgusting, praiseworthy, or ridiculous. Generalizations also diminish the claims of the particular on the moral imagination. In

7. For a theoretical discussion of a standard, see Punya Sloka Ray, *Language Standardization: Studies in Prescriptive Linguistics* (The Hague: Mouton, 1963).

8. *The Rhetoric of Aristotle,* ed. and trans. Edward Meredith Cope (Cambridge: Cambridge University Press, 1877); repr. edited by John Edwin Sandys (New York: Arno Press, 1973), 3:55n.

9. *De Oratore,* trans. W. E. Sutton and H. Rackham (Loeb Classical Library; London: Heinemann, 1942), 3.42–44.

10. John Earl Joseph, *Eloquence and Power: The Rise of Language Standards and Standard Languages* (New York: Basil Blackwell, 1987), 1–2, 16–18. Joseph questions others' emphasis on the cognitive superiority of the standard (40). See in this regard Bohuslav Havránek, "The Functional Differentiation of the Standard Language," in *A Prague School Reader on Esthetics, Literary Structure, and Style,* trans. Paul L. Garvin (Washington, D.C.: Georgetown University Press, 1964), 6. On the perceived formality of the standard in comparison to a native dialect, see Joseph, 82.

measuring life, a speaker sees not an individual but a type. His wisdom is a practical adjustment between established types and new experiences.

The standards for rational argument are powerfully enforced by verbal cleverness. Wit, says Quintilian, belongs to the conversations of men who live in the capital. *Urbanitas* in language "denotes language with a smack of the city in its words, accent and idiom, and further suggests a certain tincture of learning derived from associating with well-educated men."[11] For Aristotle, a rhetorician knows how to be clever with the "well-bred insolence" of wit (*Rhet.* 1389b). In a long section of book 2 of the *De Oratore*, Cicero recommends irony, raillery, and witticisms. As implied in Quintilian's description of wit as a "tincture" of language that comes from conversation with well-bred men, irony for Cicero also is acquired by nature and not by art (*De Orat.* 2.54.216). Wit, cleverness, and especially irony argue tonally what abstractions and generalizations argue explicitly: that language is a human tool and that human speakers themselves stipulate the standard of relevance for a particular argument.

Because rhetoric is always silently solidifying an educated class in opposition to an uneducated class, the superiority of rational analysis is a powerful tool. It is significant in this regard that Aristotle assumes that "better" rhetoric is moving closer to philosophy and away from the enchantments of storytelling and rhythm. Audiences with good taste prefer styles that are less rhythmical and repetitive and more "prose-like":

> Now it was because poets seemed to win fame through their fine language when their thoughts were simple enough, that the language of oratorical prose at first took a poetical colour, e.g. that of Gorgias. Even now most uneducated people think that poetical language makes the finest discourses. That is not true: the language of prose is distinct from that of poetry. (*Rhet.* 1404a)

Even the writers of tragedy, says Aristotle, have given up tetrameters for more prose-like iambics; they have also given up the diction that once decorated the works of dramatists and of the writers of

---

11. *Institutio Oratoria*, trans. H. E. Butler (Loeb Classical Library; London: Heinemann, 1921), 6.3.17. All further references to Quintilian will be to this edition.

hexameters.[12] Just as the tragedians have rejected rich ornamentation, so also should rhetoricians: "It is therefore ridiculous to imitate a poetical manner which the poets themselves have dropped" (*Rhet.* 1404a). The very brevity of the judgment ("it is ridiculous") and the casual acceptance of changes in style suggest collaboration with an audience who understands that rhetorical "rules" adjust to changing standards of taste and who prefers a modern, hardheaded style to an old-fashioned, ornamental one. When Aristotle says that the sophisticated rhetorician makes a clear distinction between prose and poetry and prefers rhetoric that leans toward the rigor of philosophy, he reveals philosophy's constant pressure on rhetorical speech to give up childish appeals.

Still, Aristotle has a practical streak as well. Philosophical precision is less important than winning. Thus the rhetorician's relationship with his audience is complex. On the one hand, he regards his hearers as people more or less like himself and reassures them that they, like him, are different from provincials who are ignorant of Greek philosophy and who lack the presence of mind to understand wit, let alone be witty themselves. On the other hand, the rhetorician condescends to his hearers, accepting the necessity for negotiating with their moral and intellectual limitations: "The duty of rhetoric is to deal with such matters as we deliberate upon without arts or systems to guide us, in the hearing of persons who cannot take in at a glance a complicated argument, or follow a long chain of reasoning" (*Rhet.* 1357a). Later, on the matter of winning an audience's attention on a particular point, Aristotle remarks, "It is plain that such introductions are addressed not to ideal hearers, but to hearers as we find them" (*Rhet.* 1415b). The philosopher may pursue an argument dialectically with other philosophers, but the rhetorician deals with ordinary citizens and so must consider other means of persuasion. It is only prudent to do so: there is a rich tension between Aristotle's own commitment to the truth as a philosopher and his pragmatism as a student of rhetoric in his observation that the truth is always likely to win; if it fails to do so, it must be the fault of the speaker (*Rhet.* 1355a). The truth is likely to win, but then again one must be realistic and bring that victory about.

To win demands Aristotelian *phronesis,* or, practical wisdom: "The use of persuasive speech is to lead to decisions" (*Rhet.* 1391b); a civil speaker is suspicious of the philosopher's pursuit of questions useless

---

12. For theoretical discussion of the differentiation of prose from poetry, see Ray, "The Formation of Prose," in *Language Standardization,* 138–53.

to the polity and of arguments that are governed not by the demands of the occasion but merely by "whithersoever the wind, as it were, of the argument blows," as Socrates blithely holds in the *Republic*.[13] To the man of public life, political decisions do not allow the leisure of sitting under a plane tree, as do the interlocutors in the *Phaedrus*. A civil speaker is a man of the world. Political assessment of the particular event parallels the rhetorical judgment of appropriate and effective expression (*kairos*; Isocrates, *Against the Sophists* 12).

Entrance into the political world is a sign of maturity. In the *Nicomachean Ethics*, virtuous action and deliberate choice belongs to an adult, and the lack of such capabilities characterizes the child, whose life is a merry-go-round of desire and amusement (*NE* 1095a, 1119b, 1174a, 1176b). The nobility of adults lies in their seriousness, their vigor, their self-discipline, their political activity, all of which children lack. The line between adult judgment and childish waywardness also marks the line between political and domestic justice, the private realm and the public (*NE* 1134b). The highest political activity demands a community in which human beings rule and are ruled equally. It is to be distinguished from relationships between masters and their children, slaves, and to a lesser extent, wives. The "private life" of Cicero's dialogues and letters is not the private life of the modern novel; it is the face that a political man might show to his colleagues in the forum, and like Aristotle's definition of virtue, it excludes women and children.

A pragmatic and adult man of the world does not hope for too much. The rhetorician is realistic about happiness, which is a compromise between the ideal and the exigent. The definition of happiness in the *Rhetoric* as virtue plus the ability to protect one's property (1360b) is noticeably different from the definition in the *Nicomachean Ethics*, where happiness is virtue combined with prosperity. An orator is also realistic about the supposed "mutuality" of political deliberation with his peers. He is aware that political oratory may descend to a test of will, influence, and cunning. The use of the techniques of persuasion for a corrupt purpose is a fact of life. But if the goal is to preserve collaboration in debate and to keep a polity committed to its ideals, the question becomes how to beat the sophists at their own game. Human life is not perfect and never will be. The rhetorician is levelheaded, sagacious, prudent.

13. Plato, *Republic*, trans. Paul Shorey, in *The Collected Dialogues of Plato Including the Letters*, ed. Edith Hamilton and Huntington Cairns (New York: Bollingen Foundation, 1961), 394d.

The faculty of prudence is engaged more fully in the political life than in any other. Like Machiavelli, Aristotle accepts the give-and-take of negotiation and compromise. The politician finds immense satisfaction in the calculations and triumphs of leadership. In the Isocratean tradition, rhetoric is the mode of speech of those who are dedicated to the flourishing of their own particular nation. Athens was the first, says Isocrates, "to lay down laws and establish a polity," and for that reason she is to be praised before all other cities (*Panegyricus* 40). With Aristotle, the patriotism is not so passionate, but he clearly assumes that rhetoric depends upon the health of the polis. In Cicero's *Brutus*, the careers of famous Roman orators parallel the fortunes of Rome.

Although it is possible that a rhetorician's prudence is dictated by a desire to protect his advantages, it is equally possible that his allegiances are to an ideal. He adjusts to his audience's limitations not in order to deceive them but to remind them of honor and virtue. This kind of mutuality affects an orator's "use" of rhetorical rules. Classical rhetoricians often seem to be hawking their street-smarts: human responses are easily manipulated. But their advice is also moral reflection on leadership, which, to be sure, gives a speaker power but also allows him to bring an audience to a "better self." A speaker may *want* to "save the day" or "restore a community's customary idealism" or "bring his people to good sense." Rhetorical topoi are "useful" not just because they "work" but because they reaffirm shared beliefs. Similarly, a speaker "uses" rhythm, but he also "enjoys" it. For Isocrates and Cicero, rhythm is the most powerful force in great political oratory, because it can collect a factionalized polity into a single body and recommit it to its ideals. For Cicero, rhetoric can "gather scattered humanity into one place . . . lead it out of its brutish existence in the wilderness up to our present condition of civilization as men and as citizens . . . give shape to laws, tribunals, and civic rights."[14] Rhythm celebrates the rhetorical community's understanding of virtue and human flourishing.

The twin demands for rhythm and rational clarity are the heart of rhetorical decorum. Decorum is not a static matching of subject matter to style but rather a continual adjustment between goals.

14. *De Oratore* 1.8.33. On the power of rhythm to unite an audience, see Cicero, *Orator*, trans. G. L. Hendrickson (Loeb Classical Library; London: Heinemann, 1939), 48.227–71.236. Isocrates contrasts rhythmic oratory with the speeches made in court (*Antidosis* 46), and Cicero contrasts it with the "thin and bloodless style" of the philosophers (*De Orat.* 1.13.56).

When public life consists of a multiplicity of decision makers, who, while belonging to the same society and sharing a common culture, have at least somewhat divergent interests and views, then rhetorical speech must strike a balance between articulate reason and the emotion of natural truths. As a philosopher, Plato emphasizes precision over emotion in the interest of true and undebatable knowledge. When decisions have to be made, citizens consult experts in the field: generals, architects, physicians. Isocrates, on the other hand, emphasizes the appeal to emotions, chiefly by rhythm. Decorum adjudicates the claims of logical clarity (the first requirement of a rhetorical standard) and the unification of the political body by appeals to truths regarded as self-evident;[15] it is only with the common bonds of tradition that leadership can be effective at all.

In comparison to a ceremonial mode, however, the classical rhetorical tradition emphasizes rational clarity much more than rhythmical ornament. The psychagogic power of rhythm does not license a speaker simply to tell a story; he has to make a point. Although the prescribed divisions of a speech indicate rhetoric's roots in an oral culture, the *propositio, refutatio,* and *confirmatio* remind a speaker that his utterance is not rhapsodic in the manner of Homer; it has to have sections that state the argument as a whole, and it has to meet possible disagreement.[16] Aristotle is the most severe on this point, hammering on the importance of proofs and pushing rhythm away from song: "prose . . . is to be rhythmical, but not metrical, or it will become not prose but verse" (*Rhet.* 1408b). Because Cicero is combating a current fashion for the more philosophical style of the Attics, he touts the value of a highly cultivated rhythmic style. Nevertheless, in the *De Oratore,* he follows Aristotle in putting the treatment of logical argument first. Moreover, like Aristotle, he distinguishes between a rhythm proper to oratory and one proper to poetry (*De Orat.* 1.33.151). Even when Cicero's speeches are highly rhythmical, they also have clearly laid out arguments.

Finally, the collaboration embedded in a rhetorical standard is also a cultural program: the distinction between the educated and the uneducated justifies the leadership of the educated. The collaboration of a linguistic standard reminds speakers and hearers that they share the same philosophical, literary, and most of all, political tradition.

---

15. Trimpi, *Muses of One Mind,* 5–24.
16. Compare Walter J. Ong, "Oral Residue in Tudor Prose Style," *PMLA* 80 (1965): 145–54.

Whatever the differences between an Isocratean valuation of the finely tuned sophistic speech and an Aristotelian valuation of agonistic oratory, Isocrates' speeches and Aristotle's treatise concur on this: to speak good Greek means to remember the battle of Marathon, to value Athens as a city that has promoted philosophy, to admire the achievements of her poets in epic and drama, to hold that the greatest human achievement is the formation of a community according to law, and to believe in the superiority of Greek civilization (Isocrates, *Panegyricus*). Similarly, to speak pure Latin—an ability that Cicero refers to continually in the *Brutus* when recounting the history of Roman orators—means to be acquainted with the various philosophical schools in Rome, to know the rhetorical quarrel between the Asiatics and the Atticists, to be committed to the Roman republic, and to believe in the connection between eloquence and a lawful community. To believe in the rhetorical way of life is to take for granted that men exercise their practical wisdom in the concrete reality of the polis or the forum and that political wisdom is the general consensus of educated human beings, just as good Latin is the language of educated Romans.

Not all ancient texts are informed by the practical wisdom of a civil speaker. Plato is at once more rigorously logical than the rhetorician and more mythic. When he "envisions" the truth, he turns from dialectic to accounts of the next life or of Egypt or of the realm of a lover. The attacks in various treatises on highly wrought rhythm suggest that some styles were regarded as more akin to poetry than to argument. Indeed, for rhetoricians after Isocrates, his style was considered too rhythmical for oratory.[17] Discussions of the grand style in classical antiquity associate it with tragedy and epic.[18] It is easy to forget that Longinus's *On the Sublime* is a rhetorical treatise, not only because his examples are frequently taken from poetry but also because his emphasis on wonder and emotion goes far beyond Cicero. The Stoic school of rhetoric insists upon spareness and restraint in expression, yet in separating the individual from the polity and emphasizing instead his connection with a cosmic law, Stoic rhetoric has its own kind of pathos. Moreover, in classical literature, a supernatural world (often represented by a female *magister*, as with Diotima or the *Aeneid*'s Venus) sometimes dissolves

17. Debora K. Shuger, *Sacred Rhetoric: The Christian Grand Style in the English Renaissance* (Princeton: Princeton University Press, 1988), 15.
    18. Ibid., 17–20.

the reality of the world of human action, as at the end of Plato's *Republic* or in the *Symposium*, in Cicero's *Dream of Scipio*, or in Vergil's *Aeneid*. Still, these classical visionary moments lack the intensity of similar visions in the literature of the Christian Middle Ages and are not sustained as fully and elaborately.

Rhetoric flourished both in practice and in an educational tradition until the Roman empire; it was then reduced to an educational tradition alone and withdrew from the public arena into the schools of declamation. There, because speeches had no political consequences, they were praised more for finesse than force.[19] The various philosophical schools of the empire and late antiquity also contributed to the decline of rhetoric. In the Epicurean and the Stoic rejection of political activity as the highest kind of life, public oratory lost its primary justification. In late antiquity, Plotinus regards the civil virtues that give measurement to the soul as a mere illusion of the true measurement of the divine.[20] Reality for the neo-Platonist was not only beyond the powers of the ordinary senses but also beyond articulation: Soul "dwells abidingly in the Supreme Beauty, and dwells there without deeds: for she does not govern by ratiocination, neither does she consciously redress anything, but by the mere vision of her prior [sic] she creates with marvellous power an ordered universe."[21] For St. Augustine in *The City of God*, political life on earth is a delusion.

As Neo-Platonism was absorbed into Augustinian Christianity and also into the courtly culture of the High Middle Ages, the story of setting-out-and-return became the central narrative: in Neo-Platonism, it is the descent into created nature and the return through Nature and Soul to the unself-conscious state of the One. In Christianity, it is the Prodigal Son. In romance, it is the journey away from the castle and return to it. The collaboration in which an audience could be counted on to attend to an argument but not necessarily to agree with it gives way either to communal solidarity or to a profound distrust of an audience's moral weakness. In book 4 of *On Christian Doctrine*, St. Augustine

19. On the schools of declamation, see S. F. Bonner, *Roman Declamation in the Late Republic and Early Empire* (Liverpool: University of Liverpool Press, 1949).

20. Plotinus, *Enneads*, in *The Essence of Plotinus: Extracts from the Six Enneads and Porphyry's Life of Plotinus*, trans. Stephen MacKenna, compiled by Grace H. Turnbull (New York: Oxford University Press, 1934), 1.2.2.

21. Plotinus, *Enneads*, in *Select Passages Illustrating Neoplatonism*, trans. E. R. Dodds (London: Society for Promoting Christian Knowledge, 1960), 2.9.2. On the importance of Neo-Platonism for the Middle Ages, see Erich Auerbach, *Dante: Poet of the Secular World*, trans. Ralph Manheim (Chicago: University of Chicago Press, 1961), 20.

borrows Cicero's threefold purpose of oratory: to teach, to delight, and to move, paralleled by the subdued, the moderate, and the grand style. But the consolidation of the flock as a community of believers radically alters Cicero's scheme. Self-consciousness about language can be dangerous (4.15). To delight, says Augustine, one can simply state the truth (4.12). In moving, one uses eloquence as a "hammer that breaketh the rock in pieces" so that he may "be willingly and obediently heard."[22] For classical rhetoric, the aim is to gain an audience's agreement at a particular moment; for Augustine, the aim of rhetoric is to command obedience and permanently to realign an audience's allegiances.

Symptomatic of the disappearance of classical rhetoric and its world of collaborative debate is the weak distinction between prose and poetry in medieval vernacular literatures.[23] This distinction is blurred because the prudential judgments of the rhetorical "man of the world" give way to wonder and enchantment on the one hand or to philosophical precision on the other. Indeed, in most vernacular genres of the Middle Ages, nature is so radically unstable that prudence has no "world" on which to act. The overwhelmingly superior ontological status of supernatural truth always threatens to dissolve the palpability of the natural world in the Primary Cause. It also threatens the independence of human language, which must submit to one far simpler and far truer. As the spatial, determinate categories of human argument give way to a spiritual journey, "understanding" is represented as the impressions of supernatural grace on the soul's photographic plate. The rhythms of the journey of "something unfolding" change the civil mode's generalizations from negotiable categories to fixed stages in the soul's progress.

As I argued earlier, a Renaissance humanist who analyzed classical rhetoric structurally, as Machiavelli analyzed the politics of Rome structurally, might have produced a stronger defense of rhetoric.

22. St. Augustine, *On Christian Doctrine*, trans. D. W. Robertson, Jr. (Indianapolis, Ind.: Bobbs-Merrill, 1958), 4.14–15.

23. On generic overlap in the Middle Ages, see Morton W. Bloomfield, "Episodic Motivation and Marvels in Epic and Romance," in his *Essays and Explorations: Studies in Ideas, Language, and Literature* (Cambridge: Harvard University Press, 1970), 107 and 121–23. On the overlap of prose and verse in Latin texts, see Ernst Robert Curtius, *European Literature and the Latin Middle Ages*, trans. Willard R. Trask (New York: Harper and Row, 1953), 147–54. On the overlap of prose and verse in Old and Middle English, see Elizabeth Salter, *Nicholas Love's "Myrrour of the Blessed Lyf of Jesu Christ,"* Analecta Cartusiana 10 (Salzburg: Institut für Englische Sprache und Literatur, 1974), 184; and Rosemond Tuve, *Allegorical Imagery: Some Mediaeval Books and Their Posterity* (Princeton: Princeton University Press, 1966).

Human beings, he might have said, need a combination of rational thought and emotional persuasion to stabilize a polity in certain political conditions. Rhetoric helps them articulate "what, politically, they are up against." The collaboration of rational men in making determinate meaning and controlling political instability is necessary to combat a mystified hierarchical regime that either wastes or suppresses human virtue. It tacitly "submits" that government should be carried on by the rational, pragmatic, and strong not only because a state will be better able to withstand enemies but because its citizens themselves will be exercising to the fullest their human faculties.

The Ceremonial Mode in Boethius's *Consolation of Philosophy*

With the advent of chivalric romance in the twelfth century and a greater degree of self-consciousness in the aristocratic class, the spiritual journey of Plotinus and Augustine and the fineness of courtly life coalesce in a pun on "grace": "a spiritual gift" and "courtesy."[24] A gesture's outward and visible beauty signals an inward and invisible grace. A ceremonial discourse fuses the stylization of courtly literature with the spiritual quest of the Plotinian–Augustinian tradition.

Although a ceremonial discourse begins to flourish in the twelfth century, it draws heavily on a Latin philosophical tradition stretching back hundreds of years. A paradigmatic text that shows how the philosophical tradition itself was easily absorbed into a story of setting-out-and-return is Boethius's *Consolation of Philosophy*, a sixth-century work that profoundly influenced both Latin and vernacular works of the Middle Ages and Renaissance. The existence of manuscripts of the *Consolation* in England, Italy, Germany, and France; commentaries in the ninth, tenth, and twelfth centuries; and translations of the eleventh, twelfth, and fourteenth centuries attest to its currency. In England alone, between 1556 and 1609, there were four published translations, including one by Queen Elizabeth.[25] Its

24. As in the eighth section of *The Pearl*, where Mary is called the "Queen of Courtesy."

25. Besides the translation into English in 1410 by John Walton, it was also translated by George Colville in 1556, by Sir Thomas Chaloner in 1563, by Queen Elizabeth in 1593, and by "I.T." in 1609.

numerous translators, commentators, and imitators support the claim of Howard Patch that "the content of the book permeated . . . the thought of men for at least a thousand years."[26] The *Consolation* amply demonstrates how stories of "grace"—beauty and spirit—inform other genres besides vernacular tales of conversion, knightly exploit, and amorous intrigue. Most important, it demonstrates how the abstractions and generalizations of classical argument were transformed by a "language of being."

At the beginning of the *Consolation*, Boethius, having lost his position under the emperor, is in prison. The imposing figure of Philosophia appears to him in his distraught state and banishes the "Sirens" of poetry, who, she says, have merely encouraged his emotional tumult. She will give him instead the better medicine of philosophy. First, she shows him that he trusted too much in Fortune. Then she demonstrates that true pleasure, fame, and power have their basis in goodness and blessedness. Finally, she demonstrates the compatibility of human free will and God's foreknowledge. The work is presented in regularly alternating sections of prose argument and lyric poems.

In the *Consolation*, as in Plato, the epistemological basis of knowledge is a dialectical ascent to true reality. Taking his cue from Plotinus, however, Boethius emphasizes the visionary side of Plato.[27] As a result, the *Consolation* exaggerates the "funnel effect" of Platonism, whereby the solidity of the material world gives way to the purer reality of the Forms.[28] In Plotinus, the truth of the final vision outweighs any other reality:

> And one that shall know this vision—with what passion of love shall he not be seized, with what pang of desire, what longing to be molten into one with This, what wondering delight! If he that has never seen this Being must hunger for It

26. Howard Rollin Patch, *The Tradition of Boethius: A Study of His Importance in Medieval Culture* (New York: Oxford University Press, 1935), 88. The *Consolation* was translated in the eleventh century by Notker Labeo and by a Provençal writer, in the twelfth century by Simund de Freine, in the fourteenth century by Jean de Meun, by Chaucer, and by both an Italian and a Spanish author. It influenced the work of Alain de Lille, Jean de Meun, Dante, Boccaccio, Chaucer, Gavin Douglas, Christine de Pisan, Giovanni Pontano, and Pico della Mirandola (47–113).

27. On Boethius's Platonism and Neo-Platonism, see Pierre Courcelle, *Late Latin Writers and Their Greek Sources*, trans. Harry E. Wedeck (Cambridge: Harvard University Press, 1969), 297.

28. For a description of what I call the "funnel effect" of Neo-Platonism's doctrine of Return, see Trimpi, *Muses of One Mind*, 177, 180, 188.

> as for all his welfare, he that has known must love and reverence It as the very Beauty; he will be flooded with awe and gladness, stricken by a salutary terror; he loves with a sharp desire; all other loves than this he must despise, and disdain all that once seemed fair.[29]

The contingency of argument in classical rhetoric, where a position is offered as the most opportune, dissolves into a quest for the absolute. Similarly, the contingencies of politics dissolve in the logic of universal truth. Generalizations do not establish degrees of relevance; either everything is irrelevant (compared to God), or, because an event may be a sign of God's providence, everything is relevant with a vengeance. When the journey to truth is at stake, the hesitations of verbal irony, with all of their compromises with a human world made by mutual agreements, become merely distracting noise: "disinformation."

As female *magister* to a desperate pupil, Philosophia gives this quest both panic and passion. It is she who knows the way: "'I make haste' quoth [Philosophia], 'to perform my promise, and to show thee the way by which thou mayest return to thy country.'"[30] Her relationship with Boethius is not sage-and-pupil or sage-and-sophist (as in Plato) or colleague-and-friend (as in Cicero)[31] but parent-and-child (*alumne*, 1.Pr.3). She is Boethius's nurse (*nutricem*, 1.Pr.3). She has an "amiable countenance" (1.Pr.5). She reminds him that he has been raised on her milk (1.Pr.2). She lays her hand upon his breast and dries his eyes (1.Pr.2). She will be gentle with him and soften him for stiffer remedies (1.Pr.5). The very sweetness of her speech renders him attentive (3.Pr.1). Music accompanies her catechism (2.Pr.3). She sings her verses in a "soft and sweet voice" (4.Pr.1). She knows Boethius so well that she anticipates what he will say ahead of time (5.Pr.3, 4). With the power that a child attributes to a mother, she will protect and guide him. Because his eventual acquiescence to her

29. *Enneads*, in *The Essence of Plotinus*, trans. MacKenna, 1.6.7.

30. Boethius, *The Consolation of Philosophy*, trans. "I.T." and revised by H. F. Stewart in *Boethius: The Theological Tractates and The Consolation of Philosophy*, ed. H. F. Stewart and E. K. Rand (Loeb Classical Library; Cambridge: Harvard University Press, 1918), 5.Pr.1. I have chosen this translation over the more recent one by S. J. Tester because of the rendering of Boethius's lyric sections in verse rather than prose. Seth Lerer offers an extended study of the *Consolation* as a transformation of classical dialogue into prayerful *oratio*, in *Boethius and Dialogue: Literary Method in The Consolation of Philosophy* (Princeton: Princeton University Press, 1985).

31. Cf. E. K. Rand, *Founders of the Middle Ages* (New York: Dover, 1928), 161.

authority is a foregone conclusion from the beginning, his misunder-
standings are not debates but rather psychological difficulties, caused
by faulty vision; the difficulties are sympathetic, to be sure, but still
wrong.[32] And just as all children have mothers and grow up, so must
all human beings take this journey. The parent-child metaphors
enforce the communalism of the quest.

When Boethius accedes to her argument, not only will he gain a
mother's approval but he will also reach his "home" (domum, 3.Pr.2;
4.Pr.1), a place of safety out of a world dominated by fickle Fortuna.
Full understanding of divine simplicity gives Boethius asylum from
the labor of human life (3.M.10). To arrive at the "stable simplicity of
Providence" is to look through the haphazardness of the surface
particulars of the world to rational causation and law, which, unlike
human life, are "unloosable," "unmoveable," "immutable" (4.Pr.6).
The opposition between a safe home with a nurse-mother and a
dangerous journey alone enforces a sharp split between human life
and the supernatural. Human life is a dungeon for captives, or a
storm with mists, or a journey to sea; it is being confined to "down
here" (1.M.4, M.2; 3.M.2; 1.Pr.3, M.7; 2.M.4; 4.Pr.6). "Home" is a
harbor, haven, port, or castle; it is being lifted up to a mountain, the
view from which makes all of life's troubles seem very small (1.Pr.3,
Pr.5; 3.M.10; 5.Pr.6). With Philosophia, one has wings (4.Pr.1) to get
home and a "simplicity of the highest knowledge enclosed within no
bounds" (5.Pr.5). In her refuge, one's being dilates with perfect ease.[33]
From her mouth come hymns to truth that soothe like lullabies:

> Come hither, all you that are bound,
> Whose base and earthly minds are drowned
> By lust which doth them tie in cruel chains:
> Here is a seat for men opprest,
> Here is a port of pleasant rest;
> Here may a wretch have refuge from his pains.
>
> (3.M.10)

Still, Philosophia is no auntly sort of benefactress. Of unclear
height, stern and remote, filled with "dignity and gravity" (4.Pr.1),
she comes as an emissary from another world, with strange Greek

32. Cf. F. Anne Payne, Chaucer and Menippean Satire (Madison: University of
Wisconsin Press, 1981), 55–85.
33. Patricia A. Parker, Inescapable Romance: Studies in the Poetics of a Mode (Princeton:
Princeton University Press, 1979), 54–64.

letters on her dress and symbols in her hands. At any moment, she might withdraw her attention from Boethius, "retiring" into the "secret seat of her soul" (3.Pr.2) and disdaining the *terrena animalia* who cannot put themselves through the rigors of learning.[34] The sweetness of her asylum is measured by Boethius's terror that she might throw him back once again into the turmoil of earthly life, with its "cursed crews of the wicked" and disorderly rout of furious assailants on the "castle" of truth (1.Pr.5, 3; 4.Pr.6).

   The relationship between mother and child and the journey to a place of refuge turn logical abstractions into talismans of power. As the truth made various and splendid, abstractions are the source of aureate diction, a dialect that yearns for the truth-above-all-truths. They come to the human mind like verbal refuges, as in the conclusion to the famous ninth meter of book 3: "Principium, vector, dux, semita, terminus idem." They are virtually interchangeable with concrete images. The emblematic representations of the metra (Orpheus [3.12], Ulysses [4.3], Nero [3.4], the bee [3.7]) crystallize the perfect comprehensibility of the world once it is seen through a knowing eye. Abstractions and concretions alike drive toward the "simplicity of divine knowledge" (5.Pr.4) that the confusions of human speech cannot attain. Indeed, the truth is best praised with silence, not with human speech at all.[35] C. S. Lewis characterizes the end of the *Consolation* as a whole: "We are made to feel as if we had seen a heap of common materials so completely burnt up that there remains

   34. 2.Pr.6; 3.Pr.3. The long and arduous path of true understanding has been argued to come from Augustine (Edmund T. Silk, "Boethius's *Consolatio Philosophiae* as a Sequel to Augustine's *Dialogues* and *Soliloquia*," *Harvard Theological Review* 32 [1939]: 19–39). See also Henry Chadwick, *Boethius: The Consolations of Music, Logic, Theology, and Philosophy* (Oxford: Clarendon Press, 1981), 249–51. On Boethius's debt to Cicero, especially the *Tusculan Disputations*, see Anna Crabbe, "Literary Design in the *De Consolatione Philosphiae*," in M. Gibson, ed., *Boethius: His Life, Thought and Influence* (Oxford: Blackwell, 1981), 237–74, and Lerer, *Boethius and Dialogue*, 32–45.
   35. On Augustine's rhetoric of silence and the pure language of the divinity, see Joseph Anthony Mazzeo, "St. Augustine's Rhetoric of Silence: Truth vs. Eloquence and Things vs. Signs," in his *Renaissance and Seventeenth-Century Studies* (New York: Columbia University Press, 1964), 8–9. Mazzeo's characterization of Augustine's rhetoric has been qualified by Marcia Colish, who points to the pertinence of silence to speech in Augustine's *De mendacio* and *De musica* ("St. Augustine's Rhetoric of Silence Revisited," *Augustinian Studies* 9 [1978]: 15–24). The necessity for speech as a preliminary step to full comprehension of the truth has been underlined by Lerer (*Boethius and Dialogue*, 94–123). On the apocalyptic revelations of the *Consolation*, see Pierre Courcelle, *Late Latin Writers*, 296. On the apocalyptic element in Boethius and in other works, see Michael H. Means, *The Consolatio Genre in Medieval English Literature* (Gainesville: University Presses of Florida, 1972), 7–8.

neither ash nor smoke nor even flame, only a quivering of invisible heat."[36]

Accompanying the turbulence of the *Consolation* is a formal feature that orders the emotion without dissipating it: the processional evenness of stylization. Always moving between the parallel tracks of panic and reassurance, the *Consolation* acknowledges human fears but disciplines them with parallelism, repetition, and the regular alternation of prose and verse sections. Listening to Philosophia, the human mind goes to sleep and awakens to a new power of attention. In her singing lies full understanding, full power, full pleasure (3.Pr.1, 10). It is hard to think of another work that so completely turns prose into incantation.

The Ceremonial Mode in Other Genres

Once we get past the superficial classicism of the *Consolation*—the dialogue form, the philosophical abstractions, the echoes of Plato and Aristotle—and concentrate instead on the basic motivating impulse of getting home, the parallels with other medieval genres suddenly leap to the foreground. Like the *Consolation*, romance too has a central plot of setting out on a journey, a return home, and the dual tracks of despair and reassurance.[37] As in the *Consolation*, romance's journey home is filled with intense longing and pulled by a centripetal force of a point of stability: the king's court or, for Spenser (a Renaissance author still medieval in spirit) a North star, that "firme is fixt, and sendeth light from farre / To all, that in the wide deepe wandring arre" (*Faerie Queene*, 1.1.4–5). The unstable landscape of romance and the reliability of the king define each other: the world's passions set off his impassivity, and his remote calm defines its whirlwind changes of scene: spring that turns into winter, rivers that disappear, horses riding on the clouds. The wandering knight's wandering responses legitimize a ruler's steady leadership, the heart of the "body politic"; unstable organs (subjects) need extrabodily reason (the king).[38] Erotic and religious lyrics are the lapidary forms of the

36. C. S. Lewis, *The Discarded Image: An Introduction to Medieval and Renaissance Literature* (Cambridge: Cambridge University Press, 1964), 90.

37. Northrop Frye, *Anatomy of Criticism: Four Essays* (Princeton: Princeton University Press, 1954), 93.

38. Many of Fredric Jameson's arguments about romance can be extended to a wider

same emotional weather changes and longing for closure in a supernatural body. Both share the *Consolation*'s parallel tracks of joyful reassurance and despair.[39] Both share romance's longing to join a superior body of truth.

The *Consolation*'s centripetal pull toward Philosophia is reinforced in many medieval encyclopedic works, in both Latin and the vernaculars, by a similarly sweet and stern female figure: Nature in Alain de Lille's *Complaint of Nature* and in his *Anticlaudianus*, Venus and Reason in the *Roman de la Rose*, Beatrice in *The Divine Comedy*. Even in works we think of as typically Renaissance, this womanly authority figure—both intimate and distant—still presides over confused pursuits in a confused world: Petrarch's Laura, Sidney's Stella in the sonnet sequence, Urania in the *Arcadia*, Gloriana in Spenser's *Faerie Queene*, Shakespeare's Portia and Cordelia. Where an actual female figure is not present, the femininity of authority figures is dispersed in imagery: in Cistercian texts of the twelfth century, writers refer both to Christ and themselves as mothers.[40] The same feminine imagery surrounding Christ appears in the works of fourteenth-century devotional writers and in fifteenth-century sermons.[41]

---

ceremonial discourse. One of these is Jameson's speculation that whereas comedy belongs to society's confidence that patriarchal authority will be asserted in the fathers and passed to the sons, romance is a part of the oral phase of complete dependence on the breast of the mother and terror that she will withdraw the source of nourishment (*The Political Unconscious: Narrative as a Socially Symbolic Act* [Ithaca: Cornell University Press, 1981], 142). For a Lacanian analysis of this medieval language of the body, see Louise O. Fradenburg, "Spectacular Fictions: Chaucer and Dunbar," *Poetics Today* 5 (1984): 493–517. For a reading of the language of the body and its implications in Spenser, see David Lee Miller, "Spenser's Poetics: The Poem's Two Bodies," *PMLA* 101 (1986): 170–85. For an analysis of the "text" of the female body in Renaissance and other literatures, see Patricia Parker, *Literary Fat Ladies: Rhetoric, Gender, Property* (London: Methuen, 1987). For the usefulness of the language of the female body to Elizabeth, see Louis Montrose, "The Elizabethan Subject and the Spenserian Text," in *Literary Theory / Renaissance Texts*, ed. Patricia Parker and David Quint (Baltimore: Johns Hopkins University Press, 1986), 303–40.

39. Paul Zumthor has argued that the "register" of the poetry of the *trouvères* alternates between fear of being cast out from joy in possession of the lady and ardor in expectation of that possession ("Style and Expressive Register in Medieval Poetry," in *Literary Style: A Symposium*, ed. and in part trans. Seymour Chatman [London: Oxford University Press, 1971], 263–81).

40. See Anselm, prayer 10 to St. Paul, quoted in Caroline Walker Bynum, *Jesus as Mother: Studies in the Spirituality of the High Middle Ages* (Berkeley and Los Angeles: University of California Press, 1982), 114 and 118.

41. See Richard Rolle, "A Talking of the Love of God," in *Later Medieval English Prose*, ed. William Matthews (New York: Appleton, 1963), 132. See also J. W. Blench, *Preaching*

Like the *Consolation*, romance too stylizes argument. The knight's somnambulistic awareness of the supernatural sets him apart from the earthly world, giving a ghostly resonance to his words.[42] Through him both the darkness and the light speak in oracles. The interior "pendulations" of his mind are like light reflected from water onto a wall; they tell a powerful story, yet the source is somewhere else, not perceptible to the human senses and not describable in human speech.[43] Still, belief in "a source" promises the comprehensibility of the world's turbulence; there is, somewhere, a "better telling."[44] The devices by which romance narrators authorize themselves—Malory's French book, a story told long ago, the dream vision—are witnessing signs of a consultation with the oracle, which can "explain fully" because it never degenerates ("loses its kind") to human speech. Wandering knights have to talk, but the truth can just "be."[45]

---

in England in the Late Fifteenth and Sixteenth Centuries: A Study of Engli-h Sermons 1450–c.1600 (Oxford: Basil Blackwell, 1964), 115.

42. Jameson has emphasized the uncomprehending quality of the romance hero, preferring to call attention to his bewilderment in opposition to Frye's emphasis on his power over his environment (*The Political Unconscious*, 113). But it is more accurate to say that the hero's powers come to him unconsciously than to diminish Frye's correct emphasis on his somewhat magical power over his environment. Further, Jameson's example of Stendahl's Fabrice del Dongo is complicated by the context of a nineteenth-century novel, where fallen aristocratic materialists can only highlight the bewilderment of Fabrice by contrast.

43. Auerbach uses "pendulations" to describe the interior monologue of Peter as he debates whether or not to acknowledge Christ (*Mimesis: The Representation of Reality in Western Literature*, trans. Willard R. Trask [Princeton: Princeton University Press, 1953], 42); in *Dante: Poet of the Secular World*, he attributes this word to Adolf Harnack (181 n. 10). On the various "pendulations" of romance, see Parker, *Inescapable Romance*, 138–49. Eugène Vinaver emphasizes the interiorization of experience in chivalric romance in *The Rise of Romance* (Oxford: Oxford University Press, 1971).

44. "The authoritative word is located in a distanced zone, organically connected with a past that is felt to be hierarchically higher. . . . Its authority was already *acknowledged* in the past. It is a *prior* discourse. . . . It is given (it sounds) in lofty spheres, not those of familiar contact" (Bakhtin, "Discourse in the Novel," 342).

45. Frye characterizes the romance also as a narrative that is always trying to get on top of itself, to find the full explanation, a "symbolic spread" (Northrop Frye, *The Secular Scripture: A Study of the Structure of Romance* [Cambridge: Harvard University Press, 1976], 50 and 59). "Everything we see or read about is part of a wider canvas, of a work still unwritten, a design still unfulfilled" (Eugène Vinaver, "Form and Meaning in Medieval Romance," Presidential Address of the Modern Humanities Research Association 1966 [Leeds, 1966], 15; quoted in Bloomfield, "Episodic Motivation and Marvels," 107). On romance in general, see also Frye, *Anatomy of Criticism*, 186–203 and passim; and John E. Stevens, *Medieval Romance: Themes and Approaches* (London: Hutchinson University Library, 1973).

The stylization of argument in the processional alternation of prose and verse in the *Consolation* is paralleled in romance by a steadiness of narration. Riding a tide, the hero moves forward almost in spite of his actions. The same resolute calm occurs in the slow pace of works in verse, didactic or narrative: Boccaccio's *Teseida*, Chaucer's *Troilus and Criseyde*, Hoccleve's *Regiment of Princes*, Sackville and Norton's *Mirror for Magistrates*, and Spenser's *Faerie Queene*. This processional steadiness appears also in the formulaic praise-and-request of the *orationes* of the mass, in the announcement of the participants at a tourney in Malory, in the organization of the stanzas in Spenser's "Epithalamion" around the hours of the day, and, in prose narratives, in the tonal impassivity of parataxis. The parallelism of a Petrarchan sonnet's first, fifth, and ninth lines predicts the closure of a very old story. The conflict between bodily and spiritual love does not belong to Petrarch as an individual but instead to the community of fallen creatures. Petrarch's spiritual conflict is all the more mournful and yet all the more predictable as one bound to end in disillusionment: "Che quanto piace al mondo è breve sogno."

Of all the myriad ways that romance combines emotional overflow and impassivity, panic and reassurance, the most crucial is the paradox in the representation of nature, a paradox realized at many different levels. One face of nature is the oracle from another world, like "Dame Nature," who gives her "doom" at the end of Spenser's "Two Cantos of Mutabilitie." This nature, when she enters the world, is sphinxlike: the Lady of the Lake who gives Arthur his sword, the Fisher King who first appears to Perceval as an actual fisherman, the lady who tells Balin he will kill his own brother, the three drops of blood on the snow that absorb Perceval in reverie.

But Nature has another face, this one not aloof from human life. After all, she knows human beings so well that she created a perfect environment for their pleasure and satisfaction:

> The flowery year
> Breathes odours in the spring
> The scorching summer corn doth bear,
> The autumn fruit from laden trees doth bring.
> The falling rain
> Doth winter's moisture give.
> These rules thus nourish and maintain
> All creatures which we see on earth to live.
> (*Consolation*, 4.M.6)

The blessedness of nature in its near aspects enables the easy allegorization by many medieval writers of the biblical *Song of Songs*, itself a paradigmatic "poetics of the familiar-near-and-majestic-far." The mysterious oracles of remote nature can also be friendly helpers: hermits in the *Queste* who suddenly appear to comfort, heal, and explain, the lion who helps Chrétien's Yvain in the hunt, the weasel in Marie de France's *Eliduc* who knows the resuscitative powers of herbs. Spenser's scary Dame Nature has another side in the personified figures of the months, all carrying the implements of agricultural labor: a spade, bag of seeds, scythe, ploughshare, coulter, hatchet.

A poetics of the familiar-near-and-majestic-far does not need the various stylistic and generic differentiations of classical rhetorical theory. Comic rejoicing is dignified as well as happy, in fact, dignified *because* it is happy. The languor of Malory easily becomes jolliness:

> And thus it passed on from Candlemas until after Easter, that the month of May was come, when every lusty heart beginneth to blossom and to burgeon. For, like as trees and herbs burgeoneth and flourisheth in May, in like wise every lusty heart that is any manner of lover springeth, burgeoneth, buddeth, and flourisheth in lusty deeds. For it giveth unto all lovers courage, that lusty month of May, in something to constrain him to some manner of thing more than in any other month, for divers causes: for then all herbs and trees reneweth a man and woman, and in like wise lovers calleth to their mind old gentleness and old service, and many kind deeds that was forgotten by negligence. . . .[46]

> So it befell in the month of May, queen Guenevere called unto her ten knights of the Table Round, and she gave them warning that early upon the morn she would ride on maying into woods and fields besides Westminster: "And I warn you that there be none of you but he be well horsed, and that ye all be clothed all in green, other in silk other in cloth. And I shall bring with me ten ladies, and every knight shall have a lady by him. And every knight shall have a squire and two yeomen, and I will that all be well horsed." (79)

---

46. Sir Thomas Malory, *The Morte Darthur: Parts Seven and Eight*, ed. D. S. Brewer, York Medieval Texts (Evanston: Northwestern University Press, 1972), 78. On the "languor" of Malory, see I. A. Gordon, *The Movement of English Prose* (London: Longmans, 1966), 67.

The society of the Round Table exults in its assurance that nature will purge any future invading organisms and restore fertility. Romance and comedy both have an obvious wish fulfillment and patterns of rebirth and reconciliation. In Shakespeare's *Much Ado About Nothing*, Messina casts out Don John, and in *Twelfth Night*, Illyria casts out Malvolio. When romance and comedy combine, reverence gives way to a dance of celebration. It is the formal display of figures promising rescue from turbulence combined with the intimacy of the folk that made the Tudor royal pageants so successful.

Majesty and intimacy: if home is creation itself and knights, squires, and yeomen belong to it, why differentiate styles? This is of course Auerbach's great thesis in *Literary Language and Its Public in Late Latin Antiquity*, in which he showed how the ancient separation of styles collapsed into the *genus humile et sublime*.[47] In *Mimesis*, Auerbach pursued his thesis with narratives. But it is equally well applied at a level at once more superficial and more basic. The *genus humile et sublime* not only endowed the simple man with tragedy, it also packed his speech with wisdom. The most obvious form of this sublime simplicity is the proverb (see *Consolation*, 1.M.6). The discursive political sagacity of the classics, sustained logically from sentence to sentence, paragraph to paragraph, is minced into bits, more digestible to an oral culture for whom agricultural activity is not nearly so far away as it is for the classical rhetorician. The proverb voices the wisdom of the ages: in the refrains of Lydgate's *Fall of Princes*, in Spenser's *Faerie Queene*, in Dogberry's comparison between a woman hearing her baby cry and a ewe hearing her lamb bae (*Much Ado About Nothing*, 3.3.65–66), and in the rhyming proverbs in the mouth of Lear's fool. In collections like the *Distichs of Cato* and the *Dicts and Sayings of the Philosophers*, the sayings acquire the oracular *auctoritas* of a historical past that has been absorbed in custom and nature.

In vernacular romances, the blurring of the levels of style is most obvious in diction. In Lydgate's Marian poems, as in Malory, a hypnotic evenness of stress diminishes the foreignness of polysyllables.[48] In the "Ave Regina Celorum," divine language puri-

---

47. Erich Auerbach, *Literary Language and Its Public in Late Latin Antiquity and in the Middle Ages*, trans. Ralph Manheim, Bollingen Series 74 (New York: Random House, Pantheon Books, 1965), 27–66. Although in book 4 of *On Christian Doctrine*, Augustine still holds to a separation of styles, his insistence that the Christian message can be stated in a simple style that elevates the lowliest of subjects effectively collapses classical decorum. See also Auerbach's discussion of the Gospel of Mark in the chapter "Fortunata" in *Mimesis*, 40–49.

48. When in the great joust of the "Lady Day of the Assumption" in "The Fair Maid

fies a folkish one, and a folkish language naturalizes a divine one.[49] Phrases like "O Rosa marina," "Tetragramaton," and "ut castitas lilium" sit quite comfortably next to "fostryd lying in thy lappe," and "sleyghty trappe." Although in the witty game of love, a courtly poet may self-consciously employ his "polished" and "ornate" diction, as Caxton calls aureate words,[50] part of his poetic power is to capture the whispering of an oracle. To us with Enlightenment talkiness in our heads, it is a rich fugue of lyric elegance and vatic nature.[51]

Or, on the other side, a rich fugue of vatic nature and her homely representatives. Bottom's vision at the end of act 4 of *A Midsummer Night's Dream* is a ceremonially comic oracle:

> I have had a most rare vision. I have had a dream past the wit of man to say what dream it was: man is but an ass, if he go about to expound this dream. Methought I was—there is no

---

of Astolat," the wounded Lancelot "at the last . . . sank down upon his arse and so swooned down, pale and deadly" (54–55), the word "arse" is not a descent in diction. On Malory's colloquial style, see P. J. C. Field, *Romance and Chronicle: A Study of Malory's Prose Style* (Bloomington: Indiana University Press, 1971). On the ceremony of Malory, see the introduction of D. S. Brewer to his edition of *The Morte Darthur*. According to Walter F. Schirmer, "under the influence of Latin hymnody, [Lydgate] seeks to bring about a reinvigoration of the invocatory style. . . . Zealous emulation of the Latin authors makes his style ornate with invocations until it is as heavy and stiff as rich brocade" (*John Lydgate: A Study in the Culture of the XVth Century*, trans. Ann E. Keep [Berkeley and Los Angeles: University of California Press, 1961], 197). Derek Pearsall notes the same hypnotic languor in Lydgate's prose. He describes the narrative of the "Legend of St. Giles" as "something between invocation and prayer" and also as "rhapsody and celebration"; he calls the "Life of Our Lady" an "enormously prolonged Marian hymn" that draws on the meditations of pseudo-Bonaventure (*John Lydgate* [Charlottesville: University Press of Virginia, 1970], 279 and 285).

49. "Ave Regina Celorum," in *The Minor Poems of John Lydgate*, ed. Henry Noble MacCracken, early English Text Society, 107 (London: Kegan Paul, 1911), 292. In the "Balade in Commendation of our Lady," Lydgate mixes aureation ("clennest condite of vertu soverayne," "Crystallyn welle, of clennesse cler consigned," "Fructif olyve," "redolent cedyr," "vinarye envermailyd") with "lusty leem[yng]," "oure lyfis leche," "braunchelet," and "Blisful bawm-blossum" (John Lydgate, *John Lydgate: Poems*, ed. John Norton-Smith [Oxford: Clarendon Press, 1966]), 25–29. Derek Pearsall points out that the golden Latinate words in such phrases as "clennest condite of vertu soverayne," "vinarye envermailyd" are virtual transliterations of words from the *Anticlaudianus* of Alain de Lille (*John Lydgate*, 270).

50. William Caxton, preface to *Eneydos*, in *Caxton's Own Prose*, ed. N. F. Blake (London: André Deutsch, 1973), 80.

51. The leveling of diction in a ceremonial mode creates effects similar to those in ritual. Frye characterizes ritual as a "conscious waking act, but there is always something sleepwalking about it: something consciously being done, and something else unconsciously meant by what is being done" (*Secular Scripture*, 55).

man can tell what. Methought I was, —and methought I had, —but man is but a patched fool, if he will offer to say what methought I had. The eye of man hath not heard, the ear of man hath not seen, man's hand is not able to taste, his tongue to conceive, nor his heart to report, what my dream was.

Groping for a supernatural language ("Methought I was, —and methought I had"), Bottom becomes the vessel for divine speech, even if it is a mangled version of 1 Corinthians. Shakespeare's judgment that this soliloquy could decorously close the fourth act's visionary sequence depends upon a long heritage of the imperfect differentiation between the silly and the solemn.

So far I have emphasized the sensuousness of a ceremonial prose argument, an argument that makes morality an amoral comfort. But the moral genres of meditation, complaint, and homily are easily absorbed into the parallel tracks of panic and reassurance. The meditation is latent in the *Consolation*.[52] "Boethius" is not a character; he should not be novelized. Instead he is a crystallization of a genre, of the meditation's downward spiral to despair and plea for salvation, in the same way that Rosalind in *As You Like It* is the wit of a *débat* set in motion and Bottom is a crystallization of the blessed laborer. Like the romance hero or like Dante in *The Divine Comedy*, "Boethius's" experience is the spiritual journey of the group localized in one figure.

The *Consolation* also includes homily. Philosophia argues urgently for Boethius's conversion.[53] Her goal is to cast out his human understandings and to replace them with divine simplicity. She does not persuade him to reflect on his views and then to alter them, so much as to exorcise them from his consciousness. In the same way that homiletic speech is a purification of false understanding, so also are gardens, ports, and harbors exorcisms of worldly confusion.[54] Exorcism as the reverse side of a ceremonial mode's sweet suasion is suggested in Augustine. When he persuades the people of Caesarea

52. On complaint in the Middle Ages and Renaissance, see John Desmond Peter, *Complaint and Satire in Early English Literature* (Oxford: Clarendon Press, 1956).

53. See Jonathan V. Crewe's analysis of Nashe's *Christ's Tears Over Jerusalem* as the obsessive need to punish, in *Unredeemed Rhetoric: Thomas Nashe and the Scandal of Authorship* (Baltimore: Johns Hopkins University Press, 1982), 55–64, esp. 60–63.

54. On the garden as exorcism in pastoral literature, see Richard B. Young, "English Petrarke: A Study of Sidney's *Astrophel and Stella*," in *Three Studies in the Renaissance: Sidney, Jonson, Milton*, Yale Studies in English 128 (New Haven: Yale University Press, 1958), 12.

not to fight a civil war, he is grateful that evil has been cast out: "When I saw [their tears], I believed that the terrible custom handed down by their fathers and grandfathers and from still more remote times, which had besieged their hearts like an enemy, or rather taken them, had been overcome, even before the victory had been demonstrated" (*On Christian Doctrine*, 4.24). Classical *vituperatio* has been changed into a rite of initiation.[55]

When Philosophia turns away from homiletic engagement to a lament for the *terrena animalia* condemned to blindness and ignorance, she utters a complaint:

> Alas, how ignorance makes wretches stray
> Out of the way!
> You from green trees expect no golden mines
> Nor pearls from vines. . . .
> But when they come their chiefest good to find,
> Then they are blind,
> And search for that under the earth, which lies
> Above the skies.
> How should I curse these fools? Let thirst them hold
> Of fame and gold,
> That, having got false goods with pain, they learn
> True to discern.
> (*Consolation*, 3.M.8)

The song of homily-and-complaint alternately strains for the goal and anticipates failure: human beings must be corrected and yet, because of the Fall, they are incorrigible. The combination of homiletic urgency to reform and elegiac renunciation of success is at the heart of Langland's *Piers Plowman*.

Ceremony and the Control of Deviance

The "funnel effect" of a ceremonial discourse easily transfers to authoritarian politics. To constitute the resister to truth as irrational and at the same time to whip up fear and hope, legitimize rulers as

55. Brian Vickers emphasizes the strong influence of epideictic oratory on medieval literature, stronger than the influence of forensic or deliberative rhetoric, in "Epideictic and Epic in the Renaissance," *New Literary History* 14 (1983): 497–537, esp. 501–2.

parental protectors. Without them, life is an assault from every
direction (see the martial metaphors and the castle in the *Consolation*,
1.Pr.3). The amoral distinction between inside and outside of Philosophia's embrace or inside and outside the feudal lord's castle is a strong
enforcer of the sometimes moral opposition between friend and foe:
"This cannot be evil if it makes me feel so safe." By painting loss of the
political body as loss of nourishment, loss of warmth, loss of security,
a ceremonial discourse enforces loyalty by mixing deference to
nobility with nostalgia for the protected world of the child.

Authority is insulated from criticism by representing the human
consciousness in relational terms, denying its individual autonomy
distinct from the corporate whole. Identity lies in how closely one is
united or exiled from the body of truth. The dispersion of causation
over the romance landscape accounts not only for its "strangely active
and pulsating vitality" in Fredric Jameson's phrase,[56] but also for the
inability of the hero to imagine stepping outside the patterns of
flickering reflections and analyzing them as effects with a specifiable
cause. The hero has no powers of his own; they come and go
mysteriously with changes in his environment.[57] Similarly, rather
than a tool for devising answers to questions he himself has posed,
his language is as much a given, and as little changeable, as one of his
limbs.

Authority is most effectively obscured, however, by a ceremonial
discourse's great communal myth. Obviously, the *Consolation*'s being
written in Latin ties it to a manuscript culture of the highly educated,
who preserved a scholarly dialect against the "natural" development
of Latin into the various Romance languages. Nevertheless, this
scholar still has a fantasy of communalism. The *Consolation*'s natural
metaphors argue that the truth can be perceived by unsophisticated
human faculties. In performing the seasonal activities of planting and

---

56. Jameson, *The Political Unconscious*, 112.

57. Jameson calls the romance hero a "registering apparatus for transformed states of
being, sudden alterations of temperature, mysterious heightenings, local intensities,
sudden drops in quality, and alarming effluvia, in short, the whole semic range of
transformation scenes whereby, in romance, higher and lower worlds struggle to
overcome each other" (*The Political Unconscious*, 112). This is a more potent explanation
of the apparent "individuality" of the spiritual or romance hero than those advanced
by Colin Morris in *The Discovery of the Individual 1050–1200* (1972; repr. Toronto:
University of Toronto Press, 1987) or by Robert W. Hanning in *The Individual in
Twelfth-Century Romance* (New Haven: Yale University Press, 1977). To say, as Hanning
does, that the concern of the chivalric romances with love is evidence of their concern
with individuality, because "love in its very nature is the private relationship par
excellence" (53), is to assume a universalized conception of love.

harvesting, the farmer participates with Nature and the Good (see *Consolation*, 1.Pr.6; 3.M.1). This is a comforting thought in an age when very few could read and write. It is also a comforting thought for the powerful. The trick of obscuring authority by locating it in simple people was noted by Empson in *The Second Shepherds' Play*, where the "humorous thieves" are "fundamental symbols of humanity."[58] Similarly, it is Dogberry who restores order to *Much Ado*'s Messina; it is Bottom who knows that "a most rare vision" protects the midsummer dreamers. Happily, the confused pursuits of human beings do not require kings for their resolution. In fact, when the commonwealth is in tumult and the monarch's body is itself disappearing, laborers are a substitute for the kingly hand of calm because through them, nature herself speaks. The gardeners of Shakespeare's *Richard II* know that Richard's demise and Boling-broke's usurpation are subsumed in the turning of the seasons.

There are two genres that might challenge ceremony's claim to absolute meaning. The *débat* stands aside from ceremony's pull toward a central body of truth, happily playing with mere possibility. Similarly, the literature of the carnival seems to attack ceremony simply by laughing at it. In Bakhtin's view, the carnivalesque is an important source of resistance to absolute power in the Middle Ages.[59] Both of these interpretations depend upon assessments of the power of institutions. At court, the absolute power of the feudal lord may neutralize debate as a prethreshold game preliminary to a dissolution into a truer body.[60] As long as attacks on ceremonial solemnity do not have institutional supports or are not uttered by men conceivably able to take power, they can be treated as entertainment or safely ignored. As a source of criticism within court that the court allows, the fool's criticism is tied to the powers of the lord, just as the mockery in the Feast of Asses is contained by the authority of the church.[61] The potential for folkishness to naturalize a ceremonial

58. William Empson, *Some Versions of Pastoral* (Norfolk, Conn.: New Directions, 1960), 26.

59. Bakhtin discusses the language of the folk in "Discourse of the Novel" and also in *Rabelais and His World*, trans. Hélène Iswolsky (Cambridge: MIT Press, 1968).

60. For a study of chivalric romance as a constant extension of the threshhold, see Parker, *Inescapable Romance*, 54–64.

61. "Since it [folk laughter] is securely framed off from everyday life, it can serve the function of isolating that sense of relativity in a safe place: now, and only now, may you laugh fearlessly . . . ," Gary Saul Morson, "Who Speaks for Bakhtin?: A Dialogic Introduction," *Critical Inquiry* 10 (1983): 237. The framing of folk language enables its

language often complicates interpretation, especially of parody. Although Bakhtin recognizes this difficulty, he is sure that there is parody in the French prayer: "Our father, you are not foolish, because you are placed in grand repose, you who are mounted high in the heavens."[62] But the prayer may in fact express relief that the divine father exists apart from the follies of human life. Comedy is often a release from solemnity without being a release from authority.

The "communalism" of a ceremonial discourse is an aristocratic fantasy. In the tripartite scheme of knights, monks, and "the rest," oracular beggars and maidens and dwarfs are not only vessels of a superhuman truth but also something not nearly so esteemed: *laboratores*, rustics, *servi*, peasants, the poor.[63] The problem, however, is not resolved after pointing out that a ceremonial discourse's communal story was a myth or that it was immensely useful to the legitimation of the upper class. One difficulty still remains: How much self-consciousness can we properly attribute to the aristocracy's "use" of this myth? Some literary historians portray Queen Elizabeth as the master rhetorician, fully aware of, indeed relishing, the power of Petrarchan fictions to tame restive courtiers.[64] But who knows, really, how much Elizabeth was conscious of? Peter Burke has argued that there was in fact something like a "communal story" in the culture of early modern Europe. An educated elite, which knew the classics transmitted through formal education, shared a popular, oral tradition of common people and did not regard ballads and plays and festivals as "low."[65] The inevitable distinction prompted by the rise of printing between those who could read and those who could not did not affect this participation, Burke argues, until the seventeenth and eighteenth centuries: "[E]ducated people did not yet associate ballads and chap-books and festivals with the common people, precisely

---

reinforcement of dominant institutions; so also does its absorption into ceremony, which turns folkish laughter into happy satisfaction with the status quo.

62. "Epic and Novel," in *The Dialogic Imagination*, trans. Holquist and Emerson, 78.

63. Georges Duby, *The Three Orders: Feudal Society Imagined*, trans. Arthur Goldhammer (Chicago: University of Chicago Press, 1980), 81–109.

64. See Greenblatt, *Renaissance Self-Fashioning*, 167–69; Louis Adrian Montrose, "'Eliza, Queene of shepheardes,' and the Pastoral of Power," *ELR* 10 (1980): 155, 156, 157, 159, and "The Elizabethan Subject and the Spenserian Text," 309.

65. Peter Burke, *Popular Culture in Early Modern Europe* (1978; repr. New York: Harper and Row, 1983), 23–64.

because they participated in these forms of culture."[66] The Renaissance humanist's insistence that the aristocracy must learn to read suggests an aristocracy that could not. The pageants that the Tudors "used" so successfully to consolidate their power may not have been "used" at all but happily enjoyed by aristocrat as well as commoner.

The amount of self-consciousness we can properly attribute to nonaristocratic writers is no less difficult. Feste's detachment from the golden world of Illyria at the end of *Twelfth Night* invites us to think that Shakespeare was fully conscious of "the aristocracy" as a self-enchanted group unaware of its own obsolescence. In act 2, scene 4, Orsino calls for a song from Feste. Shakespeare makes it plain that Orsino is pleased by the song's old-fashionedness:

> Mark it, Cesario; it is old and plain.
> The spinsters and the knitters in the sun,
> And the free maids that weave their thread with bones,
> Do use to chant it. It is silly sooth,
> And dallies with the innocence of love,
> Like the old age.

This is practically a thumbnail sketch of a ceremonial mode: it is plain, it is sung by powerless people, and it is "silly." At the beginning of the scene, Orsino contrasts the song of "silly sooth" with current fashion in court songs, which have "recollected" (studied) words in them, characteristic of "these most brisk and giddy-paced times." In short, Shakespeare seems to have gone out of his way to give Orsino a helpless nostalgia. But is it accurate to say that Shakespeare intends his audience to regard Orsino as an otiose, absurd figure, a representative of an out-of-date aristocracy? I doubt it. Shakespeare's "position" is better characterized as a dramatic heightening of the storytelling tools he inherited from the Middle Ages, a heightening to which the stage tends to give a political edge but which stops short of a full-scale (i.e., fully conscious, fully articulate, fully prosaic) social analysis. Shakespeare makes Orsino's passion for songs of silly sooth seem a little foolish but at the same time insulates the pathos of the song from mockery.

Further, the accusation that those who have the powers of representation create fictions that diffuse political aggression can be leveled at virtually any religion or any organization claiming to be without

66. Ibid., 27. See also Stallybrass and White, *The Politics and Poetics of Transgression*, 1–26.

hierarchy. The putative "united spirit" of a community without "betters" (or elders, or knights, or managers) will always serve some members more than others, especially those who know how the community spirit might be threatened and what steps have to be taken to prevent splintering. When a leader seeks to maintain a community without hierarchy, his knowledge is a political liability as well as a political strength; anyone who "knows" can always be accused of silently making use of what he knows. And, the argument might well proceed, nobody who can use his knowledge is likely to refrain from doing so; to hold otherwise is to be naive. In short, there is a small step between figuring out how a spiritual discourse might work repressively and the claim that it always does work repressively. (But there is always the Foucauldian question: repressive compared to what?) Built into the small step is a large claim about the general truths of human nature: whatever people may say, they do not really love something else more than themselves. It gives one pause, however, that some of the movements that have extended political rights have been driven by religious fervor: the Puritans of seventeenth-century England, and, in the United States, the pre–Civil War Abolitionist movement and the civil rights movement of the 1960s. If criticism must be a mode of action, that action often takes its force from religious belief and derives its solidity as a political movement from organized religion, that is, religious institutions with hierarchy and spiritual leaders. It also gives one pause that many of the "voices" that will be heard after an antireligious rhetoric has demystified a repressive canon belong to people who "still" have religious beliefs.

2

Early Tudor Prose and
Civil History in Thomas More's
History of King Richard III

Civil and Ceremonial Theories
of History

It is a good thing for the reputation of the first generation of English humanists that Thomas More wrote his *Utopia*. Otherwise one would be hard-pressed to see how the study of the classics altered the way educated Englishmen assessed their culture. Because of the whimsicality of its fiction, however, even the *Utopia* loses in critical bite; the analysis of historically located institutions is diffused in a wish. Criticism of aristocratic power would have been more effective if, in Bacon's words, it had been "immersed in matter,"[1] immersed in historical contingencies. As an ideal belonging too much to everyone and too little to one people in particular, More's book cannot perform the moral suasion that is peculiar to historical narrative, a "know

---

1. Francis Bacon, *The Advancement of Learning*, in *The Works of Francis Bacon*, ed. James Spedding, Robert Leslie Ellis, and Douglas Denon Heath, 7 vols. (London: Longman, 1857–59), 3:445. All further references to Bacon's works will be to this edition unless otherwise noted.

thyself" in the first-person-plural hortative: "Let us, as we are now at this juncture in our history, come to know ourselves better."[2] For Hannah Arendt, this collective enterprise is successful when the historian balances a search for the truth with a rhetorical persuasion of the obligations that the truth demands:

> The conviction that everything that happens on earth must be comprehensible to man can lead to interpreting history by commonplaces. Comprehension does not mean denying the outrageous, deducing the unprecedented from precedents, or explaining phenomena by such analogies and generalities that the impact of reality and the shock of experience are no longer felt. It means, rather, examining and bearing consciously the burden which our century has placed on us—neither denying its existence nor submitting meekly to its weight. Comprehension, in short means the unpremeditated, attentive facing up to, and resisting of reality—whatever it may be.[3]

For Arendt, the burden of history in the modern world belongs to an educated, international community that must face the political realities of the twentieth century and resist them.

English historians in the sixteenth century could not afford to face political reality in the way Arendt urges. Representation of historical events was a risky business. Well known is Elizabeth's displeasure with the production of *Richard II* on the eve of Essex's rebellion. She later imprisoned John Hayward for writing a history that, she believed, put ideas in Essex's head. But it was not just a narrative of usurpation that made monarchs narrow their eyes. In the last scene of More's *History of King Richard III*, as Bishop Morton leads Buckingham on, he casually says, "I love not much to talk muche of princes."[4] The loud understatement of this phrase would be appreciated by many Tudor historians. In a Renaissance history, simply the kind of "talking

2. This enterprise could be described as Vergilian historical epic. As Voltaire argued in his *Essay on Epic Poetry*, history and epic are closely allied. See Lionel Gossman, "History and Literature: Reproduction or Signification," in *The Writing of History: Literary Form and Historical Understanding*, ed. Robert H. Canary and Henry Kozicki (Madison: University of Wisconsin Press, 1978), 3–39, esp. 10–13.

3. Hannah Arendt, *The Origins of Totalitarianism*, 2d ed. (Cleveland, Ohio: World, 1958), viii.

4. *The History of King Richard III*, in *The Yale Edition of the Complete Works of St. Thomas More*, ed. Richard S. Sylvester, 14 vols. (New Haven: Yale University Press, 1963–76), 2:92. (Hereafter, *Complete Works of St. Thomas More.*)

of princes," quite aside from the plot, could make an enormous difference. In the next century, James I condemned Raleigh's *History of the World* neither for lazy historical investigation (not enough use of primary sources) nor for its being a boring, unplotted chronicle but rather for its tone: it was "too saucy in censuring princes."[5] The historical truth was one thing; how it was told was another, and, apparently, no less important if the telling did not harmonize with a poetics of deference.

More's *History of King Richard III* is also "saucy" in its "talking of princes." This sauciness has its liabilities, not because it is too critical but because it is too ludic. In his discussion of Erasmus's *Praise of Folly*, H. A. Mason makes a serious charge: "At bottom neither More nor Erasmus knew what to do with the overflowing of their wit, or rather they were content to let it remain in the world of *play*."[6] To define the cultural status of the playfulness in More's *Richard III* will tell us much about the configurations of English humanism under the early Tudors, when it was a novel way of decking out the medieval pageants surrounding the court and also a way for educated men to sever the ceremonial nexus between servant and lord.

For advice on history writing, the early moderns had classical texts. Had the ancient rhetoricians known they were going to be read through ceremonial eyes, they might have slanted their advice quite differently. In order to persuade later chroniclers to slow down the steep ceremonial funnel to a First Mover and to linger a little longer on the complexity of secondary causes, they might have pointed out that only in a realm not subject to the mysteries of Fortune or God can human language become a tool for rhetorical deliberation. They might also have asked their pupil chroniclers if they really thought that a new king could make the whole world over, or if they thought the triumph over discord could ever be complete. They might have asked them to consider that the heart of Aristotelian *phronesis* is knowing how large a victory can be expected and a victory over what, and that perhaps human aspirations should be limited to what is likely to happen because something similar has happened in the past.[7]

5. John Chamberlain to Sir Dudley Carleton, 5 January 1614, in *The Chamberlain Letters: A Selection of the Letters of John Chamberlain Concerning Life in England from 1597 to 1626*, ed. Elizabeth McClure Thomson (New York: Putnam's, 1965), 195.

6. H. A. Mason, *Humanism and Poetry in the Early Tudor Period* (London: Routledge and Kegan Paul, 1959), 84.

7. For classical history as a pessimistic discourse, see Nancy S. Struever, *The Language*

Above all, classical rhetoricians might have discussed the necessary adjustments in a narrative history between particulars and the generalizations that categorize them. The usefulness of generalizations, they might have observed, is to "hold the particular down" in a humanly controlled world, preventing it from transubstantiating into an omen. Generalizations also develop the skill of identifying types of people, types of events, types of decisions. Classical rhetoricians might have observed that the handling of the particular strongly affects the kind of tale being told. Dionysius of Halicarnassus touches on this question in his treatise *On Thucydides*, when he complains that Thucydides did not start his history with the true cause of the Peloponnesian War (the growth of the Athenian state) but instead with the breaking of the truce between the Lacedaemonians and the Athenians.[8] But Thucydides might well have rejoined that his purpose was not simply to explain the causes of the war but to involve the reader in the complications of political decision-making, for which a narrative of particular events would be most effective.

All this advice might have prompted classical rhetoricians to re-phrase their characterization of history's relatively dispassionate tone compared to forensic rhetoric's energetic force. Instead, emphasizing its charm, they led later chroniclers to think that history and rhetoric are similar, not because both deal with contingency but because both are finely written. For the ancients, the historian can take liberties with diction that the rhetorician cannot (Quintilian, *Inst.* 10.2.16–17); his style can have an easy and flowing placidity (Cicero, *De Orat.* 2.15.62–64). For Quintilian, it can be as loose as song (*carmen solutum* [*Inst.* 10.1.31]), a phrase in which too much weight fell on the *carmen* and not enough on the *solutum*; history is a discourse whose purpose is to record events for posterity, and for such a celebratory goal, history needs to be literarily interesting and inspiring—in short, a good read. This is not what the ceremonial chronicler needed to hear, least of all a sixteenth-century chronicler newly enchanted with the rolling parallelism of Cicero. In distinguishing history from rhetoric by allying it with poetry, the classical treatises only reassured the

---

of History in the Renaissance: Rhetoric and Historical Consciousness in Florentine Humanism (Princeton: Princeton University Press, 1970), 38; and Leonard F. Dean, "Tudor Theories of History Writing," in *Michigan Contributions to Modern Philology* 1 (Ann Arbor: University of Michigan Press, 1947): 16.

8. Dionysius of Halicarnassus, *On Thucydides*, trans. W. Kendrick Pritchett (Berkeley and Los Angeles: University of California Press, 1975), 6–7.

ceremonial author that he could successfully imitate a "classical history" by injecting a strong rhythmical pulse into his sentences and by heightening his appeals to God's providence.

It is the "looseness" of *carmen solutum* that Quintilian should have emphasized for his future, postmedieval audience.[9] Compared to medieval chronicles, Livy's preface to the *History of Rome* is almost phlegmatic in its looseness, that is, in its relaxed acceptance of difference of opinion. (This is the history, we might remember, that Erasmus told Budé was always in the hands of More's students.[10]) Livy begins by parrying with possible objections: that the subject may be overworked, that historians generally are given to extravagant claims, that they are in love either with their facts or with their style, and that audiences may after all be tired of reading about the ancient past. Livy also debates the worth of myths as historical evidence and different accounts of Aeneas's founding of Rome. He wonders matter-of-factly if the vestal virgin's claim that Mars was the father of Romulus and Remus might have been an evasion of her own sexual transgression. Small logical connectors shift the attention to other possible interpretations of the facts: *utcumque erit* (however this may be), *praeterea* (besides), *contra* (on the other hand), *tamen* (nevertheless), and *adeo* (indeed). Finally, parenthetical asides diffuse the possible flamboyance of metaphors and the indignation at contemporary Roman morality. After saying that "riches have brought in avarice, and excessive pleasures the longing to carry wantonness and license to the point of ruin for oneself and of universal destruction," Livy pauses to reflect wryly on the customary reaction to moral lessons: "But complaints are sure to be disagreeable, even when they shall perhaps be necessary; let the beginning, at all events, of so great an enterprise have none."[11] Discussion, reconsideration, awareness

9. See Quintilian's discussion of rhythm in historical prose, *Institutes* 9.4.18. Quintilian passed on to the Renaissance his phrase "lactea ubertas" (*Inst.* 10.1.32) to describe Livy's style; when in the Ciceronian controversy Livy was distinguished from Sallust and Tacitus as being too smooth, as smooth as cream, the ways in which even Livy is *not* particularly charming and milky—the ways in which he too is *solutum*—were lost sight of. For Renaissance discussions of Livy's style, see Wesley Trimpi, *Ben Jonson's Poems: A Study of the Plain Style* (Stanford: Stanford University Press, 1962), 245-46.

10. *Opus Epistolarum, Desiderius Erasmi Roterodami*, ed. P. S. Allen and H. M. Allen, 10 vols. (Oxford: Clarendon Press, 1906–41), 4:577. On the popularity of Livy in the early sixteenth century, see Leonard F. Dean, "Literary Problems in More's *Richard III*," *PMLA* 58 (1943): 25.

11. Livy, *History of Rome*, trans. B. O. Foster (Loeb Classical Library; Cambridge: Harvard University Press, 1919), 1.12–13.

of an audience's resistance to an argument and of its distaste for the virulent moralist are all built into Livy's preface. However much Livy later "stories" the particulars of the Roman tradition, his ceremonial persuasions are always inflected against the civil voice established in this preface.

The same *solutum* of debate and discussion appears in Sallust's accounts of Catiline's conspiracy and the Jugurthine Wars. In the introductory matter to *The War with Jugurtha*, Sallust debates the relative merits of pursuing public office as opposed to the quiet activity of writing history. In marked contrast to the way such a question would be posed by sixteenth-century humanists, Sallust situates it in the political circumstances of his own time (3.1); while once it was honorable to seek public office, now such pursuits are neither safe nor honorable. Furthermore, Sallust justifies his choice of the Jugurthine Wars as a worthy historical subject, not because with these wars the whole world changed but because the Roman world changed, that is, the world of Sallust and his presumed reader. It was "the first time resistance was offered to the insolence of the nobles"[12] and the beginning of the struggles that ended in civil war for all of Italy.

Very few histories written in English in the sixteenth century show classical history's internalization of debate. Few Renaissance *theories* of history do any better. The two favorite formulations of history which we find time and again in the Renaissance are Dionysius's "philosophy teaching by example" and Cicero's *testis temporum, lux veritatis, vita memoriae, magistra vitae*, and *nuntia vetustatis*,[13] formulations probably beloved because they are so unexceptionable in light of history's alleged ability to teach anything and everything. Cicero's "definition" of *testis temporum, lux veritatis, vita memoriae, magistra vitae* and *nuntia vetustatis* has the appeal of surface elegance—alliteration, parallelism, chiasmus, musical cadence—and the susceptibility to being used allegorically. In the frontispiece to Raleigh's *History of the World* in 1614, these phrases are the columns that uphold "Good Fame" and "Bad Fame" under the eye (indeed, a very large eye) of all-seeing Providence.

The descriptions of history among the early humanists are vague

---

12. Sallust, *The War with Jugurtha*, trans. John C. Rolfe (Loeb Classical Library; London: Heinemann, 1920), 5.1.

13. *De Orat.* 2.9.36. On the exemplar theory of history, see George H. Nadel, "The Philosophy of History before Historicism," *History and Theory* 3 (1964): 291–315.

mainly because for them history is part of "classical literature" and all of it opposed to medieval barbarousness.[14] Leonardo Bruni, for instance, treats history first in a list of recommended classical texts. As a moral discourse for princes and citizens, history offers "foresight in contemporary affairs," "lessons of incitement or warning in the ordering of public policy," and "moral precepts."[15] By this definition, history differs little, as a moral discourse, from rhetoric; according to Bruni, one finds the virtues "warmly extolled" and the vices "fiercely decried" in classical oratory as well. For Sir Thomas Elyot, too, history is a catchall discourse. In *The Governour*, he lumps it with other kinds of texts from which one can learn morality and true facts: Theophrastus, Aristotle's works of natural philosophy, the Bible, and Homer, all of which give information and teach both government and morality.[16] Elyot's effort to save history as both a truth-telling genre and a moral one only produces trouble. History's truth, it turns out, is like the truth of Aesop's fables ("what forceth it us though Homere write leasinges?" [2:400]). But this argument undermines history as a

14. For the remarks of William Baldwin, Roger Ascham, Thomas Nashe, John Foxe, Francis Bacon, and Edmund Bolton on the barbarousness of medieval chronicles, see Herschel Baker, *The Race of Time: Three Lectures on Renaissance Historiography* (Toronto: University of Toronto Press, 1967), 73–79. Recent histories of Renaissance historiography look for the development of resemblances to modern historical scholarship. See F. Smith Fussner, *The Historical Revolution: English Historical Writing and Thought: 1580–1640* (New York: Columbia University Press, 1962); J. G. A. Pocock, *The Ancient Constitution and the Feudal Law* (Cambridge: Cambridge University Press, 1957); Donald R. Kelley, *Foundations of Modern Historical Scholarship: Language, Law, and History in the French Renaissance* (New York: Columbia University Press, 1970). In *Tudor Historical Thought* (San Marino, Calif.: Huntington Library, 1967), F. J. Levy gives much attention to histories that are by modern scholarship naive and crude; in the end, however, he sees the glory of historical scholarship in the sixteenth century emerging when it learns to criticize sources and to leave out the passion of politics (293–94).

Studies of history that accept Renaissance notions of history as teaching moral and political lessons appear in Tillyard, *Shakespeare's History Plays* (London: Chatto and Windus, 1964); and Lily B. Campbell, *Shakespeare's "Histories"; Mirrors of Elizabethan Policy* (San Marino, Calif.: Huntington Library, 1947). Neither Campbell nor Tillyard, however, analyzes the debt of the language in which Renaissance histories are written to medieval modes. Nor do they see any distinction in More's *Richard III* beyond its being dramatically lively (Tillyard, 39–40; Campbell, 64–67).

15. Leonardo Bruni, "Concerning the Study of Literature—A Letter Addressed to the Illustrious Lady Baptista Malatesta," in *Vittorino da Feltre and Other Humanist Educators*, ed. William Harrison Woodward (1897; repr. New York: Teachers College Press, 1963), 128.

16. Sir Thomas Elyot, *The Boke Named the Governour*, ed. Henry Herbert Stephen Croft, 2 vols. (1883; repr. New York: Burt Franklin, 1967), 2:383–401. All references to *The Governour* will be to this edition. For the elasticity of Renaissance definitions of history, see Levy, *Tudor Historical Thought*, 13ff.

special kind of moral suasion, because the same defense can be made of fiction (as indeed it is later in Sidney's *Defense of Poetry*). If history's stories do not have to be grounded in the constraints of what is possible because a similar event can be demonstrated to have happened in the past, then history can turn its back on the world in dreamy hopes. Elyot's argument that the counsels of Nestor, the persuasion of Ulysses, the gravity of Menelaus, and the courage of Hector can all teach service to the public weal does not keep history in the palpable world; without a historical location, the public weal is itself merely an *imago*, threatened with ironic degeneration when it once touches concrete events.

Although for Elyot history can teach government and hence by implication, political virtue, in this context political virtue becomes purity of heart, not the steady pragmatism of a civil mode. Purity of heart is certainly the moral benefit that Jacques Amyot attributes to the reading of history, as he explains in the preface to his translation of Plutarch.[17] Cicero's *testis, lux, vita, magistra*, and *nuntia* can be interpreted through the same filter and acquire a range of significances quite foreign to the classics. Thus, history's real force, as many early humanists describe it, lies in constituting the human actor as a devoted soul. It teaches the morality of loyalty to a code: the morality of duty, honor, allegiance, and ardor for the truth (in the knightly vein) and the morality of humility, wariness, and piety (in the Christian vein). This is history-as-romance, and its flurries of hope and terror effectively vitiate the balance of the celebration of human action and the acceptance of human limitations in Quintilian's *solutum*.

With some continental thinkers, however, history is more carefully separated from the didactic intentions of poetry to make men good in their consciences; it becomes instead practice in learning to negotiate with the world and control it.[18] In the fifteenth century, Lorenzo Valla

17. The historian should portray events so vividly that "we feele our mindes to be so touched by them, not as though the thinges were alreadie done and past, but as though they were even then presently in doing, and we finde our selves caried away with gladnesse and griefe through feare or hope, well neere as though we were then at the doing of them" ("Amiot to the Readers," in *Plutarch's Lives of the Noble Grecians and Romans*, trans. Thomas North, ed. W. E. Henley, 6 vols. [London: David Nutt, 1895–96], 1:17).

18. Elyot distinguishes between the language of Livy on the one hand and the more mature Caesar and Sallust on the other when he says that Caesar and Sallust should be left to the older reader because they do not interrupt or include any "variety" that

insists that history's "truth" is fidelity to actual historical occurrences, opposing Bartolommeo Facio's belief that history should show moral *dignitas*.[19] In the sixteenth century, Patrizi opposes lying sanctioned by the ultimate goal of history to teach a moral truth, as it is in Elyot, and instead requires that "truth" be lowered to actual occurrences.[20] History now requires a submission to the world in more realistic terms than romance. Bacon puts the change succinctly when he says that poetry "raises the mind and carries it aloft, accommodating the shows of things to the desires of the mind, not (like reason and history) buckling and bowing down the mind to the nature of things."[21]

Despite some traces of the old theory of history as holding up models for inspiration, Jean Bodin's *Method for the Easy Comprehension of History*, first published in 1566, represents an important effort to separate history from moral inspiration and reverence for God. Bodin pulls history out of "rhetoric" as the early Renaissance conceived of it, contemptuously dismissing those who rattle on about exordia, narrative, and the ornaments of words and sentences, dismissing also the rhetorical niceties of fictionalized speeches. Instead, Bodin insists that praise and vituperation belong to philosophy, not history.[22] For Bodin history is primarily a discussion, not a story. To write history or to read it is to enter into a dialogue with another rational mind. The historian assesses events one way; the reader of his history has the right to assess them another way and does so by assessing the historian's predisposition to prevaricate, to misinterpret, to exaggerate. Writers should not wonder at what they find in their sources, and readers should not embrace facts as marvels (44). Bodin praises Plutarch's use of the phrase "they say" because it keeps readers from

---

would "alleviate" the pain of study, as Livy does. But this is just a pedagogical note that echoes Quintilian's recommendation of Livy over Sallust as reading for boys (*Inst.* 2.5.19); elsewhere, Livy is praised for "utility" just as much as Caesar and Sallust (*The Governour*, 1:81–86).

19. Linda Gardiner Janik, "Lorenzo Valla: The Primacy of Rhetoric and the De-Moralization of History," *History and Theory* 12 (1973): 389–404.

20. Beatrice Reynolds, "Shifting Currents in Historical Criticism," *Journal of the History of Ideas* 14 (1953): 471–92.

21. Francis Bacon, *De Augmentis*, 2.13, in *The Works of Francis Bacon*, 4:316.

22. Jean Bodin, *Method for the Easy Comprehension of History*, trans. Beatrice Reynolds (New York: Columbia University Press, 1945), 14, 51, and 53. Bodin is still influenced by medieval cosmographies, which may teach the customs, institutions, religion, and language of various people, but their final truth is still God himself (24–25). In this way, Bodin likes big histories because they are filled with the plenitude of God.

"incautiously accredit[ing] the tale" (64). He urges readers to consider dispassionately Tacitus's condemnation of the Christians by taking into account the perspective of a non-Christian Roman writer (70). Bodin himself scoffs at Caesar's report that statues in Rome sweated at certain moments during the civil war (57), and he argues with Plutarch and other historians over the Roman custom of lending wives (64). In general, Bodin praises and himself demonstrates the relaxed skepticism toward marvels that Livy shows in wondering if the vestal virgin who bore Romulus and Remus claimed Mars as the father in order to hide her own guilt.[23]

Although there are few traces of the terms of the Ciceronian controversy in Bodin's essay, nevertheless he has typical anti-Ciceronian leanings. Significantly, however, Bodin acclaims the anti-Ciceronian heroes, Sallust and Tacitus, neither for better expressing the idiosyncrasies of an individual's experience, as Croll did, nor for better expressing the tensions of intellectual inquiry, "those athletic movements of the mind by which it arrives at a sense of reality" (Croll's phrase).[24] Rather he acclaims them for the moral qualities of negotiating soberly with the contingencies of circumstance for a political end. In comparison to Elyot's escalations of terror and hope, Bodin's praise of the styles he likes suggests a distinct lack of emotion: "austere," "sagacious," "unmoved," "serious," "equable." "Sagacious" and "austere" are the two he prefers. History's distinction is having thrust off a naive distrust of experience.[25] Those who write it should have had some experience in politics. Those who read it should have one of two ends. The first is political: to learn how to negotiate between their desires and the circumstances that constrain any action. The second is intellectual: in understanding other cultures, readers should regard skeptically the statements of any witness and at the same time not discredit a witness on all matters simply because they disagree with one account.[26]

23. Although in his *History of the World*, Raleigh treats the Bible as an incontrovertible source, he shows some inclination to weigh sources against each other (Dean, "Tudor Theories," 21).

24. Croll, "'Attic Prose' in the Seventeenth Century," in *Style, Rhetoric and Rhythm*, ed. J. Max Patrick et al., 67.

25. Bodin, 43. See Ascham's distrust of experience in *The Schoolmaster (1570)*, ed. Lawrence V. Ryan (Ithaca: published for The Folger Shakespeare Library by Cornell University Press, 1967), 50–52.

26. Bodin is willing to overlook Tacitus's contempt for Christians as a bias of his era. Historians' biases are to be regarded as "normal and discountable" and not "proof of . . . depravity" (Julian H. Franklin, *Jean Bodin and the Sixteenth-Century Revolution in*

Interesting is Bodin's reluctance to renounce completely history's celebratory purpose. Some historical narratives tell of the unfolding of justice, and justice is a good thing: "When the history of all countries has thus been learned, it remains for us to inquire into the deeds of the men who achieved fame through power, or by splendor and riches of their race, or finally by their valor and conspicuous talent" (24). For Bodin, the greatest valor and talent were shown by the Romans; he praises Plutarch not for intellectual acuity or completeness but for having written of the "the most illustrious peoples" (63). Finally, he praises Dionysius for choosing a subject truly noble: "What more divine and awe-inspiring could be said, when Roman justice is under consideration, than that it was decreed by some eternal law of nature never to perish, so that the control of states might be carried over from unjust possessors to just?" (63). The best history dovetails a celebration of human capacities for justice with a discussion of the events that either destroyed it or brought it about. This understanding of the historical enterprise is surprisingly close to Arendt's.

Early Tudor Prose

An English writer in the first half of the sixteenth century who proposed to write a civil history had a difficult problem. The medieval English prose that he inherited fell into three major categories: scientific and utilitarian (e.g., medical works translated by John of Trevisa) or philosophical (e.g., John Fortescue and Reginald Pecock) or ceremonial (e.g., chronicles, devotional writing, sermons, romances).[27] But there was no tradition of civil prose. In *The Governance of England*, John Fortescue depends heavily on scholastic argument.[28] In *The Repressor of Overmuch Blaming of the Clergy*,

---

the Methodology of Law and History [New York: Columbia University Press, 1963], 147).

27. A recent collection of essays announced by its editor as an "authoritative guide to a number of important authors and genres of Middle English prose" includes devotional writings, chronicle prose, sermon literature, romance, medical prose, and utilitarian and scientific prose. According to these authors, vernacular civil prose did not exist in the Middle Ages (*Middle English Prose: A Critical Guide to Major Authors and Genres*, ed. A. S. G. Edwards [New Brunswick: Rutgers University Press, 1984]).

28. For instance, Fortescue starts his argument about possible means of increasing

Reginald Pecock repeats rigid abstractions. Pecock is explicit about his procedure: for an argument to be "ful and formal and good," it should be philosophical, laid out with "logik bi ful faire and sure reulis."[29] Instead of adjusting to the intellectual inadequacies of his audience, Pecock feels he must combat them. He wishes a book about good argument were written in the mother tongue for the common people, "for thanne thei schulden therbi be putt from myche ruydness and boistosenes which thei han now in resonyng" (9). This is hardly a civil speaker's collaboration with others who speak his linguistic, social, and rhetorical standard. Indeed, if any English standard is developing in the fifteenth century, it is not a shared linguistic norm among educated men but rather one created by the administrative needs of court.[30]

The prologues and epilogues to the books that William Caxton printed at the end of the fifteenth century show the other side of the coin; where medieval prose is not philosophical, it is ceremonial. A ceremonial mode generates Caxton's choice of material, his elliptical and digressive manner of presenting it, and most of all the welter of emotion that his books evoke from him: confusion, despair, bewilderment, hope, ardor, and reverence. As in a ceremonial mode generally, the particular is infused with significances that provide stability in a mutable world. Aristocratic patrons are described as the only source of meaning in an incomprehensible flux.[31] Where the particular is not

---

the king's revenue with a universal definition of kinds of governments: *dominium regale* and *dominium politicum et regale*, a definition justified by citations to Aquinas, to the *Compendium Morale* of Roger of Waltham, and to Aegidius Romanus (*The Governance of England: Otherwise Called the Difference between an Absolute and a Limited Monarchy*, ed. Charles Plummer [Oxford: Clarendon Press, 1885], 110–11 and 173–75).

29. Reginald Pecock, *Repressor of Overmuch Blaming of the Clergy*, ed. Churchill Babington, in *Chronicles and Memorials of Great Britain and Ireland During the Middle Ages*, Rolls Series 19, 2 vols. (London: Longman, 1860), 1:9.

30. According to Wyld, a spoken standard does not exist until the sixteenth century (Henry Cecil Wyld, *A History of Modern Colloquial English* [New York: E. P. Dutton, 1920], 98–99). E. J. Dobson agrees ("Early Modern Standard English," in *Approaches to English Historical Linguistics*, ed. Roger Lass [New York: Holt, Rinehart and Winston, 1969], 419–39). John Hurt Fisher argues for the existence of a *written* standard in the fifteenth century, based on the documents from the court of Chancery. This written standard should be distinguished, he argues, from Wyld's, which was derived from literary sources ("Chancery and the Emergence of Standard Written English in the Fifteenth Century," *Speculum* 52 [1977]: 870–99). Malcolm Richardson sees the Chancery standard as originating specifically with Henry V ("Henry V, the English Chancery, and Chancery English," *Speculum* 55 [1980]: 726–50).

31. See the treatment of the Earl of Rivers in Caxton's prologue to the *Cordial* and of

interpreted through romance or homily, it is interpreted through the folk anecdote. In the prologues and epilogues generally, "subjects which could have given rise to a general discussion are treated in a practical, almost anecdotal, way."[32] For Caxton, prose may be free of the old alliterative tradition,[33] but, still allied both with gracefulness and spiritual ardor, it is chiefly a new courtly entertainment, as if it were a different meter.[34] When Caxton is not writing prose ceremony, he uses the law. A servant-printer defers to a worshipful aristocrat in the language of the court recorder, as in the prologue to *King Arthur*.[35]

Much English humanist prose of the early sixteenth century is still in the effusive, heraldic vein of Caxton. Elyot's *Governour* frequently figures as a prime example of early humanist assimilation of classical texts, largely because of the use of classical terms for government (*res publica*) and classical exempla. It is true that Elyot discusses some matters with intellectual detachment. He first introduces "magnanimity," defines it, and then comments:

---

the dead Earl of Worcester in the Epilogue to the *Declamation of Noblesse* (*Caxton's Own Prose*, ed. Blake, 71 and 125).

32. N. F. Blake, "Caxton's Language," *Neuphilologische Mitteilungen* 67 (1966): 122–32, esp. 127.

33. N. F. Blake, "Caxton and Courtly Style," *Essays and Studies*, n.s. 21 (1968): 29–45.

34. See the noticeable failure to distinguish prose from poetry in the prologue to the *Distichs of Cato* and in the epilogue to book 2 of the *History of Troy* (*Caxton's Own Prose*, ed. Blake, 63–66 and 99–100).

35. "Thenne to procede forth in thys sayd book whyche I dyrecte unto all noble prynces, lordes and ladyes, gentylmen or gentylwymmen, that desyre to rede or here redde of the noble and joyous hystorye of the grete conquerour and excellent kyng, Kyng Arthur, somtyme kyng of thys noble royalme thenne callyd Brytaygne, I Wyllyam Caxton, symple persone, present thys book folowyng whyche I have enprysed t'enprynte; and treateth of the noble actes, feates of armes of chyvalrye, prowesse, hardynesse, humanyte, love, curtosye and veray gentylnesse, wyth many wonderful hystoryes and adventures" (*Caxton's Own Prose*, ed. Blake, 109). Compare a fifteenth-century petition: "Besecheth mekely youre humble liege Andrew Ogard knight, that where as by succession there is fallen unto him in the reaume of Denmark where he is born and in other places of the King of Denmarks obeissance, certaine lifloode and landes and other goods meubles, plese hit your highnesse to shewe unto youre saide liege that he may have knowlache if it bee the good plesour of your excellence that he joysse the saide enherytance and other goods and theruppon send into the said reaume of Denmark and other places his procurours for him with suffisant pour to obteine possession and joyssance of the said enheritance and other goods and to doo the services and duetez required therupon, after the lawes of the cuntrees, whiche thing how be hit the saide Kinge of Denmark is of your alliance, yit the saide besecher wol not in noo wise attempte nor doo hit withouten your gracius licence in that partie" ("Petition to the King," 14 March, 23 Henry VI, 1445, *Proceedings and Ordinances of the Privy Council of England*, ed. Sir Harris Nicolas, 7 vols. [London: G. Eyre and A. Spottiswoode, 1834–37], 6:38).

> But nowe I remembre me, this worde Magnanimitie beinge yet straunge, as late borowed out of the latyne, shall nat content all men, and specially them whome nothing contenteth out of their accustomed Mumpsimus, I will adventure to put for Magnanimitie a worde more familiar, callynge it good courage, whiche, hauynge respecte to the sayd definition, shall nat seme moche inconvenient.[36]

"Their accustomed Mumpsimus" is the conservative fondness for a garbled *sumpsimus* from the Latin mass. Immediately after this passage, Elyot turns to Aristotle's discussion of "magnanimity." To adopt new ways of expression from the Latin is to move the discussion beyond traditional clichés.

But such passages are rare in *The Governour*. As with Caxton, Elyot has difficulty rising to a level of generalization that might permit him to discuss particulars rather than celebrate them or relate them anecdotally. The "good things" that Elyot hopes to instill in his young pupils are treated as if they were concrete particulars, even when they are not. Like a good lord, the virtues are harbors of refuge in a mutable world and clothed in superlatives: "Of the most excellent Vertue named Justyce," "Of what excellence benevolence is," "Of the noble vertue Fortitude." "Placabilitie . . . undoubtedly is a vertue wonderfull excellent." Wise men too are treasures: the "noble philosopher and moste excellent oratour, Tullius Cicero" (2:351); the "very delectable" orations in Tacitus (1:90); the "incomparable swetenes" of Xenophon (1:84); the "incomparable swetnesse of wordes and mater . . . in the saide warkes of Plato and Cicero; wherin is joyned gravitie with dilectation, excellent wysedome with divine eloquence, absolute vertue with pleasure incredible, and every place is so infarced [stuffed] with profitable counsaile, joyned with honestie, that those thre bokes be almoste sufficient to make a perfecte and excellent governour" (1:93–94). Elyot's descriptions are fervid or fearful. In reading Homer "reders shall be so all inflamed, that they most fervently shall desire and coveite, by the imitation of their [the heroes'] vertues, to acquire semblable glorie" (1:59). If grammar is introduced too soon in a child's education, it will kill "the sparkes of fervent desire of lernynge," which should be the fruit of "the most swete and pleasant redinge of olde autours" (1:55). Even when he wants to reflect on a virtue rather than praise it, Elyot slips from discussion into praise and horror (see

36. *The Governour*, 2:288–89.

the treatment of "Placabilitie," 2:55). A virtue is a paradisiacal refuge from monsters (2:92).

The fear and despair of this prose undermine the collaboration of associates on a political problem. In arguing the necessity for kings and magistrates, Elyot laments the chaos that would follow without them: "O what mysery was the people than [*sic*] in; O howe this most noble Isle of the world was decerpt and rent in pieces" (1:22). He cries out in prayerful perplexity at the end of book 1: "O mercifull god, howe longe shall we be mockers of our selfes? Howe longe shall we skorne at our one calamitie?" (1:303). When at the end of *The Governour*, he groans, "Suerly I am in more drede of the terrible vengeaunce of god, than in hope of amendement of the publike weale" (2:256–58), he is acquiescing to the old suspicion of complaint that it is better to be afraid of evil than to "collude" with it by understanding it. *The Governour* is a series of medieval "dicts" amplified by exclamations of wonder, admiration, and despair from a good servant who wishes to inspire devotion and obedience.

In Cavendish's *Life of Wolsey* (written between 1554 and 1557), the particular is still storied by romance and homily. Wolsey is lauded in lavish descriptions, as in the dinner for the French ambassadors at Hampton Court, which lingers with a Malory-like relish over the details of knightly accoutrements.[37] But once Wolsey has fallen, Cavendish switches his allegiance to a higher Lord, and Wolsey is homiletically displayed as a deluded man who forgot his place: "Here is the end and fall of pride and arrogancy of such men, exalted by Fortune to honor and high dignities; for I assure you in his time of authority and glory he was the haultest man in all his proceedings that then lived" (186). Wolsey either enjoys solid ontological status in creation or disappears into an omen.

At a moment ripe for civil discussion, Cavendish's habits of thought demonstrate the tendency of a ceremonial mode to fly from the particular to an abstraction. He wants to defend Wolsey against the complaints of commoners, but instead of describing his talents as an administrator, Cavendish reviles "commoners" generally (a "wavering and newfangled multitude") on behalf of "lords" generally and laments the necessity for "governors." "Wolsey" dissolves into an abstraction forced on a fallen world: "And yet such ministers must be, for if there should be no ministers of justice, the

---

37. George Cavendish, *The Life and Death of Cardinal Wolsey*, in *Two Early Tudor Lives*, ed. Richard S. Sylvester and Davis P. Harding (New Haven: Yale University Press, 1962), 75–76.

world should run full of error and abomination and no good order kept ne quietness among the people" (104–5). As in Elyot, Cavendish's chief response is resignation. The common people will complain and magistrates will be corrupt. Ceremony's appeal to chaos as the terrifying Other, here used to justify magistrates and implicitly to defend Wolsey, is not a defense of hierarchical government as opposed to another kind of government or of Wolsey's administration as opposed to another kind of administration. The power of generalizations to compare particulars is lost in a rush to primary abstractions, here order itself, which, like the talismanic abstractions in Boethius's *Consolation* (truth, life, author, path, goal), has no acceptable alternative.

The Ceremonial Narrative of the Chronicle

Just as Caxton "romances" his aristocratic patrons and Elyot "romances" his virtues, the chroniclers too turn historical events into the *aventures* of knights or into splendid tableaux.[38] The narrator fixes his attention on a spectacle with dazed, obsessive concentration and then without commentary switches to another. This continuous and complete realignment of sympathies is a problem not in the handling of sources, however, but rather in the chronicler's constitution of the particular.[39] Human figures are cast on a two-dimensional background, successively appearing to the eye as the attention happens to

38. In his verse prologue, John Hardyng says he writes his fifteenth-century chronicle for his lord's "pleasaunce and consolacion" (*The Chronicle of John Hardyng. Containing an account of public transactions from the earliest period of English history to the beginning of the reign of King Edward the Fourth. Together with the continuation by Richard Grafton, to the thirtyfourth year of King Henry the Eighth*, ed. Henry Ellis [London: F. C. and J. Rivington et al., 1812], 16). In his prose *The New Chronicles of England and France (1516)*, Robert Fabyan sounds very much the romancer as he uses a verse prologue to reach into his memory for the pageant that is to follow (*The New Chronicles of England and France in Two Parts*, ed. Henry Ellis [London: F. C. and J. Rivington et al., 1811], 2).

39. Stephen Booth has called attention to this sudden and complete realignment of sympathies in Holinshed's chronicle. But these unmotivated reversals are not peculiar to Holinshed; they are part of the chronicle's inheritance of romance, romance's dependence on a ceremonial mode, and a ceremonial mode's handling of one particular as no more or no less significant than any other (*The Book Called Holinshed's Chronicles: An Account of Its Inception, Purpose, Contributors, Contents, Publication, Revision and Influence on William Shakespeare* [San Francisco: Book Club of California, 1968], 42–45).

swerve one way or another. When they are organized into a pattern, it is a homiletic explanation so all-inclusive that the distribution of emphasis is still more or less equal; people and events are just gazed at from a farther perspective.

The narrative integrity of a single *aventure* becomes a special problem in sixteenth-century accounts of the Wars of the Roses, as the English chroniclers switch impassively from Henry VI as the pitiable king to Edward IV's prospects as an adventuring knight. When for instance in Polydore Vergil's *Anglica Historia*, Edward IV returns from France, lands at Ravensport, and rides to York, the narrative concentrates wholly on the adventures of Edward as a knight in an alien landscape, bravely defending himself and his followers. But it was Henry VI, not Edward, on whom Polydore (and hence both Grafton and Hall, who follow him closely) had earlier concentrated as the figure of sympathy, and it was Edward who was "storied" as the monster that a baleful landscape had spewed up.[40]

Women can even more powerfully realign sympathies, almost like the sudden rearranging of mirrors in a kaleidoscope. They are irresistible when they are beautiful, like Froissart's Countess of Salisbury, by whom Edward III is "stryken . . . to the hert" (1:193); or when they show up with a man's determination and power, like Froissart's Countess of Montfort, who, when her husband is in prison, leads her people in defense of the town of Hennobont, with "harnesse on her body," riding "on a great courser," and urging the women to cut off their skirts and carry stones and pots full of chalk to throw at the assailants.[41] In Polydore's chronicle, the narration chugs along cheerfully with the adventures of Edward IV, his repossession of the throne, and his imprisonment of Henry VI, when suddenly the figure of Margaret—Henry's queen—appears on the landscape. Although Polydore cannot keep himself from finger-wagging (after all, she might have remembered that all her troubles had to do with her part in the death of Humphrey, Duke of Gloucester), he also invests her tale with pity (the misfortunes of this queen) and tenderness (her hopes for her son). When Polydore describes her reaction to the news

40. Polydore Vergil, *Polydori Vergilii Urbinatis Anglicae Historiae Libri Vigintisex* (Basileae: Mich. Isingrinium, 1546), Book 24, 512–26.

41. *The Chronicle of Froissart*, trans. John Bourchier, Lord Berners, ed. W. E. Henley, 6 vols. (London: David Nutt, 1901–3), 1:199. All further references to Froissart will be to this edition.

that Warwick has been slain and her husband taken prisoner, he is fully sympathetic with a grieving woman.[42]

When aristocrats are not pursuing *aventures*, then they stabilize the baffling flux of human time in a moment of radiant meaning. Time in a romance is always just about to stand still, as the surface of the palpable world suddenly gives way to the beyond. In Berners's translation of Froissart, the bravery of the wounded Charles of Luxembourg fixes a moment in a lyric oracle: "Sirs, ye ar my men, my companyons, and frendes in this journey, I requyre you bring me so farre forwarde, that I may stryke one stroke with my swerde" (1:298).

In a chronicle-style coronation, the imminent apocalypse has arrived, and time comes to a dead halt. Edward Hall describes London's decking itself out for the crowning of Henry VIII, from the array of "base and meane occupacions" up to "the worshipfull craftes."[43] Hall then says that his "lacke of cunnyng" prevents him from adequately describing the physical features with which God endowed the king, but he nevertheless describes his velvet, ermine, raised gold, diamonds, rubies, emeralds, pearls, and then the attire of the knights, esquires, gentlemen, officers, and household servants. In Hall's amazing opening paragraphs of this history, a kingdom damned by civil war (division, depopulation, calamity, misery, discord, execrable plagues) is rescued by the "concord" of the marriage of Henry VII to Elizabeth: new king, new age, new state of being for the whole world. In Holinshed's account of the coronation of Henry VII, the apocalyptic inclinations of romance are explicit: "it was hoped, that now the quiet orders and good lawes of the land . . . should now be renewed and brought againe in use."[44] Each ritualistic crowning promises an everlasting harmony. When in 1649, Edward Herbert writes his history of Henry VIII, he waves his hand dismissively at the chronicle's love of pageantry: "Thus, upon the third of

---

42. "His auditis, misera mulier metu corruit, dolore disrumpitur, intercluditur, torquetur, tempus calamitosum, fortunam adversam, aerumnam deplorat, fatum Henrici incusat, quod iam venisse pro certo habebat, et denique se afflictat, ac prae morte vitam aspernatur, quod fortasse animo provideret deteriora, quae supra caput erant, iamque impendebant" (Polydore Vergil, *Anglicae Historiae Libri Vigintisex*, Book 24, 528).

43. Edward Hall, *Hall's Chronicle; Containing the History of England During the Reign of Henry the Fourth, and the Succeeding Monarchs, to the End of the Reign of Henry the Eighth* (London: J. Johnson et al., 1809), 507–8.

44. See, for example, *Holinshed's Chronicles of England, Scotland, and Ireland* [1587], 6 vols. (London: printed for J. Johnson et al. 1807–8), 2:713. The first edition of *Holinshed's Chronicles* appeared in 1577.

June, being about six weeks after his Fathers death, he [Henry VIII] espoused the Lady Katharine. Their Coronation yet was diferr'd till the 24. of the same moneth. The magnificences thereof, being by *Hall, Hollinshed*, and others set downe, are by me purposely omitted."[45] A historical mode has become a genre.

When the chronicle stories the particular by homily instead of romance, enchantment gives way to absolute judgments. Fabyan every once in a while shakes his finger at errant human beings; Joan of Arc is eventually punished by God for her "sorcery and develysshe wayes" (*New Chronicles*, 642). In his account of the corruption of Richard II, Holinshed first acknowledges the faults of the king but then, locking into homily, furiously condemns the multitude for desiring a new sovereign (2:868–69). Polydore's argument that the troubled reign of Henry VI was caused by the sin of Henry Boling-broke in usurping the throne—an argument for which he has received great plaudits as a humanist historian—is basically a homily: when men commit evil, God punishes them.[46] When in 1501 Henry VII rounds up some conspirators and has them executed, Polydore interrupts: "But see now how God remembers all the crimes we have committed! At length even James Tyrrell came to the scaffold."[47] In recounting the harshness of Henry's two informers, Empson and Dudley, Polydore sighs: "the king claimed that he tolerated these exactions [of Empson and Dudley] . . . in order thereby to maintain the population in obedience. Thus we mortals, relying on our reason, are accustomed to excuse our sins to God, who is the most unerring witness of our minds and who cannot be deceived."[48] Romance moves from one pitiful figure to his pitiful enemy; homily moves, just as rapidly, from denunciation to complaint's futility. The impulse in romance to assume that significance lies in the particular—with numinous, polysemous revelations—appears in homily as the assumption that God or Fate will eventually assign full significance.

Besides romance and homily, the particular is also storied by the folkish anecdote, whose jolliness reinforces hierarchical power as

45. Edward, Lord Herbert of Cherbury, *The Life and Raigne of King Henry the Eighth* (London: printed by E. G. for Thomas Whitaker, 1649), 8.
46. Polydore could have learned the mode from the gloomy Gildas, an edition of whose *De calamitate, excidio et conquestu Britanniae* Polydore published in Antwerp in 1525 (Denys Hay, intro. to *The Anglica Historia of Polydore Vergil A.D. 1485–1537*, ed. and trans. Denys Hay, Camden Society, 3d series, 74 [London: Royal Historical Society, 1950], xiii).
47. *The Anglica Historia of Polydore Vergil*, trans. Denys Hay, 127.
48. Ibid., 131.

successfully as romance *aventures* and tableaux. In the description of
The Great Chronicle (attributed to Fabyan) of the marriage of Henry VII
to Elizabeth Woodville, the king is a typical bridegroom, parading his
horsemanship before his new bride (a "lusty and Jocant ffayt"), then
turning to the Queen and making "a lowly obeysaunce"; "shortly
afftyr he was seen In the Quenys Tent kyssyng and clyppyng hyr In
moost lovyng maner."[49] The king deserves to be king because he
shares the affections of the lowliest of his subjects. Even when the
mysterious "folk" show up with actual criticism of the sovereign, a
potential severity dissolves into affirmation of the king's authority. In
The Great Chronicle, Fabyan tells of "one woodhows" in the court of
Edward IV, who was "in good ffavour . . . ffor his manerly Raylyng
and honest dysportys." One day in a "hoot and drye Somyr," he
came into the king's chamber wearing high boots and carrying a pike,
and delivered a riddling speech about the "rivers" in the kingdom.
Understanding quite well that the jester is referring to "the lord
Ryvers and his blood," the king receives the warning as a great
"dysport" (*Great Chronicle*, 208). The jester is an emissary from
nature's reliable order of seasonal change. In constituting the body
politic, Woodhouse the jester and his amiable garrulousness are
equally as effective as the Tudor myth.[50]

Folkishness also appears in the form of the proverb. In its raw
cunning, it shares with homily a knowing superiority to the figures in
the landscape. When Henry VI retakes the throne and Edward IV is
forced to flee to France, Hall purses his lips: "He [Edward] forgat the
olde adage, saynge, in tyme of peace provyde for warre." The only
excuse Hall offers for Edward's folly is "he so much trusted fortunes
flatteryng, that he thought never to see her chaunge, nor yet to have
at dyce any yll chaunce, or at chestes [sic] any checke mate"
(*Chronicle*, 284). Hall also clucks over Empson and Dudley: "and yet
they had warnynge of greate and sage persons to close their handes
from suche uncharitable doynges and cruell extremitie, accordyng to
the Adage, the extremitie of justice, is extreme injurie" (*Chronicle*,
499). In *The Great Chronicle*, Fabyan uses the proverb oracularly. He
reports Edward V's riding with his uncle Richard of Gloucester from
Stony Stratford to London, where he was met by the Mayor of

49. Robert Fabyan, *The Great Chronicle of London*, ed. A. H. Thomas and I. D. Thornely
(London: George W. Jones, 1938), 370.
50. On the natural and divine bodies of the king as legal doctrine, see Ernst
Kantorowicz, *The King's Two Bodies: A Study in Medieval Political Theology* (Princeton:
Princeton University Press, 1957).

London and his brother. The duke was clothed in blue velvet and Gloucester and all the king's servants in black, "In soo much that than was myendid and spokyn of an old prophecy sayyng. When the blak fflete of Norwaye, is cummyn and goon, Than buyld ye yowir howsis / Of lyme and of stoon" (*Great Chronicle*, 230). The folk proverb also allies with aristrocratic shrewdness. Hall describes how Edward IV mustered allies to fight the Earl of Warwick, gathering the earl's in-laws, his own in-laws, and his trusty friends, "knowing perfitly that if he had once mastred the chief belwether, the flocke wolde sone be dispercled" (283). Political conflict is a fight between foxes; leadership is knowing how the sheep trot.

Cooling the Passions: Dialogue, Proverb, and Irony

Some Tudor writers who seem remarkably unliterary are nevertheless more keenly conscious of the importance of debate than those who mastered Cicero's *De Inventione* and the third book of the *De Oratore*. Some so-called drab prose writers of the midcentury know that a ceremonial mode's abhorrence and devotion do not encourage pragmatic solutions. In contrast to Elyot's contests between a sweet, incomparable, and salvific virtue and a detestable surrender to evil, the arguments in Thomas Starkey's *Dialogue between Reginald Pole and Thomas Lupset* (c. 1534) have precise and variable oppositions that a reasonable man might hold: that England should institute Roman law in place of common law because Roman law orders the common- wealth more fairly and thereby helps the citizens become prosperous;[51] that the kingship should be an elective office rather than inherited (99–101, 154); that there should be public school for those who will govern instead of haphazardly allowing children to pick up their education where their parents decide (169); that the people could be encouraged to have more children by taxing bache- lors and remitting the taxes of those with children (141); that there should be a restriction on imported luxuries (144). This constitution of evil as a difficulty that can be met by carefully considered legislation

51. Thomas Starkey, *A Dialogue Between Reginald Pole and Thomas Lupset*, ed. Kathleen M. Burton (London: Chatto and Windus, 1948), 174.

rather than as a monstrous eruption increases throughout the century, and its prosaic dispassion marks a clear departure from ceremonial reverence.[52]

Starkey also confronts a ceremonial writer's tendency to polarize choices. Pole, the modern man in this dialogue, argues that happiness will always be measured in degrees and not in an either/or choice between the fullness of joy or the emptiness of fear. Lupset, the traditionalist, protests that perfect felicity admits of no degree—a position strongly implied by the emotionalism of ceremony and homily (54). Pole rejoins that happiness admits of no degree if the human being is a soul only; but if the human being is a soul and body together, then felicity will admit of degrees because worldly circumstances (happiness of the body) are so very different (55). Therefore worldly happiness will always be relative. To refuse to accept a relative happiness in the interest of a pure one is to withdraw from the world, to be frail and imbecile; monks who have retired to monasteries are "like to fearful shipmen which for dread of storms and troublous seas keep themself in the haven, and dare not commit themselves to the dangerous tempests of the same" (53). Better is the man who "in great tempest and troublous time governeth well his ship." Here, the ceremonial image of a saving force providing "haven" to a lost soul is redone in praise of an active virtue. Starkey does not wish to scorn monks who retire to monasteries, "which thing surely is not amiss done of them which perceive their own imbecility and weakness." Nevertheless, he does call them frail and weak and imputes a moral childishness to those who are "prone and ready to be oppressed and overthrown with these common and quiet pleasures of the world" (53). If human beings suffer tyrants, Pole argues, the cause is partly their willingness to suffer them (154). In the discussion of England's poverty, Lupset argues that England is richer than any other country and therefore its poverty should not be a source of complaint. Pole rejoins that Lupset speaks "like a man of the old world" (88). To want reform is to be modern.

Starkey's argument sounds like a familiar laud of the active life over the contemplative. But more significant is the attack on the passivity that characterizes the various forms of ceremony. In the *Discourse of the Commonweal* (c. 1549), Thomas Smith also rejects the futility of meditation and the desperation of homily. The "universal dearth" is

---

52. Arthur Ferguson has described the increasing realism in sixteenth-century approaches to economic and political problems in *The Articulate Citizen and the English Renaissance* (Durham: Duke University Press, 1965).

"caused by ourselves and not by the sending of God." The benefit of thinking that human beings cause economic swings is that then "help" can be "devised by man." Otherwise human beings have nothing but "prayer and amendment of life."[53] Smith also consciously avoids homily's exorcisms. We cannot "devise that all covetousness may be taken from men . . . no more than we can make men to be without ire, without gladness, without fear, and without all affections" (118). Human greed is a given; the best human beings can do is to find institutions to curb it.

For Starkey, management of the world requires aggressive debate. The "student" in his dialogue should not acquiesce as if he were talking to a Boethian Philosophia. Pole reproves Lupset: "Master Lupset, you are in these matters very easy to persuade. You make no objections, after your manner in other things, wherefore I somewhat fear that we admit over-quickly these fauts [faults] in the Church for some private hate that we bear again[st] the priests and prelates therein" (126). But the objections must not be attached to persons ("some private hate"), and they must not give way to homily's compulsions. Even the heretic Luther and his disciples are "not so wicked and foolish that in all things they err." "Hating heresies" should not lead one to "fly from the truth" (128–29). Pole here draws a distinction between raising objections and "abhorrence." Despite the usual matter for complaint in this dialogue (people are idle, envious, gluttonous), Starkey shows a conscious effort to reduce emotionalism by formulas of tentativeness: "It is not convenient" (126), "such an idle train displeaseth me" (124), "it is not unreasonable" (120), "it should also be no small furtherance many ways" (159), and "thus, Master Lupset, you may see how that both your reasons and mine also may have place, if they be well applied and indifferently weighed" (108). Procedures for discussion delimit argument by enforcing a split between the visionary, tumultuous world of private bonds and the world of public considerations. Those who want reform (what Starkey calls "meddling in the affairs of the commonweal") should carry on dialogues in which, indifferently weighing reasons, they are "conspiring togidder in . . . virtue" (27, 34, 35). At the end of More's *Richard III*, there is a similar sort of "conspiracy" of the modern, the rational, and the purposeful.

53. Thomas Smith, *Discourse of the Commonweal of This Realm of England*, ed. Mary Dewar (Charlottesville: published for the Folger Shakespeare Library by the University Press of Virginia, 1969), 116.

Of the various prose modes available to an early sixteenth-century vernacular writer struggling to free himself from romance reverence, the most useful were the proverb and the folk anecdote. At the end of the fifteenth and beginning of the sixteenth centuries, folkishness in the form of proverbs had an ambiguous cultural status, in part belonging to an oral culture, in part belonging to an age of writing.[54] In the prefatory material to his *Adages*, Erasmus distinguishes the proverbial adage from the wittier apothegm. Although the adage is a mark of an educated writer, it contains very simple wisdom.[55] Erasmus quotes Aulus Gellius's proverbial reflection on the proverb: "Even a gardener oft speaks to the point." Indeed, "it sometimes happens that a man of lowly position and of no account, or of very little education, says something that even persons in high place should not despise."[56] The proverb also expresses the humble piety of a good Christian. "Between friends all is common" leads to the ceremonial truth that we are "the same body."[57] But, as Erasmus's plundering of classical sources suggests, proverbs also belong to the man of classical letters; their difficulty commands respect.[58] The "difficult proverb" or apothegm could be used for intellectual incisiveness, as it is in Bacon. It economically defined the scope of a question, and its tonal neutrality contrasted ironically with the effusions of a ceremonial mode. Some of the ironic detachment of the proverb appears in More's *Richard III*.

For an early-sixteenth-century vernacular writer, however, the most readily available means to internalize debate was to contrast the equanimity of a folkish mode—its volubility even in the midst of disasters—with the chronicle's wonder, horror, and bald statement of the record. In Fabyan's *Great Chronicle*, one Thomas Cook is brought before Edward IV's council for treason. Legal proclamation states the hard facts:

> . . . tyll oon Jury by the meanys of sir John Fogg and othyr endygthid hym of treason, afftir which Indygthment, An Oyer determyner was set at Guyldhalle, In the which wyth the mayer then was appoyntid The duke of Clarence Therle of

54. Ong, "Oral Residue," 147.
55. Erasmus, *Adages Iil to Iv100*, trans. Margaret Mann Phillips and annotated by R. A. B. Mynors, in *The Collected Works of Erasmus*, 49 vols. (Toronto: University of Toronto Press, 1974–), 31:3–28.
56. Erasmus, *Adages Ivil to Ix100*, 32:3.
57. *The Collected Works of Erasmus*, 31:15.
58. Ibid., 8–9.

warwick The lord Ryvers sir John Fogg wyth othyr of the kyngys Counsayll, To the which place the said sir Thomas was browgth and there aregnyd upon lyffe and deth[.]

So far the recorder. Immediately, there follows the tale which explains the event to Fabyan's satisfaction:

> In tyme whereof the mayer beyng a Replete and lumpysh man satt ffor chyeff Juge and slept, wherffor the duke syttyng upon his Rygth hand seeing his myssdemeanure said opynly In his derysion, sirs spekyth sofftly ffor the mayer Is on slepe.

Without any comment on the comedy of this, the legal record continues: "This daye was the said Sir Thomas acquytid of the fforesaid Indygthtement" (Fabyan, *Great Chronicle*, 206). The anecdote swallows up the authority of the law in the biological rhythms of wake and sleep. The only response to the law's possible harshness is to claim, as folkishness does, that the disasters of nature can be dissolved in lightheartedness: life is short; life is incomprehensible; there is little point getting excited about it. If we had any reason to think that Fabyan was a cunning narrator, we might interpret this passage as an ironic comment on legal authority: those who speak "law-talk" will always sound as if they had no notion of ordinary living.

In Fabyan's juxtaposition of the proclamation style and the cheerfully curious and affectionate teller-of-anecdotes, there is an enormous potential for irony. Edward IV calls his councillors before him and asks for their advice about "a voyage over see into Fraunce." He then asks for advice from "the mayer of London and his brethren the aldermen" and for their assistance. "And after that he rode about the more parte of the lande, and used the people in suche fayre maner, that he reysed therby notable summes of money."

Edward then sends for "all the trusty commoners" and exhorts them too for funds. Fabyan concludes this account with a statement that the ear schooled in a classical style could only find astoundingly unaware of its rhetorical modalities: "the whiche way of levyinge of this money was after named a benyvolence" (*New Chronicles*, 664). Again, if we had any signal that Fabyan was a cunning narrator, we might hear in this passage the irony for which Sir Thomas More is famous—straightfaced and sly.

More's *Richard III*: A Ceremonial Mode Both Vestigial and Parodic

Sir Thomas More's *History of King Richard III* has been interpreted in the context of Tudor historiography, early humanist prose, and humanist thought. It is best considered in a context that combines all three, for the significance of this remarkable work is More's objectification of a ceremonial mode as a useful political tool. The *History of King Richard III* is thus closely allied with the "talking of princes" in the *Utopia*, not so much with the famous dialogue between Hythlodaeus and More about the moral danger of serving princes but rather with the consideration of how kings rule, how they raise money, how they react to counselors, how they use splendor to consolidate their power.[59] Unlike the *Utopia*, however, *Richard III* brings politics into the actual world of events so recent that they were still in the memory of More's readers. Ultimately, it asks a question not about the tyrant Richard III but about national identity: How should we Englishmen talk of our princes?

Apparently written at the same time as the *Utopia* in the second decade of the sixteenth century,[60] *Richard III* was conceived at a fluid moment in English culture. The pageants of Henry VII's and Henry VIII's court were fully medieval in their splendor, their allegorical images, their ritual. When Henry VII arrived in London after his victory at Bosworth Field, he presented "his three standards, the banner of St. George, the red fiery dragon of Cadwaladr on a white and green ground, and a dun cow painted upon 'yellow tarterne' [rich silk]."[61] The accounts of his coronation list the amounts paid for scarlet, blue, and black cloth, ermine, red roses, dragons, ostrich feathers, and fringes and tassels of gold and silk. The coronation ceremonies, which lasted three days, included the bestowing of honors, a procession from the Tower to Westminster Hall (in which the king wore a long gown of purple velvet trimmed with ermine and rode under a canopy carried by four knights), and the celebration of

59. On the *Utopia* as an argument that sociological analysis is a necessary preliminary to political analysis, see George M. Logan, *The Meaning of More's "Utopia"* (Princeton: Princeton University Press, 1983), 59–61.

60. On the date of composition of *Richard III*, see Sylvester, *Complete Works of St. Thomas More*, 2:lxiii–lxv.

61. J. D. Mackie, *The Earlier Tudors, 1485–1558* (Oxford: Clarendon Press, 1952), 54.

a mass.[62] Afterwards there was a banquet with the lords of the realm and the citizens of London. Henry's progress to the north in 1486 to quell supporters of Richard was also accompanied by elaborate pageantry. At Lincoln, he "celebrated Easter in time-honored fashion: by receiving twenty-nine poor men whose feet he washed, and to whom he donated alms," by distributing sums of money to the poor and sick, and by attending religious services throughout the week.[63] These displays of the ruler as beautiful protector continued throughout the sixteenth century in the coronations of successive kings, in civic pageantry staged by various towns in England, and in royal progresses.

Much of the humanists' new learning served as rhetorical adornment at these court pageants. During the fifteenth and early sixteenth centuries, humanism was chiefly an Italian import, starting with Poggio's visit to England in 1418 and followed by the recurring sojourns of papal bureaucrats.[64] Their interest was collecting manuscripts (a disappointing endeavor in England), stylistic elegance, and the study of Greek. Among Englishmen themselves, humanism was largely the patronage of Italian visitors, study in Italy, and the introduction of humanistic learning in the schools. William Grocyn and Thomas Linacre both lectured on Greek at Oxford. Linacre was a tutor to the young Prince Arthur. John Colet and William Lily, with advice and encouragement from Erasmus, reformed the curriculum at St. Paul's, teaching schoolboys some good Ciceronian Latin and some Aristophanes, Homer, Euripides, Plautus, Vergil, Ovid, Horace, and Sallust.[65]

The admiration for the classics was often accompanied by a rejection of the native tradition. In the *Utopia*, Hythlodaeus's preference for Lucian, Aristophanes, Homer, Euripides, and Sophocles is not countered by an alternative list of native English writers or any of the books printed by Caxton. Given More's obvious concern for the effect of English laws on the behavior of English subjects (in the discussion of stealing), one would expect him to fill out the *Utopia*'s debate between himself and Hythlodaeus with the observation that the classics are inaccessible to an uneducated audience and that

62. Sydney Anglo, *Spectacle, Pageantry, and Early Tudor Policy* (Oxford: Clarendon Press, 1969), 14.

63. Ibid., 21.

64. On humanists in England in the fifteenth century, see Roberto Weiss, *Humanism in England During the Fifteenth Century*, 3d ed. (1941; repr. Oxford: Basil Blackwell, 1957).

65. T. W. Baldwin, *William Shakespere's "Small Latine & Lesse Greeke,"* 2 vols. (Urbana: University of Illinois Press, 1944), 1:75–133.

although most thieves cannot read, they might be persuaded to a more wholesome life if some vernacular books with woodcuts were more available, like Caxton's *Golden Legend* or the *Biblia Pauperum*.[66] But he does not do so. In the *Utopia* at least, More is a man of the new learning.

With other prominent figures, humanism has a more popular and piously Christian aspect. Although John Colet in part studied the New Testament as a historical document, checking its facts against Suetonius,[67] the final drift of his lectures at Oxford was a living Christianity, for which the Bible was a devotional text. Erasmus's knowledge of classical languages resulted not only in books of literary wit (translations of Lucian, epigrams, *Colloquia*, *Adagia*) and in the monumental edition of the Greek New Testament with Latin notes and introductory *Paraclesis* but also in a wish that vernacular translations and a laymen's guide to Scripture be available to those who did not know Greek and Latin. In his famous vision of the farmer singing versified sections of the Bible as he follows his plow, Erasmus is thinking of a community reinvigorated by a new piety.

A third side of humanism is its connection with the Tudor dynasty. The humanists' articulateness made them useful to the Tudors' creation of a court drawing all eyes to the king. Under Henry VII were created the posts of "Latin secretary" and "Royal Librarian."[68] In the Tudor pageants, displays of the new Latin accompanied the allegorical representations of Christian virtues (Mercy, Grace, Seven Gifts of the Holy Ghost). Latin panegyrics celebrating the marriage of Henry and Elizabeth were presented in the pageants during the royal progress to the north in 1486.[69] In 1518, Cuthbert Tunstall and Richard Pace delivered Latin orations at the Field of Cloth of Gold.[70] Tunstall orated again in 1527 during the negotiations for the proposed marriage of Princess Mary.[71] In 1522, William Lily was commissioned to write verses for the festivities surrounding Henry's discussion with Charles V of the foreseen war with France. On the same occasion, More delivered an oration in Latin.[72] The first five of More's epi-

---

66. John N. King, *English Reformation Literature: The Tudor Origins of the Protestant Tradition* (Princeton: Princeton University Press, 1982), 40–42.

67. Frederic Seebohm, *The Oxford Reformers: John Colet, Erasmus, and Thomas More*, 3d. ed. (1887; repr. London: Longmans, 1911), 35.

68. Weiss, *Humanism in England*, 7.

69. Anglo, *Spectacle*, 19–20.

70. Ibid., 129 and 130.

71. Ibid., 211.

72. Ibid., 187 and 190.

grams, printed in 1518 and 1522, heralded the accession of Henry VIII
to the throne. The humanist involvement at court extended even
beyond occasions of state: Colet, Pace, Tunstall, and More all served
on the King's Council.[73]

Besides talking to kings, however, humanists talked to each other.
More's correspondence (which includes letters to Colet, Erasmus,
William Budé, Tunstall, John Fisher, references to Polydore Vergil,
Grocyn, Linacre, Pace, Palsgrave, Reuchlin, and descriptions of
gatherings where letters were passed around for comment) defines
the humanists as a literary group. Their camaraderie is reinforced by
a common battle against the "unlettered," who do not know how to
argue decorously, who foolishly value disputation for its own sake,
and who object to Erasmus's edition of the Greek New Testament.[74]
Erasmus's *Colloquies* include references to Budé, Busleiden, Colet,
Peter Gilles, Linacre, More (and his pet monkey), and Reuchlin. This
humanist coterie is figured in the *Utopia*'s prefatory network of letters:
More to Gilles, Gilles to Busleiden, Busleiden to More, Budé to
Lupset, Erasmus to the printer John Froben, and Joannes Paudaunus
to Gilles. Ironic slights at the literarily *passé* celebrate the literarily *au
courant*. Some of More's epigrams attack Germain de Brie's hyperbolic
account of a naval battle and the unmetered verses of a monk. In the
letter to Peter Gilles that prefaces the *Utopia*, the joke about the exact
length of the bridge in that "no place" country separates those who
can read classical "sauciness" and the naive, who will drink in the
story as a travel narrative.

Humanist literature also defines the newly learned men as public
servants. Book 1 of the *Utopia* praises various men for their political
skill. Georges de Themsecke, provost of Cassel, commands a thor-
ough knowledge of the law and diplomacy. Peter Gilles holds an
important position in the city of Antwerp. John Morton, then lord
chancellor of England, is eminently suited for public office. Book 1 of
the *Utopia* is a representation of how such public men might use
classical learning to analyze a political culture.

But besides the mutual congratulations on worldly success, humanists also remind each other that service to kings is merely a necessary

73. J. A. Guy, *The Public Career of Sir Thomas More* (New Haven: Yale University Press,
1980), 8–9.

74. *The Correspondence of St. Thomas More*, ed. Elizabeth Frances Rogers (Princeton:
Princeton University Press, 1947). For More's reaction to Martin Dorp's objections to
Erasmus's New Testament and the public communication of letters, see "Letter to
Martin Dorp," in *St. Thomas More: Selected Letters*, ed. Elizabeth Frances Rogers (New
Haven: Yale University Press, 1961), 4–64.

fact of life, not a career fulfilled; such service should always be measured against their own superior moral standards. The famous "Dialogue of Counsel" in book 1 of the *Utopia* shows More's uneasiness in being a party to royal self-aggrandizement. In a letter to John Fisher, More explains his ambivalence in taking a position on Henry VIII's council in 1517: he keeps his place, he says, "as precariously as an unaccustomed rider in his saddle."[75] More's decision to serve the Tudor court apparently dismayed Erasmus, who felt compelled to assure other humanists that More took the post against his will.[76] In an epigram, More debates whether a senate is better than kingship; one of the virtues of a senate is its being elected by the "reasonable agreement" (*certum . . . consilium*) of the people.[77] A history in a civil mode could consolidate the humanists' sense of themselves as the group that deserved to have power because it had the linguistic tools most suitable for such a "reasonable agreement."

For More's own humanist discourse, the importance of his allegiances with London cannot be overemphasized. Humanism in England started at the universities, but by the first decade of the sixteenth century, its center was the London community. Colet followed the other Oxford reformers to London in 1504, where there was a network of teachers, students of the classics, literary men, public servants, clerics, and patrons. More's literary relationship with Erasmus, who came to England in 1499 with the patronage of Mountjoy, is well known. More's activities as a lawyer also drew him into circles with other humanists; in 1514 he was listed in Doctors' Commons, whose members included Colet, Grocyn, and Tunstall.[78] More was elected from London to the parliament of 1504, and in 1510, he was appointed undersheriff. We know that he did legal work for the Company of Mercers, and he may have done some for the Merchants of the Staple. In 1509–10 he worked for both the crown and for the city in a number of official capacities.[79] It was More who calmed the turbulent multitude in the riots of 1517, but then it was also he who obtained a pardon for the rioters. More's service to the

75. Ibid., 94.

76. Guy, *The Public Career of Sir Thomas More*, 6–7.

77. St. Thomas More, *Epigrams*, in *The Yale Edition of the Complete Works of St. Thomas More*, ed. Clarence H. Miller, Leicester Bradner, Charles A. Lynch, and Revilo P. Oliver (New Haven: Yale University Press, 1984), vol. 3, pt. 2:228–29.

78. James Kelsey McConica, *English Humanists and Reformation Politics Under Henry VIII and Edward VI* (Oxford: Clarendon Press, 1965), 51–52.

79. Russell Ames, *Citizen More and his Utopia* (New York: Russell and Russell, 1949), 43–44.

city in its various conflicts with the crown and his literary talents motivated him to find a discourse that would reify the perspective of a London community defined partly by the humanism of some of its members and partly by the political hostility of others to royal policies. Certainly in a crucial passage in *Richard III* the London citizens get a dramatic moment on center stage.

The History of King Richard III was written in this crucible of secular medieval pageantry hardly separated from religious rituals, fancy learning in the "new" way, and a critical detachment from certain aspects of the past. It is partly a *de casibus* story of a king who forgets that evil does not go overlooked and that power always submits to fortune,[80] partly a humanist debunking of the verbal pageantry by which monarchs stun their subjects, and partly a groping for a new civil discourse. It was not printed in More's lifetime. It appeared first in Richard Grafton's prose continuation of John Hardyng's verse chronicle in Grafton's edition of 1543 and again in 1548 and 1550 when Grafton inserted it in his edition of Edward Hall's *Union of the Two Noble and Illustre Families of Lancaster and York*. Grafton found *Richard III* good material for a commercial enterprise because it was a well-told tale, not because it had something new to reveal about the reign of the last Yorkist king. Indeed, by the time More started to write it, there was a firmly established tradition of Richard as a cruel tyrant who had murdered his nephews in the Tower and perhaps poisoned Queen Anne, a tradition that More's history did nothing to contradict.[81]

The ready conclusion is that *Richard III* was another piece of humanist propaganda intended to bolster Tudor legitimacy. Elizabeth Donno rejects this view.[82] The More family, she argues, had too much of a tradition of loyalty to the Yorkists suddenly to start toeing the Lancastrian line. For her, More's history is a humanist epideictic piece, designed to display wit in *vituperatio*. Its failure to reveal anything new about Richard and its careful pacing, dramatic dialogue, and irony indicate More's intention to be magnificently

80. Leonard Dean argues that *Richard III* is a Christian humanist history, regarding politics both from the moral point of view of the *de casibus* tradition and from the amoral point of view of *Realpolitik* ("Literary Problems").

81. Richard appears as a monster in the histories and chronicles of Robert Fabyan, John Rous, and Bernard André (Alison Hanham, *Richard III and His Early Historians: 1483–1535* [Oxford: Clarendon Press, 1975], 104–7).

82. Elizabeth Donno, "Thomas More and *Richard III*," *Renaissance Quarterly* 35 (1982): 408.

clever.[83] More radically, Alison Hanham sees *Richard III* as a Lucianic parody of contemporary chroniclers, exposing their acceptance of hearsay as the gospel historical truth.[84] This interpretation has the virtue of taking into account the satiric bent of More's other literary activity at the time of writing *Richard III*. In 1505–6, he had engaged in a friendly contest with Erasmus in imitating Lucianic declamations, and from 1509 to 1519, he was writing epigrams. But Hanham does not acknowledge those sections of *Richard III* that are unmistakably in traditional chronicle style. Daniel Kinney's interpretation of the Latin version as a text that resists clear generic definition, thereby "invit-[ing] and exploit[ing] contradictory responses to establish a new dialectical space of its own,"[85] has the virtue of seeing the politics of the text's sauciness. But how much this interpretation depends on a notion of "irony" that assumes More's full control of an English civil mode remains a question.

None of the above interpretations addresses the relationship between the English and Latin texts. Neither version is a translation of the other, and More seems to have shifted between languages at different stages of composition.[86] It is not unreasonable to surmise that one of More's purposes in writing in two languages simultaneously was to bring to English historiography the civil detachment that was so much more easily achieved in the language of the classical historians.[87] In certain places, the Latin has an aggressive precision and irony lacking in the English. In the famous sultan-and-shoemaker passage, the Latin includes the ironically cautious phrase *intempestiva veritate*, which is not attempted in English.[88] In other scenes, the

83. Ibid., 418.

84. Hanham, *Richard III and His Early Historians*, 155–61.

85. "King's Tragicomedies: Generic Misrule in More's History of *Richard III*," *Moreana* 86 (1985): 132. Other studies of the genre of *Richard III* appear in Walter M. Gordon, "Exemplum Narrative and Thomas More's *History of King Richard III*," *Clio* 9 (1979): 75–88 and Patrick Grant, "Thomas More's *Richard III*: Moral Narration and Humanist Method," *Renaissance and Reformation*, n.s. 7 (1983): 157–72.

86. Sylvester, *Complete Works of St. Thomas More*, 2:liv–lvi. See also Daniel Kinney's introduction to the Latin version discovered in the Bibliothèque Nationale in Paris, *The Yale Edition of the Complete Works of St. Thomas More*, ed. Daniel Kinney (New Haven: Yale University Press, 1986), 15:cl n. l.

87. Daniel Kinney finds the Latin a more coherent and more rhetorically effective text than the English because it ends with Richard's accession to the throne. See his discussion of the new Latin text of *Richard III* in *The Yale Edition of the Complete Works of St. Thomas More*, 15:clii.

88. P. 54. See the description of the proclamation announcing Hastings's death and the Latin of the Louvain edition (54). On the inclination of vernacular writers to focus

English omits the Latin's pointed allusions to classical texts.[89] Certainly the sharp change in style at the end argues for the dependency of the English on the Latin if it was not to break down into anecdotal horror and pathos.

Significant in this regard is More's friendship with Polydore Vergil, whose *Anglica Historia* More may well have seen in manuscript.[90] Although, as I have argued earlier, Polydore often vacillates between romance wonder and homiletic absolutes, in other places his Latin handles generalizations with ease and flexibility. In discussing Henry VII's agents Empson and Dudley, Polydore feels no compulsion to defend or judge the king; he simply criticizes Henry's injudiciousness at this particular time in his life as a character trait with greater or lesser usefulness in centralizing his power.[91] In Polydore's account, the conflict in 1517 between native apprentices, whipped up by the speeches of two monks, and foreign merchants is a struggle between commerce and misguided Christian zeal, which interferes in the good of the country (with a quotation from Cicero's *De Officiis*).[92] Here at least, the power of generalization to control the welter of emotion in vernacular narrative is so apparent that it is odd that More did not develop further Polydore's analysis of a king's administrative efficiency. Rational administration in the interest of national prosperity is certainly one of More's chief concerns in the *Utopia*. But in *Richard III*, More's primary interest may have been to hold up for examination the way discourses constitute kings as leaders, not to assess a particular king. If More appeared to be denouncing the current ruler's predecessor, then no one was likely to be angered by the refusal to revere, and More could thereby have a free hand in experimenting with the

---

on the emotion in passages translated from the Latin, compare for example Polydore's description of Elizabeth's grief as she seeks sanctuary (*Anglicae Historiae Libri Vigintisex*, Book 24, 540) with the rendering by an anonymous English translator (*Three Books of Polydore Vergil's English History Comprising the Reigns of Henry VI., Edward IV., and Richard III. from an Early Translation*, ed. Sir Henry Ellis, Camden Society 29 [London: J. B. Nichols, 1844], 175). Compare also Polydore's description of Edward's landing at Ravensport (*Anglicae Historiae Libri Vigintisex*, Book 24, 523), with the anonymous translation (138), and then the still more emotional rendering in Grafton (*The Chronicle of John Hardyng . . . Together with the Continuation by Richard Grafton*, 451) and the even more emotional version in Hall (*Hall's Chronicle*, 291).

89. A quotation from Terence appears in the Arundel manuscript (*Complete Works of St. Thomas More*, 2:131); see Sylvester's note, ibid., 228.

90. Ibid., lxxv–lxxvi.

91. *Anglica Historia*, trans. Denys Hay, 131.

92. Ibid., 243.

vernacular's ability to analyze princely power—as it had not in earlier chronicles and would not until Bacon's *History of Henry VII*, Raleigh's *History of the World*, and Daniel's *Collection of the History of England*. "Experiment" is the right word. Although for some, the suggestion that More did not fully achieve what he intended is a slap in the face of a great writer, adequate interpretation of this text must forego the modern desire to find stable meaning (or significant instability of meaning, as the case may be) and instead negotiate between the intentional choices of an author and the pressure of the discourses he inherited.

The pressure of the chronicle tradition on More's history cloaks much of the action in mystery. The elegiac lament of complaint appears in the customary summarizing epitaphs and in the eulogy for Edward IV (3–4). In the summation of Hastings's character after his death, More homiletically exhorts the pious flock: "O good god, the blindness of our mortall nature" (52). The omens leading to Hastings's death— Stanley's dream, the stumbling of the horse, the joke about not needing a priest, the encounter with a man of the same name on Tower Wharf—evoke the workings of fortune, to which the speaker bows with the humility of the proverb: Hastings was "trusty ynough, trusting to much."

The events are heavily storied by romance and the folk tale. The queen's decision to take sanctuary with her second son, her face-off with the Archbishop of Canterbury,[93] and her sorrowful farewell to the boy tell a sad tale of a woman struggling to defend herself in a world of power and in the end baffled by it:

> And therewithall she said unto the child: farewel my own swete sonne, god send you good keping, let me kis you ones yet ere you goe, for God knoweth when we shal kis togither agayne. And therewith she kissed him, and blessed him, turned her back and wept and went her way, leaving the childe weping as fast. (42)

Not only the pathos of the situation, but the balladlike monosyllables in delicately even stress ("let me kis you ones yet ere you goe," "turned her back and wept and went her way"), the near rhyme

---

93. In the English version, More calls this figure the Archbishop of York, confusing him with the archbishop who took the seal from the Queen, a mistake not made in the Latin (Sylvester, *Complete Works of St. Thomas More*, 2:194).

("kissed him, and blessed him"), and the parataxis all echo romance. The deaths of the two princes in the tower is also a sorrowful tale of two innocents. After they are shut up in the tower, Edward V "never tyed his pointes, nor ought rought of hymselfe, but with that young babe hys brother, lingered in thought and heavines til this tratorous death, delivered them of that wretchednes" (85), and when the murderers come to find them, the boys are described as "the sely children lying in their beddes" (85).

The account of Edward IV's wooing of Elizabeth Woodville is a comic folk-tale. It has the determined son (comedy's protagonist), an outraged mother (comedy's blocking figure), the pathos of the first affianced Lady Lucy, who thought that the king had made secure promises to her ("And that if it had not ben for such kind wordes [of the king], she would never have shewed such kindenes to him, to let him so kindly get her with childe" [65]), the coy self-possession of Elizabeth, who, when she sees just how eager Edward is to have her, protests that "as she wist herself to simple to be his wife, so thought she her self to good to be his concubine" (61), and the man of power's admiration for a woman who can so stiffly say him nay. The folk-storyteller's affection for the high spirits of his characters becomes in More a congratulation of people who manage to withstand the tempestuous world, as when Elizabeth is crowned the queen of a man who was the enemy of her first husband (65), or a pitying sigh for those lost in the tempestuous world, as when the same Elizabeth thought to ensure the security of her sons by keeping them close to the Duke of Gloucester (15). In the famous description of Jane Shore, folkish pride in a survivor leads More to admire her beauty even in doing public penance and to protect her from her accusers by reminding them of her generosity when she was the king's mistress. Indeed, the very dramatic liveliness of this history, which some readers have found its chief virtue, depends upon a romance combat between radical innocence, which establishes clear moral norms, and radical monstrousness. Elizabeth Woodville, Jane Shore, Hastings (who turns out to be an innocent), the citizens of London, and the children in the Tower are all transgressed by a romance beast.

But besides the traditional storyteller, there are also signals of a narrator who capitalizes on the incoherences of the traditional chronicle. The chief signal of this knowing author lies in *Richard III*'s being "well-written": the skillful plot, the insinuations that slowly condemn

Richard, and most of all the parody.[94] In the scene at Baynard's castle, where Buckingham solicits Richard to take the throne, the frequency of the doublets and the fluidity of the indirect discourse—as if Buckingham's speech was only a tissue of clichés—make it impossible not to hear parody of the legal reportage in Fabyan:

> And much mater was ther in the proclamacion devised, to the slaunder of the lord chamberlain, as that he was an evil counsellor to the kinges father, intising him to many thinges highlye redounding to the minishing of his honor, and to the universal hurt of his realm, by his evyl company, sinister procuring, and ungracious ensample, as wel in many other thinges as in the vicious living and inordinate abusion of his body, both with many other, and also specialli with shores wife, which was one also of his most secret counsel of this heynous treson, with whom he lay nightli, and nameli the night last passed next before his death. (53)

The free indirect discourse of this speech, self-confidently jeering at homily's threats, is highly unusual in English prose at this point in the development of the language.

The politician's use of folkishness is also parodied. At the Guildhall, the Duke of Buckingham is coy with the citizens of London, assuring them that he is aware of their fears under Edward and the harshness of Edward's taxes. He laces this speech with ingratiating concretions: "wote," "certes," "grennes and trappes," "pilling and polling," "goodes to be lashed oute among unthriftes," "every thing . . . hawsed aboue the mesure" (69–70). He remarks sarcastically on Edward IV's benevolences: "as though the name of benevolence, had signified that every man shold pay, not what himself of his good wil list to graunt, but what the king of his good will list to take." This text is best described as one in which romance, homily, and folk-tale of a ceremonial mode are alternately vestigial and parodic.

More's Cunning Narrator and Civil Irony

How does one define the consciousness in back of the parody in *Richard III*? A parodist is, after all, not necessarily a civilist. The choice

94. On the parody, see Hanham, *Richard III and His Early Historians*, 163–64.

can be briefly put: if More is parodying different kinds of human speech with the assumption that God is in control, then the political manipulation becomes the chicanery to which all fallen human beings are inclined but which is irremediable. This parody belongs to the *débat*. If More is parodying different kinds of human speech with the assumption that human beings are in control of most aspects of their lives, then he is asking what is the Good for the community and what actions should be taken in consequence. This parody belongs to satire.

The famous sultan-and-shoemaker passage has often been called ironic in a satiric sort of way:

> But muche they talked and marveiled of the maner of this dealing, that the matter was on both partes made so straunge, as though neither had ever communed with other thereof before, when that themself wel wist there was no man so dul that heard them, but he perceived wel inough, that all the matter was made between them. Howbeit somme excused that agayne, and sayde all must be done in good order though. And menne must sommetime for the manner sake not bee a knowen what they knowe. For at the consecracion of a bishop, every man woteth well by the paying for his bulles, that he purposeth to be one, and though he paye for nothing elles. And yet must he bee twise asked whyther he wil be bishop or no, and he muste twyse say naye, and at the third tyme take it as compelled ther unto by his owne wyll. And in a stage play all the people know right wel, that he that playeth the sowdayne is percase a sowter [shoemaker]. Yet if one should can so lyttle good, to shewe out of seasonne what acquaintance he hath with him, and calle him by his owne name whyle he standeth in his magestie, one of his tormentors might hap to breake his head, and worthy for marring of the play. And so they said that these matters bee Kynges games, as it were stage playes, and for the more part plaied upon scafoldes. In which pore men be but the lokers on. And thei that wise be, wil medle no farther. For they that sometyme step up and playe with them, when they cannot play their partes, they disorder the play and do themself no good. (80–81)

Here, the folkish idiom ("there was no man so dul," "all must be done in good order though," "know right wel," "can so lyttle good," "might hap to breake his head," "pore men be but the lokers on," and "do themself no good") expresses the stubborn and dependable perspective of a nonaristocratic audience. When More has the people refuse to cheer when the fellow planted in the rear of the crowd shouts, "King Richard! King Richard!" or when he has them laugh at the dire seriousness with which Richard denounces Jane Shore, he short-circuits the responses assumed by the chronicle tradition. Their *sotto voce* mutterings frame the rhetoric of aristocrats, whose threats hang ludicrously in the air. These folk know perfectly well that what is being performed in front of them is a stage play, even if they lack the ability to write histories of changes in political power with proper Ciceronian elegance.

But their lacking the ability to write changes in political power makes all the difference. This passage is in fact a reversion to an old principle of a ceremonial mode: the simple are a vessel for God's solemn truth. The irony of this passage does not belong to satire. It is not the civil irony of Bacon in the *Essays*:

> Truth may perhaps come to the price of a pearl, that showeth best by day; but it will not rise to the price of a diamond or carbuncle, that showeth best in varied lights. A mixture of a lie doth ever add pleasure. Doth any man doubt, that if there were taken out of men's minds vain opinions, flattering hopes, false valuations, imaginations as one would, and the like, but it would leave the minds of a number of men poor shrunken things, full of melancholy and indisposition, and unpleasing to themselves?[95]

Nor is it Gibbon's in his description of the monastic saints:

> The favourites of Heaven were accustomed to cure inveterate diseases with a touch, a word, or a distant message; and to expel the most obstinate demons from the souls or bodies which they possessed. They familiarly accosted, or imperiously commanded, the lions and serpents of the desert; infused vegetation into a sapless trunk; suspended iron on the surface of the water; passed the Nile on the back of a crocodile; and refreshed themselves in a fiery furnace.[96]

95. Francis Bacon, *The Essayes or Counsels, Civill and Morall, 1625*, in *Francis Bacon: A Selection of His Works*, ed. Sidney Warhaft (New York: Odyssey, 1965), 47. All further references to Bacon's *Essays* will be to this edition.

96. Edward Gibbon, *The Decline and Fall of the Roman Empire*, ed. Oliphant Stephens (New York: Modern Library, 1932), 2:17.

The irony of both of these writers depends upon a highly developed language of exposition and the silent agreements written into the "contract" of a civil standard. With these agreements, writer and reader can count on a shared sensitivity to the meanings in certain stylistic registers, to the pressure of skilled articulateness as it comprehends the particular according to rational categories, and to the deflection of that pressure in wit. Through a standard, they silently corroborate each other's acceptance of the increasing secularization of moral values, the knowledge of classical literature as a mark of status, the withdrawal of religion from the public sphere, and the separation of private feeling from public decisions. Bacon and Gibbon both know well how rich in meaning (and how much fun) is irony's silent exchange of glances.

Then too the contracts of a civil standard make a claim to authority. These men claim their fitness to hold power. Gibbon's articulateness and disdain enlist a reader's agreement that his linguistic sophistication legitimizes him as a cultural governor; indeed, when the reader understands that Gibbon is tipping him the wink, both are legitimized as cultural governors. Theirs is a discourse whose detachment is necessary to civilization because it can analyze the effectiveness of institutions. The articulateness of these writers is an advertisement for their social usefulness; a humanly made polity needs them.

By contrast, the stubborn simplicity of the London citizens in the sultan-and-shoemaker passage expresses most clearly a condemnation of all institutions as a meaningless charade in a fallen world. This irony, of the *débat*, is courtly, folkish, and homiletic all together. It is courtly insofar as the disagreements are often stylized (sometimes in verse, as in *The Owl and the Nightingale*). It is folkish insofar as disagreements are regarded as the happy variety of God's creation (the mutual insults of the owl and nightingale are charming). Both the stylization and the folkishness dissolve the necessity for choice. It is homiletic when the text's surface charm implodes to the seriousness of a superhuman truth (the nightingale says that her happy song reminds human beings of the heaven they long for). In a debate, human language is speech, a tool and an artifact. In the *débat*, human language is song, always about to give way to divine voice.

The most famous representative of this form in the English Middle Ages is Chaucer, who does not show Bacon's and Gibbon's disdain. Whether Chaucer is a traditional Christian or an unorthodox Christian, *The Canterbury Tales* accept the full range of human life as God's wonderful or mysterious intentions. Chaucer does not believe, as do Bacon and Gibbon, that his own explicit statement of disdain for the

Pardoner could "help" society, as Gibbon believes that the expression of his personal contempt for early Christianity provides the model of an improved moral posture. Irony for Chaucer derives from the *débat*, which enjoys a security that Gibbon does not; whatever the human foible, God can be trusted to take care of it.[97] For the civilist, there is always something to be done, an argument to be made, a judgment to make up one's mind about. The civilist cannot wholly trust language to represent the world correctly.

In the interpretation of Renaissance texts, it makes a considerable difference whether the irony derives from a classical debate or from a *débat*. It has been argued that Castiglione's *Book of the Courtier*, Erasmus's *Praise of Folly*, More's *Utopia*, and Sidney's *Arcadia* are all built on the structure of classical rhetorical debate.[98] But these "debates" are of radically different cultural status. The neo-Platonic ascent to the divine in book 4 of the *Courtier* and the *Arcadia*'s opening lament for a lost Urania ground these works in a ceremonial mode. Hence, their "debates" are not the probable arguments of political leaders; neither are they the narrative "discussions" of Livy's history nor the kind of social improvement programs implied in Bacon's and Gibbon's aggressive definitions. In their inflection of human disagreements against the supernatural, these works are primarily celebrations of God's plenitude. That they borrow from the classical rhetorical tradition cannot be denied. But they are not "explorations of experience." In fact, they are closer to Chaucer's elaborate *débat* in *The Canterbury Tales* than they are to Ciceronian dialogue.

Even with this distinction, however, sixteenth-century irony is still

---

97. Beryl Rowland notes seven kinds of irony: (1) verbal irony; (2) the Socratic fictional character; (3) dramatic irony or irony of fate or fortune; (4) philosophical irony, where the ironist assumes a God-like stance; (5) irony of values, which obliquely points out the contradictions between stated ideologies and actual behavior; (6) thematic irony, as in "The Pardoner's Tale"; (7) structural irony, as in "The Miller's Tale" ("Seven Kinds of Irony," in *Essays in Chaucerian Irony*, ed. Earle Birney [Toronto: University of Toronto Press, 1985], xv–xxx). Rowland characterizes Chaucer's irony as "urbane" (xviii), but if it is "urbane," it is not Bacon's or Gibbon's. Rowland implicitly admits the distinction between the irony of the medieval *débat* and the irony of Cicero: "urbane in the Ciceronian sense, this kind of irony [verbal irony] totally lacks the thundering *saeva indignatio* with which the great rhetorician denounced Catiline in the Roman senate. Untouched by a reforming spirit, making no more than a furtive derisive comment on the major social conflict of his time, he [Chaucer] produces an irony that stings like the hairs of a common nettle rather than the tail of the legendary scorpion" (xxvii).

98. Joel B. Altman, *The Tudor Play of Mind: Rhetorical Inquiry and the Development of Elizabethan Drama* (Berkeley and Los Angeles: University of California Press, 1978), 64–106.

difficult to interpret because the civility of early modern English is only imperfectly differentiated from the parodic wit of the *débat*. Perhaps, as has been argued, the purpose of the consideration and reconsideration in Bacon's *Essays* is to induce the "healthy perplexity" of the scientific mind.[99] But Bacon's essayistic "reconsiderations" often invoke a text with special authority. "Of Death" starts with the superciliousness of, "Men fear Death, as children fear to go in the dark; and as that natural fear in children is increased with tales, so is the other"; it ends, however, with, "But above all, believe it, the sweetest canticle is *Nunc dimittis*" (*Essays*, 49). The quotation from Luke (the Bible as the Real Word) does not invoke scientific "reconsiderations." In Bacon, civil debate is imperfectly differentiated from *débat*-turned-somber. In *The Merchant of Venice*, Shakespeare also asks for a hard look at self-serving aristocrats and an equally hard look at a conniving alien (whose complaints are not illegitimate). After converting the alien, however, he dissolves the difficulty of choice in the moonlight of Belmont, from which height all the universe exists in "sweet harmony." That Shakespeare was satisfied with this ending, which seems to us evasive and perplexing, measures our distance from his sense of adequate resolutions.

Most of More's detachment in *Richard III* comes from the *débat*, as he parodies the patently manipulative speech of aristocrats. Still, passages in *Richard III* have the distance of civil rhetoric. In the description of the three mistresses of Edward IV, More says of the two besides Jane Shore:

> The other two were somwhat greter parsonages, and Natheles of their humilite content to be nameles, and to forbere the praise of those properties. (56)

The neutral circumlocution in "of their humilite content to be nameles" and in "forbere the praise of those properties" civilly deflects the emotional pressure of the particular on the moral imagination. It also asks for degrees of outrage relative to the polity: that a king should have mistresses is part of the ways of the world and, besides, a private matter; compared to faults of leadership, it does not warrant much attention.

When More summarizes the history of Edward's coming to power,

---

99. Stanley E. Fish, *Self-Consuming Artifacts: The Experience of Seventeenth-Century Literature* (Berkeley and Los Angeles: University of California Press, 1972), 91.

an oblique understatement invokes the collaboration of intelligent men:

> Al three [the brothers Edward, George, and Richard, sons of the Duke of York] as they wer great states of birthe, soo were they greate and statelye of stomacke, gredye and ambicious of authoritie, and impacient of parteners. (6)

In the last phrase—"impacient of parteners"—the tone casually shifts from admiration to outrage, and finally to cool assessment of the typical traits of ambitious men. Again, there are degrees of outrage: that there are ambitious people and that they should be disinclined to friendship should not raise a moral fever. More describes in a similar fashion the sort of people Buckingham and Richard gathered as allies in their plot:

> Of spiritual men thei toke such as had wit, and were in aucthoritie among the peple for oppinion of ther lerning, and had no scrupilouse consience. (58)

The compression of the Latinate "no scrupilouse consience" brings the sentence to a satiric close.

However, the instability of civil irony in the vernacular at this point in the development of the language makes some passages of *Richard III* almost uninterpretable. The death of Clarence may be either a macabre joke or a sad tale:

> For were it by the Queene and the Lordes of her bloode whiche highlye maligned the kynges kinred (as women commonly not of malice but of nature hate them whome theire housebandes love) or were it a prowde appetite of the Duke himself entendinge to be king: at the lest wise heinous Treason was there layde to his charge, and finallye wer hee fautye were hee faultlesse, attainted was hee by parliament, and judged to the death, and therupon hastely drouned in a Butte of Malmesey, whose death kynge Edwarde (albeit he commaunded it) when he wist it was done, pitiously bewailed and sorrowfully repented. (7)

Here, More's irony runs uneasily between an apparent mockery of Edward IV in particular and a darkly ironic view of kings in general. At the beginning of this history, Edward is a good king. Here, however, More has either changed his mind or switched to the far view of the Christian homilist, who lumps all kings together in worldly corruption. Civil wit has escaped More's control, and a steady moral point of view is abandoned for sheer linguistic fun.

So also, in the description of Richard, the sentence again seems to set up the irony at the end:

> He slewe with his owne handes king Henry the sixt, being prisoner in the Tower, as menne constantly saye, and that without commaundemente or knoweledge of the king, whiche woulde undoubtedly yf he had entended that thinge, have appointed that boocherly office, to some other then his owne borne brother. (8)

More could be implying that a king might very *well* appoint that butcherly office to his own born brother; it is the way of kings. But again, if More is now satirizing Edward, he is either contradicting himself or has abandoned the civilist's independent judgment in favor of a homiletic irony that condemns all kings. The "sauciness" that James found offensive in Raleigh's history is not parody of anything and everything. It is a tacit demonstration of how educated subjects might "talk [to each other] of [their] princes." For More, wishing to separate himself from the apolitical pathos of romance and the apolitical fury of homily, the problem was to find a dispassionate note. But because this dispassion was so difficult to achieve in the vernacular, More's solution was a parody that too easily tipped over into a *débat*-like giddiness standing in marked contrast to Raleigh's sobriety.

Not being able to sustain a civilist's stance, More finally turns to two different "authorities" to govern the text. One is the citizens of London, whose criticism of political chicanery is mute, giving way to the "voice" of divine truth. The second is Bishop Morton, who dominates the last section of the history, the same Morton who figures as a wise leader in the first book of the *Utopia*. More seems unclear which authority he finds most reliable. The citizens, the people, are the spokesmen for a traditional ceremonial mode, where truth is truth, piety is simplicity, the polity should be well ordered, and kings should care for their subjects. The end of the history reverts to their simple norms. After Buckingham decides that Richard has been acclaimed king, the London citizens, "not able to dissemble theyr sorow, were faine at his backe to turne their face to the wall, while the doloure of their heart braste oute at theyr eyen" (77). The contrast between the crafty speech of wicked politicians and the sorrowful silence of the good folk condemns speech itself. In the end, homiletic formulas take over and firmly condemn Richard as a wicked, wicked man.[100] If one is looking for a civil mode, then one is likely to find this section a failure.

The other political governor of this text is Bishop Morton, spokesman for the new class of humanists and servants to the Tudors. Like the simple citizens, these men also believe that truth is truth, piety is simplicity, the polity should be well ordered, and kings should care for their subjects. The difference is that men like Morton know all about political "dealing [it]self."[101] They are not given to repeating homiletic formulas and weeping over pitiful women and babes. They know about political constraints on human life, and they are prepared to deal with those constraints pragmatically. The figure of Morton cuts through ceremony's centripetal gaze toward authority and

---

100. Indeed, in places the sentences seem to be exercises in political language, where, ultimately, the language of pragmatism eludes More's control. Buckingham muses on getting rid of Hastings: "And of trouth the lord Chamberlen of very trust shewed unto Catesbye, the mistrust that other began to have in the mater. And therfore he fering lest their mocions might with the lord Hastinges minishe his credence, wherunto onely al the matter lenid, procured the protectour hastely to ridde him. And much the rather, for that he trusted by his deth to obtaine much of the rule that the lorde Hastinges bare in his countrey: the only desire whereof, was the allective that induced him to be partener and one specyall contriver of al this horrible treson" (46). The diction of Buckingham's calm deliberation ("might . . . minishe his credence," "procured," "obtaine much of the rule") and of the writer's clear assessment of his motives ("the allective that induced him") suddenly gives way to frightened complaint: "al this horrible treson." If one thinks that vigor and raciness are the great glory of sixteenth-century prose, as many literary historians have, then one will congratulate More for finding in this last section, not paralleled in the Latin, a rapid, colloquial style that assumes unambiguous moral judgments of virtually all politics. (See for example, A. W. Reed, "Philological Notes" in *The English Works of Sir Thomas More, Facsimile Edition of William Rastell's Edition of 1557*, ed. W. E. Campbell [London: Eyre and Spottiswoode, 1931], 1:189). When Sylvester speculates that More did not finish his history because it was too much of a "charter" legitimizing the Tudors, he imagines a civil More rereading his manuscript and dissatisfied with its ceremonial division of rulers into kind protectors and evil monsters (*Complete Works of St. Thomas More*, 2:ciii). Sylvester also speculates that More did not finish the work because the third Duke of Buckingham, son of the Duke of Buckingham in the last scene of the history, was in 1514 the next heir to the throne of a still sonless Henry VIII (lxix).

101. "Dealing self" is Rastell's phrase in his interpolations to the English version in his 1557 edition (*Richard III*, 44). In Donno's view, Morton is being satirized here (435). She argues that a humanist like More would be unlikely to find a man praiseworthy for worldly experience. But Ascham's preference for theory over experience in *The Schoolmaster* is not the official humanist position. In *The Laws of Ecclesiastical Polity*, 5.7.1–2, Richard Hooker has great praise for men of experience.

instead redirects the alliances of the educated to other men like themselves. In the concluding scene of *Richard III*, More suggests such an alliance when he describes Buckingham's secret plotting against the king as a "conspiracy or rather good confederacion" (87).

But something fails More in the vernacular handling of this man who might lead a "confederacion." Morton's Aesopian story about the lion-king who decreed that all horned beasts should leave the wood and the scurried departure of one animal out of fear that the bunch of flesh on his forehead might be called horns is not an articulate critique of power. The final moral lesson is cast in the form of folkish cunning and quiescence, not in the form of articulate sagacity, assuming mastery of the world. Although in its point that a king may define the world just as he pleases, the fable resists romance reverence, at the same time it assumes with a shrug that kings will always have to be suffered. It is the same kind of cheerful folkishness on which More so much depended in the *Dialogue of Comfort Against Tribulation*, supposedly written at the end of his life in the Tower of London. There the "solution" to injustice is to trust in God and regard human follies with serenity.

The pull between the London citizens and Morton reflects not only More's own ambiguity but the ambiguous goals of early English humanism: an educational mission to enlighten all members of society, primarily through vernacular translations of the Bible (of which, of course, More was suspicious because of the errors in translation); an educational mission aimed at an aristocracy that enjoyed too much its horses and hounds; a happy "confederacion" of educated wits whose greatest pleasure was to talk to each other in good, classical Latin; and a more serious "confederacion" of political criticism. When the wit and the rational analysis combined to render irrelevant both the wisdom of Christianity and the wisdom of the simple, then a secularity emerged that humanists themselves found threatening. The shrillness of Ascham's complaint, "ye know not what hurt ye do to learning that care not for words but for matter, and so make a divorce betwixt the tong and the heart"[102] stems from a half-perceived knowledge that humanism has within it the possibility of a much worse divorce, between a world where the coincidence of human action and God's word still counts and a world where it does not. After all, the Machiavelli of *The Prince* is a humanist too.

102. Roger Ascham, *The Schoolmaster*, ed. Lawrence Ryan, 6. On this conflict in other humanists, leading to Hobbes, see Victoria Kahn, *Rhetoric, Prudence, and Skepticism in the Renaissance* (Ithaca: Cornell University Press, 1985).

Let us go back to More himself, who is a singular figure in the windy politics of the Tudors. In *Renaissance Self-Fashioning*, Stephen Greenblatt has painted More as vacillating between the eager bureaucrat and the pious Catholic—on the one hand pleased with his success at court, on the other longing for the body of the church.[103] But the picture may be more complicated and less focused on the solitary individual who one day sees politics as an exciting career and the next as "absurd" and "mad." (Greenblatt's language echoes with existentialism touched up with romantic alienation.) However, between "More" as constituted by the homily-with-fool and "More" the successful bureaucrat at the court of Henry VIII, there is "More" the civilist, a man who casts a suspicious eye not on all politics but only politics under kings like Henry Tudor. It is significant that except for the metaphor of the stage-play in the sultan-and-shoemaker passage, *Richard III* plays a small role in Greenblatt's account. Consideration of this text, however, might have led to reflection on the instability of civil rhetoric at this point in the history of the language and also in the history of the conditions that support such a rhetoric. In fact, the instabilities of civil rhetoric in *Richard III* explain why Aristotle connects rhetoric with debate protected by the law; only with such protection can a speaker claim to pronounce for others like himself. Otherwise, his stance may easily become the pleasurable *sound* of criticism, the delights of Tacitean ironies for those who have been brought up on Ovid (and for the Tudors, humanists could be interesting but ignorable pets), or the eruptions of the alienated wanderer. When in the *Utopia* More criticizes the practices of European kings, he does not speak for himself but instead shifts the burden of authority onto a solitary sage, not unlike Hoccleve's Beggar in *The Regiment of Princes*.

Although the conclusion is ready to hand that More would have been more of a civilist had he been born into a civil culture, the alternative conclusion has to be considered: More failed to write a fully civil history not because he *could* not but because he did not *want* to. If the choice comes down to the claims of piety against the claims of reason, we might dwell on it a little longer and, out of respect for More, overcome the peculiar transformations that religious belief undergoes in the hands of More's latter-day sympathizers.

No writer of the sixteenth century evokes the rhetoric of piety as much as Thomas More: here was a man who was ready to go to the block for his convictions. Even the "embarrassing" facts of his

103. Greenblatt, *Renaissance Self-Fashioning*, 11–73.

opposition to a vernacular Bible and his persecution of heretics are outweighed by the circumstances of his death. Now the trouble with this rhetoric of piety is its disbarring all objections: "More was willing to die for what he believed in; what is it but arrogance in a moral posture that claims it can judge whether or not More's convictions were worth dying for?" But this is just what a civil "rhetoric of seriousness"—as opposed to a rhetoric of piety—might hold: "People die for lots of reasons; surely it makes good sense to decide if the reasons were worth the price; the tympani of solemnity merely interfere with clear thought. Besides, you should not be so taken with that sultan-and-shoemaker passage. The view of things *sub specie aeternitatis* is always going to make deliberate political action look trivial, even when it is performed in the name of justice." Because in classical rhetoric piety is connected to the *patria*, compromise with rational human judgment is fairly easy. But when piety is connected to transcendent truth backed up by a story of mysterious birth, unjust condemnation, willing submission to death, and a supernatural justification, the accommodation is almost impossible.

The struggle between these two generates the deep unsteadiness of *Richard III*. For More, some things are not just "serious questions," they are the Solemn Truth. One of those truths is Christian fellowship, which is deeply threatened by any declaration of an independent national church. To understand this fellowship requires neither clear thought nor serious argument but rather belief in God's revealed word and attention to the promptings of reason as God put them in human nature and his church. Civil prose has the virtue of analyzing political "dealing" without being terrified by it, but its excitement with the give-and-take of politics obscures the incontrovertible Christian truth that justice starts with goodwill toward one's fellows, not with clever speeches and bold actors. Whatever the obvious political and rhetorical limitations of the silent folk in the sultan-and-shoemaker passage, their simple judgment is utterly reliable because in fixing on human motivation, they judge as God does.

In the modern liberal democracies, we do not master tyrants by threatening them with hell anymore. But we still have the problem of what we are going to be serious about, how serious we will be, and how society will encourage this seriousness. Some may hold that there is no truth beyond accurate description anyway and certainly no truth that justifies grand, emotional gestures. Others, holding that human happiness is the only truth, may "believe" in freedom or therapy or the play of art; but, happily, because the suppression of freedom or the failure of therapy or the frustration of play are failures of structural systems (political or psychological) rather than of the individual's goodwill, we can be serious without threats of punishment. Others, believing only in a rhetoric of literary criticism, regard solemnity in historiography as just one of several attitudes that has to be carefully handled, as if to say: "Let's face it. Audiences secretly love solemnity, but because they want it to come from a 'tough sensibility,' the trick lies in the rhetorical pitch of the preliminary toughness. With a subject like Thomas More, this management is unusually ticklish because too strong a note of admiration might make one sound pious. A nonbeliever has then to shift the slant of his solemnity toward More's 'courage' in the abstract [the historian knows what it is to stand up to the world] or toward the 'terrible choice' between his life and his belief [the historian knows the demands of a Sartrean existentialism] or toward the 'appalling tyranny' of Henry [the historian is of the sort who will fight for justice]. It's difficult, but then civil prosaicists writing literary history should relish the challenge."

These rhetorical managements have the pomp of serious reflection. They do not, however, confront the central difficulty of More's belief in God and a unified Christendom. They have simply shifted the "solemn" onto more acceptable categories: the sanctity of the individual over any institution and the sanctity of freedom of choice over human—and certainly over extrahuman—authority. Contemporary criticism of premodern texts enacts these shifts over and over again; we do not like to admit that writers who left such compelling works were also deeply religious. Still, when even nonbelievers are moved by the silent folk in the sultan-and-shoemaker passage, they are acknowledging some kind of belief in a Radical Serious: politicians should be leaders, not power-seekers; virtue is not cleverness. Such nonbelievers could conceivably hold the following position: that there is a Radical Serious; that people need to be brought up with love of it, a desire to define it, and humility before it; that the church teaches these kinds of love and desire as well as they can be taught by any institution; and that successful teaching depends upon a love for the church that cuts across national boundaries. To a believer, of course, such an attitude sounds fairly cold-blooded, the church having been stripped of the heartbeat of revelation. But the position shows more respect for More than cheapening him with a rhetoric of heroism and individual "rights" that would have left him perplexed or amused. More should not too easily be made "one of us."

3

The Recovery of Ceremony at the End of the Sixteenth Century: Sidney's *Defense* and Hooker's *Of the Laws of Ecclesiastical Polity*

Both Sidney's *Defense* and Hooker's *Laws of Ecclesiastical Polity* are defenses or apologias. The two unauthorized versions of Sidney's work of 1595 bore both titles: an *Apologie for Poetrie* and *The Defence of Poesie*. Hooker's *Laws* is an apologia for the Anglican church. Sensing, like Ascham, a divorce between the tongue and the heart, both Sidney and Hooker defend traditional supports of the communal quest, ceremonial poetry and ceremonial ritual. Although much of the defensiveness of these works derives from the familiar battle with creatures who do not naturally seek the home of spiritual truth, another motive is political, to justify hierarchical authority. The defensiveness is itself telling, for in a ceremonial *family*, after all, there should be no need for *politics*.

The need for these defenses and apologias was prompted by attacks on a ceremonial mode from various quarters. One source, as we have seen, was the humanists' attack on royal pageantry as expensive and stupefying. The second was no less direct: the Puritan attack on the pageantry of the church—the vestments and decorations of which Queen Elizabeth was especially fond. The stories of Wolsey's suggesting to Pole that he might read Machiavelli and of Essex's pulling a Marprelate pamphlet from beneath his robes and waving it tauntingly in front of Elizabeth point to a third and extremely powerful assault on ceremony's communal myth, whether in spectacular pageants or oral stories: the printed book.

In her monumental study *The Printing Press as an Agent of Change*, Elizabeth Eisenstein appropriately warns against exaggerating the effects of print on the culture of early modern Europe. Instead, she cautions, print emphasized tensions already in existence before Gutenberg's invention of 1452. The spread of books did not destroy an oral and visual tradition; printed woodcuts spread the image far more widely than before.[1] Luther's dramatic challenge of 1517 was not the first protest against clerical abuse; print made Protestantism a powerful social movement because it could mobilize sympathizers far away from Wittenberg. While the widespread availability of printed scholarship consolidated an international humanism, numerous printed originals or translations in the vernacular also increased national identity. Print did not create but rather exaggerated an already existing gap between classical scholarship and native traditions; the same machinery that could produce great editions of the classics could also turn out the ballads and broadsides once communicated orally. Print also gave the scholar a new independence; he could, like More, stay at home and work for one throne, or, like Erasmus, promote himself as a freelance scholar and writer.[2]

One of the most lasting effects of print was in the social arena. Print distinguished between entrepreneurial authors pursuing a career in books and aristocratic authors still circulating their poems in manuscript. For Sidney in the *Defense*, the printing press is the most readily identifiable culprit in a new and unbecoming self-display. It has, in his view, given ambition to "base men with servile wits . . . who think it enough if they can be rewarded of the printer."[3] The press has

1. Elizabeth L. Eisenstein, *The Printing Press as an Agent of Change: Communications and Cultural Transformations in Early-Modern Europe*, 2 vols. (Cambridge: Cambridge University Press, 1979), 1:66–69.

2. Ibid., 1:331, 355–56, 359–60, and 396. On Erasmus, see "Erasmus' Relations with His Printers," in P. S. Allen, *Erasmus: Lectures and Wayfaring Sketches* (Oxford: Clarendon Press, 1934), 109–37.

3. Sir Philip Sidney, *A Defence Of Poetry*, in *Miscellaneous Prose of Sir Philip Sidney*, ed.

brought forth mere "bastard poets," who instead of being "content to suppress the outflowings of their wit" have "by publishing them" thought to be "accounted knights of the same order" as aristocrats (111). But print is just one of many kinds of usurpation. Historiography too is an "underling" (109), and philosophers who pick out the "sweet mysteries of poetry" are like "ungrateful prentices [who were] not content to set up shops for themselves, but sought by all means to discredit their masters" (107). In the hands of these sophists, who "trimmeth . . . their garments with guards of poesy" (109), poetry and good learning are debased.

In this confusion of print and marketable status, poetry carries the force of wise tradition. For Sidney, it is an aristocratic calling. His famous defense of the poet against the philosopher and the historian defines the argument intellectually: effective poetry versus ineffective philosophy and history. But the attacks on would-be poets rushing off to the printer also define the argument socially: aristocratic poets versus climbing professionals. By the late sixteenth century, the literary skills of men like More, Tunstall, and Pace have been drawn into a tighter courtly circle, which prefers pastorals, romances, and sonnets to essays on education. Sidney, as we know, was in the midst of this courtly current. Even before being knighted in 1583, he was the model of chivalry at Elizabeth's court. In 1575, he was present at Leicester's famous festivities for Elizabeth at Kenilworth. In the same year, he participated in the formalities arranged for the christening of Lady Russell's daughter. In 1578, he wrote a pastoral drama, *The Lady of May*, for Elizabeth's entertainment. In 1581, he was one of several knights in a pageant in which "Four Foster Children of Desire" assaulted the Fortress of Perfect Beauty—the gallery in which Elizabeth sat at one end of the tiltyard at Whitehall—and, after a two-day battle, were overcome by the Queen's virtue.[4] Sidney's playful refurbishing of the old Aristotelian triad of philosophy-history-literature, and of Ciceronian defenses of rhetoric against philosophy is no more central to the *Defense* than his defense of the poet-knight and his chivalric activities.[5] More memorable and more visually striking

Katherine Duncan-Jones and Jan van Dorsten (Oxford: Clarendon Press, 1973), 111. All references to the *Defense* are to this edition.

4. James M. Osborn, *Young Philip Sidney: 1572–1577* (New Haven: published for the Elizabethan Club by Yale University Press, 1972), 325, 371, 501, 505; William A. Ringler, Jr., ed., *The Poems of Sir Philip Sidney* (Oxford: Clarendon Press, 1962), 518 n. 4.

5. For a reading of Sidney's "poetry" as a mediator in a "body politic" torn by "civil

than prose, poetry reinforces a communal society by allying truth with the affect of personal relationships, crucial to which is the oral word. Learned books can put goodness before human eyes, but only love can turn subjects into ceremonial beholders.

The Romance Leader: Silent Overseer and Amiable Display

In defending the poet as a superior leader and social exemplum, Sidney articulates the implied argument of medieval romance: the knight is the best persuader to virtue because his own beautiful adoration of the truth draws subjects to him (as in *Astrophil and Stella* 71, "So while thy beauty draws the heart to love"). In a ceremonial mode, justification of the oracular teacher is unnecessary; if the world is chaotic and meaningless, then any figure not from this world carries authority, and if it is a mother or father, a comforting authority. When knightly leaders, however, remain firmly *in* this world, then more work has to be done to authorize them; the relationship in feudalism between knights joined in fellowship and the right of one knight to land and power is not without conflict. The Other of romance is not just a mysteriously appearing enemy, or a boar, or a dragon but also the ruling lord himself, who must be "storied" as different from ordinary knights in order to legitimize his claim to be the best protector.[6]

The ruling lord's difference is marked not by his superior political theory but by a wisdom that is virtually silent. Romance leaders— Mark in the Tristan story, Theseus in "The Knight's Tale," Arthur in the *Morte D'Arthur*—are not the central figures of the narrative. Nevertheless, their power pervades the romance world;[7] they give other journeyers an identity; Perceval, Bors, and Galahad all announce themselves as members of Arthur's Round Table. In Chaucer's "Knight's Tale," Theseus's final speech on change, order, and human patience answers the questions posed earlier by Palamon and

---

war among the Muses," see Margaret W. Ferguson, *Trials of Desire: Renaissance Defenses of Poetry* (New Haven: Yale University Press, 1983), 137–62.

6. Cf. Jameson, *The Political Unconscious*, 118–19.

7. Tuve, *Allegorical Imagery*, 316.

Arcite about the purpose of human suffering. But Chaucer feels compelled to authorize Theseus even more emphatically by the sudden introduction of Theseus's father, Egeus, a character not mentioned before his first appearance late in the narrative. Egeus's wisdom, however, is not an elaborate political theory; it is the simple knowledge that life is sorrow and that human beings are "pilgrymes passynge to and fro." After this interview with a wise-man-who-says-very-little, Theseus is transformed from the superior warrior to the true father of his courtly "children," fit to deliver a sermon from Boethius.

The mediation that turns a silent and potentially dreadful lord into a lovable one is provided by ceremony's innocents. One of these innocents is a woman, the lady of the castle who holds power only by consent of her husband and who is the erotic cynosure of potentially restive knights.[8] Another innocent is nature. In the medieval *Secreta Secretorum*, an alleged letter of Aristotle to his pupil Alexander containing advice on ruling, the king's knowledge of governing is analogous to the knowledge of caring for botanical "offspring." "Aristotle" advises the prince to care for his subjects as if they were trees in a garden and to regard himself as their keeper and savior.[9]

8. The romance of courtly love functions politically to contain the restlessness of landless knights who must attach themselves to another leader. See Erich Köhler, "Les Romans de Chrétien de Troyes," *Revue de L'Institut de Sociologie* 36 (1963): 271–84; also Herbert Möller, "The Social Causation of the Courtly Love Complex," *Comparative Studies of Society and History* 1 (1958): 137–63 and "The Meaning of Courtly Love," *Journal of American Folklore* 73 (1960): 39–52; Duby, *Three Orders*, 302–3. For romance as a controller of deviance, see Jameson's somewhat fuller version of the chapter in *The Political Unconscious*, "Magical Narratives: Romance as Genre," in *NLH* 7 (1975): 135–63. On the courtly mistress as an extension of the king's power, see C. Marchello-Nizia, "Amour Courtois, Societé Masculine et Figures du Pouvoir," *Annales. Économies. Sociétés. Civilisations* 36 (1981): 969–82. The rise of romance in the twelfth century is paralleled by the rise of the cult of the Virgin—another powerful intercessor between a lord who can sometimes be threatening and a devoted servant. It is also the period of the rise of the literature giving advice to princes (Lester K. Born, "The Perfect Prince: A Study in Thirteenth- and Fourteenth-Century Ideals," *Speculum* 3 [1928]: 470–504). The split between stern lord and interceding knight appears in religious works as well. See in *The Ancrene Riwle*, the analogy between the soul saved by Christ and a lady in a castle besieged by a tempting lord and rescued by a good and true knight (trans. M. B. Salu [London: Burns and Oates, 1955], 172–73).

9. "Thow shalt lewe [believe] well that thy subjectis bene lyke a gardyn, in wych bene dyvers maneres of trees, and thou shalt noght holde ham as londe berrynge thornes wythout frute. Whyle that thy Subjectis duryth in estate, shall dure the defense of thy realme and of thy Powere [.] And therfor the be-hovyth hame to governe wel, and fro wronges ham defende, and that thou ham helpe in al hare nedys. And therfor

Moreover, just as in a ceremonial discourse the language of truth is accessible to the farmer and herder, so here the lord's knowledge is allied to the wisdom of the folk. In the *Secreta Secretorum*, the language of ruling is analogous to the language of the body.[10] Following the Pythagorean scheme that linked the four elements, the four seasons, the four humors, and the four ages of man, the author of the *Secreta* admonishes the king to know the four seasons of the year, which are allied to the four elements and to the four bodily humors.[11] Spring is a young man at a wedding; summer is a "spowse ful woxen of body [,] and Parfite age, in ful vertue of natural hete" (243–44). "Hervest" is a "woman of grete age, that nowe wox a colde and hade nede to be hote clothyde, for that the yowuthe is Passyde, and age neghyth, Wherfor hit is no mervaile yf beute she hath loste" (245). Winter is "an olde katte, al overcome wyth age and travaill, that lyve ne myght, for she is al dispoylit of beute and of Streynth and vertue" (246). The ruler's knowledge is extraordinarily simple: it is the wisdom of weddings and old age, of gardens and trees.

The *Secreta* does not place great emphasis on the king's eloquence; much more important is his vigilance with the bodies of his subjects, which signify character traits (226–36). In this vigilance, the king should maintain a silence that distinguishes him from the talkers around him. He should keep his thoughts secret from his counselors, disguising his approval of their advice (209). He should "assay" his advisers by telling them that he needs money and watching whether they suggest he get it from his people or offer it themselves (210). His aloof reticence will make his people burn with desire to hear his speech (12). He should refrain from mingling with the rural folk and appear before all his people only once a year. When he does so, his political "speech" should be a performance, not human talk: he should dress in "royalle and excellent . . . array . . . in riche and

---

the nedyth to have a Constabil that shal not bene a destruere of thy trees, but a kepere and a Savere" (*Three Prose Versions of the Secreta Secretorum*, ed. Robert Steele, Part I, Early English Text Society, Extra Series 74 [London: Kegan Paul, 1898], 213).

10. The king's knowledge of physiognomy enables him to distinguish good and evil people (216–36); he must also know about the four elements of the earth and the four humors (236–38); he must know how to care for his own body with proper sleeping, walking, cleaning his teeth (238–39); he must know the right hours and times of eating and drinking (240–41). On the connection of power to the order of the universe, especially the order described by pseudo-Dionysius, see Duby, *Three Orders*, 111–12.

11. *Secreta*, 243. On the Pythagorean tetrad, see S. K. Heninger, Jr., "Some Renaissance Versions of the Pythagorean Tetrad," *Studies in the Renaissance* 8 (1961): 7–33.

precious clothyng, and . . . of the most straunge cloth that may oughwhere be founde" (12), and he should have all his barons and knights about him in their "bright armoure," himself sitting "on a stede with his septre in his hond, and the Crowne on his hed, and on his body his cote Armure of his royalle armes" (13). The Tudors' powerful "discourse of sovereignty" in their pageants, tournaments, progresses, and masques splendidly fulfilled the *Secreta*'s advice.[12]

The *Secreta*'s one exception to a king's stunning silence is in the interest of morale-building. "In tyme of warres and batayles," a king should be "a fayre and a swete spekere with amyable and gracious wordis" (12). The king's watchfulness should not infect his royal discourse, which, when it is uttered at all, should persuade subjects that everything is just as it should be and that the king loves them. Generally, however, a king should only *appear* as if he were talking. Instead, he should create his royal performative statement out of the trees, bushes, grass, and flowers that he attends to so carefully, the rich robes that drape his body, the trappings on his horse, and the array of his knights.

When Renaissance schoolmasters decided that a command of classical rhetoric was necessary for government, they saw its chief use in displaying to full advantage the king or his worshipful subjects. If, says Elyot, a noble man "shall happe to reason in counsaile, or shall speke in a great audience, or to strange ambassadours of great princes" (1:76), it is good for him to have his rhetorical house in order; otherwise he will embarrass himself or the king. For Thomas Wilson in *The Arte of Rhetorique*, however, Ciceronian articulateness is not an ambassadorial display of the home court but a technique in political control. As others have observed, Wilson's *Arte* is paradoxically motivated.[13] In the preface Wilson says that eloquence is for those in authority, but in printing his *Arte* he made eloquence available to the very audience that authority had to control. On this score, Sidney is less muddled than Wilson: the enemy are the purveyors of a bastard

12. On the politics of Tudor and Stuart pageants, see Anglo, *Spectacle, Pageantry, and Early Tudor Policy*; David Bergeron, *English Civic Pageantry, 1558–1642* (London: Edward Arnold, 1971); Stephen Orgel, *The Illusion of Power: Political Theater in the English Renaissance* (Berkeley and Los Angeles: University of California Press, 1975); Roy Strong, *The Cult of Elizabeth: Elizabethan Portraiture and Pageantry* (London: Thames and Hudson, 1977); Frances Yates, *Astraea: The Imperial Theme in the Sixteenth Century* (London: Routledge and Kegan Paul, 1975).

13. Whigham, *Ambition and Privilege: The Social Tropes of Elizabethan Courtesy Theory* (Berkeley and Los Angeles: University of California Press, 1984), 2.

eloquence—the "prose-printers" and imitators of Cicero with their "Nizolian paper-books" (117) and "herbarists" with the "tedious prattling" of certain "printed discourses" (118). The rhetorical dilemma for aristocratic authority compelled to make "defenses," "apologies," and "justifications" is to outtalk these linguistic climbers and at the same time maintain an air of perfectly self-justified silence. In the *Defense* Sidney solves this problem by offering many articulate reasons why poetry has a superior epistemology and superior psychagogic powers but finally by relying on his own songlike charm as the most powerful, and, in the end, silent, reason of all.

Sidney's Silly Poetry and Grave Governor

In the brilliance of Elizabeth's court, a Maloryesque nostalgia for an aristocratic past would hardly serve, and Sidney found a less bewildered attitude in the playful rhetoric of Neo-Platonism.[14] The "ravishing prose" of the *Defense* is not, however, a surface feature of style.[15] It is generated by a ceremonial discourse's fundamental opposition between an earthly quest and a spiritual home and the identification of the authoritative language of truth with the simple language of nature. To be sure, the *Defense* has civil-sounding arguments. Sidney acknowledges that he must listen to objections lest his own reasons carry weight merely because they have no opposition (99). In announcing the poet as a "maker" (77) of "what may be and should be" (81), he seems to hold that language is a

14. For arguments that Sidney was not the exemplary knight he portrayed in the *Defense*, see Richard A. Lanham, "Sidney: The Ornament of his Age," *Southern Review; Australian Journal of Literary Studies* 2 (1967): 319–40; F. J. Levy, "Philip Sidney Reconsidered," *ELR* 2 (1972): 5–18; Louis Adrian Montrose, "Celebration and Insinuation: Sir Philip Sidney and the Motives of Elizabethan Courtship," *Renaissance Drama*, n.s. 8 (1977): 3–35; Alan Hager, "The Exemplary Mirage: Fabrication of Sir Philip Sidney's Biographical Image and the Sidney Reader," *ELH* 48 (1981): 1–16. On Sidney's connection with the politics of his time, see Andrew D. Weiner, *Sir Philip Sidney and the Poetics of Protestantism: A Study of Contexts* (Minneapolis: University of Minnesota Press, 1978); Alan Sinfield, "Sidney and Du Bartas," *Comparative Literature* 27 (1975): 8–20 and "The Cultural Politics of the *Defence of Poetry*," in *Sir Philip Sidney and the Interpretation of Renaissance Culture: The Poet in His Time and in Ours*, ed. Gary F. Waller and Michael D. Moore (London: Croom Helm, 1984), 124–43.
15. Paul Alpers, *The Poetry of The Faerie Queene* (Princeton: Princeton University Press, 1967), 282.

human tool for constructing reality, language authorized not by God but by the poet's independent imagination. Nevertheless, even if we were to qualify the now-accepted argument that the organization of the *Defense* imitates a classical judicial oration[16] by characterizing Sidney's apology as judicial in form but epideictic in spirit, the implication that it has assimilated classical debate cannot be accepted. The heart of this work is not the agon of classical oratory but ceremony's spiritual quest.

As a result, the old Ciceronian *movere*, Sidney's chief justification for poetry's superiority, has an exaltation it never had in Cicero. For Sidney, poets have a "delightful vein" (75) and a "charming sweetness" (74); poetry has "sweet delights" (76); after the divine and philosophical, the third kind of poets is "the first and most noble sort," waited on in "the excellentest languages and best understandings" (81); the poet delivers forth his ideas "in such excellency as he had imagined them" (79); the divine poets "both in antiquity and excellency, were they that did imitate the unconceivable excellencies of God" (80). The conclusion of the famous "golden world" passage ends in a Boethian home. In short sentences, Sidney first marches the other claimants to the imitation of nature through the court: "So doth the astronomer. . . . So doth the geometrician and arithmetician. . . . So doth the musicians. . . . The natural philosopher thereon hath his name, and the moral philosopher. . . . The lawyer saith. . . . The grammarian . . . and the rhetorician and logician. . . . The physician . . . and the metaphysic." But when the poet steps on the scene, the·passage moves from confinement to expansiveness ("freely ranging only within the zodiac of his own wit"), from a brazen nature to a golden one, from earthly gardens to floral tapestries of paradise (78).

Along with the general ceremonial exaltations is a ceremonial mother. Poetry is a mistress who must be defended against the poet-haters of the world: "Alas, Love, I would thou couldst as well defend thyself as thou canst offend others" (103). The perfect freedom of poetry is a pastoral landscape of mother's milk and honey, presided over by a woman who "hath been the first light-giver to ignorance, and first nurse, whose milk by little and little enabled them [human beings] to feed afterwards of tougher knowledges" (74); the *architektonike* of learning is "mistress-knowledge" (82); poetry is a serene matron untroubled by an unruly child, who "like an unmannerly daughter showing a bad education, causeth her mother Poesy's honesty to be called in question" (116); diction is the apparel of "that

---

16. Kenneth Orne Myrick, "The *Defence of Poesie* as a Classical Oration," in *Sir Philip Sidney as a Literary Craftsman* (Cambridge: Harvard University Press, 1935), 46–83.

honey-flowing matron Eloquence" (117). Just as Philosophia rescues Boethius from darkness, captivity, constraint, and storms, here poetry the mistress-singer lifts Sidney above mere historians and philosophers, who are "sullen" (83), "captived" (90), "manacled" (90), "tied" (85), "laden" (83), "compassed within the circle of a question" (78), "wrapped within the fold of the proposed subject" (80), inclined to fall in ditches, and blind (82). Instead she shows him the picture that "doth . . . strike, pierce, [and] possess the sight of the soul," satisfying the "inward conceit" (85).

The force of the passages that break loose from parrying with opponents is to testify to poetry's home in innocent nature. One hardly has to mention it before even the most articulate courtier is singing in adoration. "Silly" poetry (74) holds "children from play, and old men from the chimney corner" (92). Its silliness enables it to speak to "the inward light" which "in nature" teaches us "it is well to do well" (91). Those unaware that the famous passages in Plato are flowers of poetry "did never walk into Apollo's garden" (75); the poet leads you to virtue "as if your journey should lie through a fair vineyard, at the first giv[ing] you a cluster of grapes, that full of that taste, you may long to pass further" (92). For poetry, literacy is not necessary; its powerful images move the low as well as the high: "See whether wisdom and temperance in Ulysses and Diomedes, valour in Achilles, friendship in Nisus and Euryalus, even to an ignorant man carry not an apparent shining" (86). Free of the philosopher's and historian's mature insistence on logical precision and levelheaded realism, the poet is, like Perceval or Galahad, a lovely youth, inspiring hope of salvation for the Christian community. He offers release from the fallen feelings of "professors of learning": fear, exasperation, anger, despair, and, above all, the very defensiveness of "defenses." The deepest informing influence on Sidney's syntax, hyperbolic diction, visionary prosopopoeias, and longing for a golden world opposed to history is neither the Renaissance Neo-Platonism of the Florentine Academy nor Renaissance Aristotelianism; it is a ceremonial mode that had absorbed the Neo-Platonic quest at least by the time of St. Augustine and then had become the basic structure of romance narrative and the lyric.[17]

17. Studies of the classical and continental influences on Sidney's *Defense* include A. C. Hamilton, "Sidney's Idea of the 'Right Poet,'" *Comparative Literature* 9 (1957): 51–59; O. B. Hardison, Jr., "The Two Voices of Sidney's *Apology for Poetry*," *English Literary Renaissance* 2 (1972): 83–99; D. H. Craig, "A Hybrid Growth: Sidney's Theory of Poetry in *An Apology for Poetry*," *English Literary Renaissance* 10 (1980): 183–201. On Platonism

It is this naturally lovable leader that is Sidney's strongest defense against the philosopher and the historian. As has often been observed, Sidney borrows the Ciceronian argument that rhetoric is superior to philosophy because it has greater psychagogic power. But his poet-rhetorician is not so much forceful as amiable. His competition, the philosopher, is obviously not fit to be at court: he is "rudely clothed," he egotistically displays the book he has written, and, with his "definitions, divisions, and distinctions" and his somber fixation on "vice," he is altogether lacking in grace. In a later distinction between "professors" of learning, who labor over their "art," and courtiers, who are "naturally artful," the scholar-philosopher is sent packing back to Oxford. The historian is equally boorish: he lives in another age, he is "curious" and "inquisitive"; and he dominates conversation, tending to "chafe[s]" and playing the "tyrant" at dinner (83–84). With the natural "amiability" recommended in the *Secreta*, the poet shines more brilliantly than these two defensive and self-conscious egomaniacs. Sidney is just as "homely and familiar" (93) in his description of Pugliano's enthusiasm for horsemen and horses as Menenius Agrippa is later with the nonaristocratic Romans. His tastes are unpretentious; he likes the rudest of poetry, the old song of Percy and Douglas, "and yet is it sung by some blind crowder, with no rougher voice than rude style" (97). So amiable is he that he can graciously condescend to the philosopher and historian—those curmudgeons!—with affectionate irony. The aristocratic prose writer of defenses can lead the feudal family because he has connections with silly poetry, and both have connections with nature and with the silly-idle and the silly-blessed. In being innocent of the need for self-justifications, the poet, like all romance knights in their natural simplicity, appears naturally justified.

This natural justification overrides the definition of the poet as a secular maker. Sidney's claims for poetry are apparently contradictory. On the one hand, the poet is a secular craftsman whose purpose is to delight. On the other, he is something of a priest, whose purpose is to save souls. At the beginning of the *Defense* poetry is a "making," but at the end, it is "a divine gift, and no human skill" (111). At one

---

in the *Defense*, see Irene Samuel, "The Influence of Plato on Sir Philip Sidney's *Defense of Poesy*," *Modern Language Quarterly* 1 (1940): 383–91 and F. Michael Krouse, "Plato and Sidney's *Defence of Poesie*," *Comparative Literature* 6 (1954): 138–47. On Neo-Platonism in the *Defense*, see John P. McIntyre, S.J., "Sidney's 'Golden World,'" *Comparative Literature* 14 (1962): 356–65.

moment, the end of all learning is "virtuous action" (83), but at another, it is to "lift up the mind from the dungeon of the body to the enjoying his own divine essence" (82). Poetry teaches the secular "headaches" of life, but it also shows "the weakness of mankind and the wretchedness of the world" (95). Ultimately, the balance is tipped toward religion: the "heavenly Maker of that maker" is the poet's final justification (79). The return to a religious ground colors many of the arguments. It has been maintained, for instance, that in the second part of the *Defense*, Sidney rehabilitates the philosopher and historian in a strong reader who knows good from bad, truth from falsehood.[18] But these schoolmasterly *magistri* are not so easily rehabilitated. The poet's grace is the outward sign of his devotion to a religious truth. The philosopher and the historian do not have "devotions." They have "intellectual preferences"—and badly disposed habits to boot: the philosopher inclines to streamlined "method," and the historian habitually forgets that human misfortune will be redeemed in paradise.

The religious ground also turns all contest into a *débat*, in which "secularity" is not opposed to religion but, just a little further away from the center of religious truth than the Bible, churches, and priests.[19] Sidney says as much when he describes the merriment of Erasmus and Agrippa as having "another foundation than the superficial part would promise" (100), that is, a religious ground. Because nothing is untouched by God's power, the *débat* welcomes the apparent contradictions of the world. In fact, everything can be rendered good if properly motivated by reverence (103–5). Even the commonplaces of a classical, secular tradition can join the party. Language as a humanly made tool poses no threat because the poet's independent imagination, inspired by a heavenly maker, always seems to bring forth images that will conduce to a ceremonial society: a "true" Theagenes, a "constant" Pylades, a "valiant" Orlando, and "so right a prince as Xenophon's Cyrus" (79). With this comfort, Sidney can easily extend his genial condescension from Pugliano to the philosopher and historian, despite their secular crankiness. The argument-by-demonstration ("Are you enchanted when I, a poet, talk about poetry? I rest my case.") and the argument-by-invitation ("I am

18. Ferguson, *Trials of Desire*, 146–51.

19. On the court as an inspirer of playfulness in poetry, see Daniel Javitch, *Poetry and Courtliness in Renaissance England* (Princeton: Princeton University Press, 1978). On Sidney's persuasion by irony, see Catherine Barnes, "The Hidden Persuader: The Complex Speaking Voice of Sidney's *Defence of Poetry*," *PMLA* 86 (1971): 422–27.

having an enormously good time praising poetry, and I would be even more enchanted if I could share my pleasure with you.") circumvent the necessity for giving reasons. Certainly Sidney is more serenely confident than are classical rhetoricians like Aristotle or Cicero that the highest human ideal is the best persuader. As with the self-delighted interlocutors in Castiglione's *Courtier*, a social and religious security dissolves antagonism in affectionate laughter.[20]

The real contradiction in the *Defense* lies in the nature of the human will. Poets are the best leaders because the love of poetry is natural— and yet it is not. There are, alas, natural disbelievers.[21] Outside of the courtly circle, deriders "seek a praise by dispraising others . . . prodigally spend[ing] a great many wandering words in quips and scoffs, carping and taunting at each thing"; by "stirring the spleen," they interfere in the purity of a ceremonial "through-beholding the worthiness of the subject" (99). Some understand delight, which is being "ravished . . . to see a fair woman" (115). But others know only laughter, which is a mere "scornful tickling" (115) and linked with the "itching tongue[s]" (100) of idle fools. In the peroration, the enemy to the aristocratic poet's freedom, his upward gaze, his lightness, and his sensitivity are "earth-creeping . . . mind[s]" that live too near the "dull-making cataract of Nilus" to hear the "planet-like music of poetry" (121). In its Latin root of *rus*, the adjective "rustical" splits the pastoral feudal family into opposing groups. The defender of poetry who earlier maintained that poetry is the best persuader because she can speak even to the ignorant man with an apparent shining here separates the ignorant and willing from the ignorant and unwilling. "Rustical" metonymically alludes to the antipastoral characteristics of the philosopher's "thorny" arguments (85) and the "stony and beastly" (74) people who at the beginning of the *Defense* could be charmed by ceremony's images but who now interfere with the

20. Thomas M. Greene's remarks on Urbino's "game of autocontemplation" in Castiglione's *Courtier* have interesting applications to Sidney's *Defense*; both depend on the *débat* ("Il Cortegiano and the Choice of a Game," *Renaissance Quarterly* 32 [1979]: 173–86, esp. 179).

21. The *Defense* is after all an "argument to the incredulous" (79). The textual problem in the word "incredulous" is significant. The word appears as "incredulous" in Ponsonby's edition of 1595 (*The Defence of Poesie*, facsim. ed. [London: Percy Lunc, Humphries, 1928], v). Van Dorsten emends it to "credulous": "with no small argument to the credulous of that first accursed fall of Adam, since our erected wit maketh us know what perfection is, and yet our infected will keepeth us from reaching unto it." The sentence makes more sense, however, if the word is left as Ponsonby's "incredulous," the phrase "of that first accursed fall of Adam" modifying "arguments," not used as the object of "incredulous."

shepherds' singing. To move with the desire to know is indeed an *opus* and a *labor*, but there are those on whom all the *opera* and *labores* in the world will not be effective. It is here that we have come to the paradox in the romance king's two faces: silent overseer and amiable display. While the ambivalent status of the *débat*—half divine, half secular—will save poetry as delightful *and* religious, it cannot so easily solve the necessity for the ruler to be a cunning psychologist as well as splendid knight.

There are five sagacious leaders in the *Defense*. The first two are the philosopher and the historian, the one prudent about "cumbersome . . . passion" and the other about the dismal spectacle of history. The three others are Menenius Agrippa, the prophet Nathan (who in his seriousness about sin is much like the philosopher), and finally an unnamed "Goth." Menenius Agrippa and the Goth are the only two who are engaged in the active life, the one a senator and the other a captain in the army. Menenius Agrippa is brought into the *Defense* as an example of how the "homely and familiar" fable of the belly can calm a populace and bring it to good order.[22] He is the knight in his other courtly role—that of the magistrate—a role that Sidney knew well in his father's service to Elizabeth as governor of Ireland and to which he probably aspired himself.

While the courtier-poet serves the state by his exquisite demonstration of deference to a superior "mistress-knowledge," the governor-poet serves the state by a remarkable expedience. Agrippa's homely and familiar tale does not appeal to a ravishingly lovely mistress-knowledge but to the people's self-interest: if the stomach is not given central importance, then the arms and legs will get no food. Agrippa is not performing Sidney's trick in most of the *Defense* of demonstrating poetry's power by showing how it "draws" his devotion. Agrippa captivates his audience by *feigning* affability, *playing* the homely and familiar poet. As such, he is consistent with the definition of a poet as a maker of images that will skillfully lead stubborn hearers to loyalty. But he is not consistent with the poet as a charming youth.

22. The fable of the belly itself probably originated as a didactic folk tale in the fourth century B.C. but was preserved in Aesop. Menenius Agrippa's use of it appears in Livy and Plutarch (David George Hale, *The Body Politic: A Political Metaphor in Renaissance English Literature* [The Hague: Mouton, 1971], 26–27. Hale argues that the conservative metaphor of the "body politic" was used in the Renaissance in appeals for social change (59–61). But the aggression of these appeals belongs to homily, and indeed to homiletic protestations that the body should be natural: neither two-headed, nor diseased, nor giving food to one finger more than another. Ferguson also overemphasizes the radical possibilities of the metaphor (*Trials of Desire*, 209 n.7).

Sidney's ambivalence about rhetorical shrewdness surfaces in the unsteady semantic sense of the word "gravity." *"Similiter cadenses"* (the chiming of clauses) at the end of a sentence, he says, hardly befits the "gravity of the pulpit" (118). That is, the pulpit is a serious platform; a preacher should not indulge in jingling *homoioteleuta* at the end of a sentence. But when Sidney imagines the philosopher and historian coming to their famous debate "with a sullen gravity" (83), the word seems to mean "full of ponderous and boorish warnings about the difficulties of life." Here, the Latin root of *gravity—gravitas*, heaviness, weightiness—allies it with dungeons of the body and clayey lodgings and earth-creeping minds. Like the world that is hostile to the dreamy idealism of the knight, the "gravity" of the philosopher and historian is heavy, weighed-down, earth-creeping, and incapable of rising to the visionary heights of poetry.

Sidney's ambivalence about gravity crystallizes in the story of Agrippa's counterpart in the active life—the Goth who wins a war by not burning the enemy's library. Here, Sidney is defending poetry against the accusation that it distracts knights from virtuous deeds. That poetry might be distracting is indeed a question to be asked, for the very worth of ceremonial romance is precisely its ability to distract by lifting one out of a gray and inequitable world. But Sidney does not hesitate in denying the charge that poetry is a sidetrack:

> Marry, this argument though it be levelled against poetry, yet it is indeed a chainshot against all learning, or bookishness as they commonly term it. Of such mind were certain Goths, of whom it is written that, having in the spoil of a famous city taken a library, one hangman (belike fit to execute the fruits of their wits) who had murdered a great number of bodies, would have set fire in it: no, said another. . . .

Sidney has set this hangman up as your model barbarian: he is a murderer, he wants to set fire to books, and he is a Goth. Therefore when his Gothic superior speaks next, something even more barbaric should follow. But the Goth's rejoinder is not brutish and far from stupid:

> [N]o, said another very *gravely*, take heed what you do, for while they are busy about these toys, we shall with more leisure conquer their countries. (105, emphasis mine)

Neither "reverend" nor "with boorish caution" fits the meaning of "gravely" here. Rather, it seems to mean "shrewdly." That this scheme to destroy the enemy without losing any more soldiers should be the last line of the story is a jarring note. Sidney does not diminish the Goth's perspicacity with a statement that he eventually lost the war. Indeed, the Goth is left standing firm, having convincingly demonstrated that poetry (and all book learning) is very distracting.[23] The same ambivalence about shrewdness appears in the treatment of Philanax in the *Arcadia*, at once a minister who serves his king devotedly and also, at the end, in his prosecution of the two noble princes, a cunning, busy, vigilant, vengeful man.

One of the most noteworthy facts about English political theory at the end of the sixteenth century is that there is little of it. Although Sidney knew the work of François Hotman, Philippe de Mornay, and Hubert Languet, he emphatically rejected their political theories (and indeed, the implications of writing any political theory) when in the *Arcadia* he chose to "commit a fiction."[24] Similarly, in the *Defense*, Sidney does not feel compelled to formulate a full-fledged political theory because whatever his objections to the Queen's foreign policy and her proposed marriage to Alençon, his politics are so deeply informed by ceremonial deference that he can assert that poetry best leads to the "ethic and politic consideration" without wondering if he has made any leaps. Reverence holds the community together without the need of constraints; poet-knights best inspire this reverence. What could theory add to this? The closest Sidney gets to a reasoned position on politics is the implication that society is best held together by tradition. Besides philosophers, historians, preachers, and shrewd Goths, the final figures of "gravity" in the *Defense* are the "grave forefathers" (100) who have always known who was wise and who foolish. This blithe self-assurance makes the *Defense* both lovable and exasperating. It is lovable because the spectacle of human happiness is infectious in its vitality, just as Pugliano's love of horsemanship bubbles over to Sidney. It is exasperating in its opening

23. That Sidney realizes the inappropriateness of this story to his purpose is suggested by his subsequent rhetorical maneuvers. He starts to talk rapidly and expeditiously, airily repeating points as if they had already been demonstrated. This rhetorical strategy also occurs in arguments that reply to Gosson (Arthur F. Kinney, "Parody and Its Implication in Sidney's *Defense of Poesie*," *Studies in English Literature, 1500–1900* 12 [1972]: 11–19).

24. Martin N. Raitiere, *Faire Bitts: Sir Philip Sidney and Renaissance Political Theory* (Pittsburgh: Duquesne University Press, 1984), 17. Raitiere acknowledges the important article of Irving Ribner, "Sir Philip Sidney on Civil Insurrection," *Journal of the History of Ideas* 13 (1952): 257–65.

the door to difficult problems and then quietly shutting it before we get more than a glimpse of the trouble inside.

If we allow Sidney his religious premise, however, then the connection between poetry and coercive leaders is inevitable. All human beings wish to achieve "as high a perfection as [their] degenerate souls, made worse by their clayey lodgings, can be capable of." Social order is necessary to provide the conditions for reaching that perfection. Because the human will is weak, social order will not "naturally" follow from a beholding of the good. And because reason is even weaker, social order will not follow from citizens' rational perception of the link between social order and salvation for all (or most). Instead, reason must be persuaded by first attracting the will. The will, which does not respond to religious truth as readily as it should, can be helped along by the poet's beautiful images; in responding to them, the listener's soul will become composed. If the amiable poet-knight sometimes becomes the shrewd poet-governor when he contrives the images that are put before the weak souls in the polity, he is not manipulating his followers but responsibly "esteeming" their capabilities.

This disjunction between social governors and poetic makers of attractive images goes back to Plato. In the *Republic*, the visionary poet's images are censored by the guardians if they encourage the wrong passions. The disjunction between amiable knight and politician also appears elsewhere. In Shakespeare it is a painful choice between manipulative prudence and fantastic chivalry without any true leaders (the Greeks and Trojans in *Troilus and Cressida*) or between successful prudence and failing amiability (Caesar and Antony in *Antony and Cleopatra*). In other plays, Shakespeare attempts a reconciliation. In *The Tempest*, the manipulative Prospero is balanced by the gentle Ferdinand, the next heir to the throne. In *1 Henry IV*, the amiable Hal, who at Shrewsbury is reborn as the perfect chivalric knight, absorbs the vital honor of Hotspur and the shrewdness of his father. If we find the reconciliation suspicious, our quarrel must necessarily be not with disguise of power in an erotic and pastoral discourse but rather with the premises (1) that there is a higher truth; (2) that human beings *want* to be brought to it (even if they sometimes forget themselves, as they themselves admit); (3) that they are best brought to this higher truth by the gentle persuasion of communal tradition, embodied in stories; and (4) that when the gentle persuasion of tradition fails, the responsible leader will rightly exercise force.

Not so easy to defend, however, is Sidney's failure to assimilate moral "gravity" into his defense of the affective tie between truth and the lovers of truth. Without the acknowledgment that, in the quest for the good, human beings do the best they can in a heavy world, the *Defense*'s airy optimism can sound "silly" in the modern sense of the word, idiotically making grander promises of success than reality will bear. By comparison, Shakespeare and Spenser seem properly to pause in humility. Even in as giddy a play as *A Midsummer Night's Dream*, Shakespeare acknowledges the fears that surround his little world of lovers and players. At the end of the "Epithalamion," Spenser concedes that all human beings, himself included, are "wretched, earthly clods." If the aristocrat has a responsibility to lead his fellows to the truth, we might want him to do it with a greater sense of solicitude for the weakness of humanity in general.

Sidney's failure to absorb political "gravity" in the voice of the *Defense* is even more of a problem. In the mockery of the philosopher and historian and in the blithe dismissal of earth-creeping minds, the poet's security in his own skill is not clearly distinguished from his security in his aristocratic status. If the aristocratic poet-governor must stoop to a less-than-beautiful manipulation of recalcitrant subjects, his paternalism might have greater self-consciousness of the liability to error. Shakespeare's handling of this figure in Duke Vincentio in *Measure for Measure*, in Prospero in *The Tempest*, and most of all in Prince Hal acknowledges just this difficulty.

Then too Sidney's failure to absorb intellectual gravity has political ramifications. He claims that poetry's function is to submit experience to the "imaginative and judging power" (86), but inasmuch as the discursive "judgment" of poetry is subsumed in music and images, it amounts to a stockpiling of commonplaces, accumulated but not debated. The tradition of classical philosophy and rhetoric is displayed, but its insistence on choice is dissolved in a defense of aristocratic amateurishness against the very social types that might not find the Accession Day Tilts quite so wonderful as Sidney did and whose "graceless" learning might slice to the heart of aristocratic legitimacy. Shrewd leaders, methodical philosophers, realistic historians might successfully resist the poet's enchantment. Some readers would dearly love to ignore the political argument because they can then accept Sidney's charming invitation to join the dance. A generic distinction in defense of his bonhomie ("This is a defense of *poetry*, not a work of political theory; you should not expect it to sound like Plato's *Republic* or Aristotle's *Politics*") will not help, because Sidney himself invites the connection between the beautiful poet-knight and a hierarchical society.

Poetry's ambivalent status between the secular realm and the religious also bears dwelling on; it might allow Sidney to have things two ways. If poetry is secular, then it can be a holiday plaything, and the coterie of aristocrats can continue to enjoy it without harming anyone. Secular poetry also justifies Sidney's display of artful competence. Here is a man who has mastered his "field," and he floats lightly above it with the breathtaking assurance that no unsolvable problems will arise. Poets have their mysterious craft; what a pity others cannot levitate so freely as they! But if poetry is religious, then it is not only not harmful but beneficial, a great salve for the soul's hurts, inspiring devotion as much as glee.

In considering this charge, we must return to the relationship between ceremony's solemn truth and the happiness of the *débat*. The invitation to the tone-deaf in Sidney's peroration to hear the performance (as long as they keep quiet) sounds less hollow if the performance leads ultimately to the divine. Having earlier conceded that the inspirational source of the music is God himself, the tuneless might suppress their distaste for it in the interest of a greater social good: "It does not move or delight me, but it apparently moves and delights others and creates the kind of community I want to be a part of. For the sake of the whole, I will keep my mouth shut." Moreover, the religious premise might justify a considerable amount of lay participation; if the right poets are virtual priests and if the society as a whole believes that the worst of human ills is despair, then truth's pageant can only continue to be compelling when there is a sizable crew of people redoing the sets. Human beings need all the consolations they can get, from priests or from semi-priests.

But then what about Sidney's enthusiasm for secular shoptalk—the problem of Spenser's language, the glories of *Gorboduc*, the delights of Surrey? Are these the interests of someone eager to save souls? Perhaps the worst of human ills is not the community's despair after all but a social condition inflicted on the artificer. Put this "silly" poet (who is not nearly so silly as he likes to portray himself) among the rustics (not with a colleague like Sir Edward Wotton), and you will condemn him to a secular hell, the excruciating boredom of having no one to talk to about his "makings." Or worse, let the balcony fill up with catcallers who obstinately reject the invitation to be charmed, and the poet is condemned to another secular hell, the frustration of creating beautiful objects that human "beasts" cannot appreciate. The one protection from these hells—the inertia of tradition—does not save Sidney from the charge of preening. If there is "nothing of so sacred a majesty but that an itching tongue may rub itself upon it," Sidney's recommendation to deal with the catcallers by "laugh[ing] at the jester" (100) does not answer the charge. It merely pits tradition saturated with religious truth against reasoned argument. Here, the blurred line between the religious and the secular works too much to Sidney's advantage. On the other hand, if the images a poet fashions do in fact lead to God and do in fact lead others to God, then he has a right (1) to be happy and (2) to protect his calling; that he himself happens to enjoy its privileges (and its "shop") is a side-issue.

The combination of self-deprecating irony and giddiness that makes Sidney so exasperating may be, after all, the best defense of an activity virtually indefensible. If poetry is a natural good and naturally beloved, the best defense is to sing a song, not break a butterfly on the wheel of discursive argument. Poetry is either so obviously enchanting that justifications are superfluous or so obviously merely one enchantment among others that special claims for it are heavy-handed. The argument that the weak souls of most human beings cannot be lifted up by reason and hence require some other inspiration (or discipline) can be made for music, painting, dancing, and sport. Even if Sidney is defending inspiring leadership, not just poetry, a "grave" defense would still be unnecessarily heavy artillery. Surely, if one with great gifts should arise in the midst of a right-minded community groping for direction, the response would be to rejoice, not to scrutinize the basis of his authority. In the end, Sidney's competence in "discursive song," which pricks up the ears of suspicious readers, ultimately enables the tonal range necessary to an argument that poetry both is and is not religious, is and is not natural. As self-evidently lovable, poetry is not likely to disappear from the face of the earth, and we may all "follow St. James's counsel in singing psalms when [we] are merry" (80). Yet, the miseries of the Fall being what they are, poetry is still something to be grateful for, celebrated ceremonially.

Richard Hooker's *Of the Laws of Ecclesiastical Polity:* The Rhetoric of Gravity

Sidney's confession that he fears being "pounded" for straying from poetry to oratory is made with such self-assurance that we can hardly take his professed apprehension seriously. Similarly, power is so obviously a part of poetry's "ethic and politic consideration" that Sidney can introduce senators and generals with little apparent worry. His real fear is being pounded for admitting that his poet-knight will sometimes have to talk gravely. Richard Hooker shares none of Sidney's skittishness on this score; he is confident that gravity is the primary requirement for leadership.[25]

Now in "esteeming" a ceremonial discourse, Richard Hooker is a thinker worth coming to terms with. He *knows* that it assumes a hierarchical polity. He *knows* that a ceremonial discourse mixes love with power. It is the responsibility of the priest to bring his flock to a spiritual home that they themselves are too childish to understand how to get to. It is his responsibility to protect the communal rituals his flock has known since childhood; out of love for them, the flock might be induced to strive for a spiritual home it might otherwise find too laborious.

For Hooker, only extraordinary naiveté would lead religious leaders to deny that they are also magistrates. The Anglican church is necessarily bound up with the political body of England. England is threatened by hostile powers. Priests therefore have a spiritual duty to uplift the hearts of their parishioners and a political duty to persuade them to defend their queen and their religion. To the priest, "religion unfainedly loved" exalts the soul and unites it with the ceremonial "home" of the universe; but to a wise priest-magistrate, religion also "perfecteth mens habilities unto all kindes of vertuous services in the common wealth" (5.1.5). In this argument, Hooker is on the edge of outright Machiavellianism: it is best to have a true religion, but, because no religions are without a glimmer of truth, better to have even a false one than none at all. The straightforwardness is something to be thankful for. If the exposure of power in a Renaissance discourse of love is entirely too easy, as if one were to push over a painted stage-set to discover a monster director behind it, in Hooker we encounter a thinker who is prepared to push back.

Hooker's intentions in writing the *Laws* are not at all clear. Some have argued that while he thought he was writing a philosophical work, his advisers and collaborators thought he was writing—or

25. Egil Grislis notes Hooker's fondness for the epithet "judicious" to characterize "the wiser sort" ("The Hermeneutical Problem in Hooker," in *Studies in Richard Hooker: Essays Preliminary to an Edition of His Works*, ed. W. Speed Hill [Cleveland: Press of Case Western Reserve University, 1972], 173–74). But Hooker is equally fond of "grave" and "gravity." See in book 5 alone: 25.2,3; 30.4; 31.2; 32.2; 33.1; 38.1; 41.2; 42.5; 65.4; 65.6; 81.6.

thought he should have been writing—a polemical one, defending Whitgift's earlier *Answer to the Second Admonition* (1574) by answering the Puritan Thomas Cartwright's reply to Whitgift point by point.[26] Others have argued that Hooker's intention to justify Elizabeth's right to decide in church matters conflicted with the philosophy of natural law he borrowed from Aquinas.[27] Studies of Hooker's style, on the other hand, have concluded that his argument, though complex, is nevertheless coherent. His orderly syntax, with Ciceronian subordination of lesser points to main points, reflects his belief in a purposeful universe and in reason redeemed by grace.[28] This position

26. C. J. Sisson argues that from as early as 1585 when Hooker was appointed Master at the Temple, the *Laws* was Whitgift's idea and was eventually carried out as a collaborative effort with Edwin Sandys, Hooker's pupil, and George Cranmer (C. J. Sisson, *The Judicious Marriage of Mr. Hooker and the Birth of "The Laws of Ecclesiastical Polity"* [Cambridge: Cambridge University Press, 1940]). Sisson's arguments have been challenged by Hardin Craig, "*Of the Laws of Ecclesiastical Polity*: First Form," *Journal of the History of Ideas* 5 (1944): 91–104. For the view that Hooker's philosophical arguments in book 2 are themselves polemical—a defense of Whitgift's *Defense* against Cartwright's *Reply*—see Rudolph Almasy, "The Purpose of Richard Hooker's Polemic," *Journal of the History of Ideas* 39 (1978): 251–70. W. D. J. Cargill Thompson agrees that the political theory is consistent but argues that throughout Hooker has his eye to the necessities of the immediate political circumstances ("The Philosopher of the 'Politic Society': Richard Hooker as a Political Thinker," in *Studies in Richard Hooker*, ed. W. Speed Hill, 3–76).

27. On the contradictions of Hooker's argument, see Peter Munz, *The Place of Hooker in the History of Thought* (London: Routledge and Kegan Paul, 1952). D. W. Hanson sees the work as a tissue of paradoxes, contradictions, and reconciliations (*From Kingdom to Commonwealth: The Development of Civic Consciousness in English Political Thought* [Cambridge: Harvard University Press, 1970], 265–80). F. J. Shirley argues that book 3's contention that Scripture specifies no one, immutable form of church government is contradicted by book 7's contention that an episcopal form of government is authorized by the *ius divinum* (*Richard Hooker and Contemporary Political Ideas* [London: published for the Church Historical Society by the Society for the Promotion of Christian Knowledge, 1949], 109). Arthur S. McGrade has argued that the political arguments of books 7 and 8 should be read in light of the arguments from natural law in book 1 ("The Coherence of Hooker's Polity: The Books on Power," *Journal of the History of Ideas* 24 [1963]: 163–82). For an important answer to Shirley, setting Hooker's warrants for an episcopal form of government in the context of contemporary theological controversy, see M. R. Sommerville, "Richard Hooker and his Contemporaries on Episcopacy: an Elizabethan Consensus," *Journal of Ecclesiastical History* 35 (1984): 177–87. Robert K. Faulkner has justly emphasized that Hooker's polity is a religious, not a political one. He argues that Hooker's insistence on Convocation as a check on the Queen's authority was a criticism of royal supremacy in church matters (*Richard Hooker and the Politics of a Christian England* [Berkeley and Los Angeles: University of California Press, 1981]).

28. Georges Edelen, "Hooker's Style," in *Studies in Richard Hooker*, ed. W. Speed Hill, 241–77. For the argument that Hooker's style reflects coherent philosophical positions, see, for example, 262 and 266. W. Speed Hill's analysis of Hooker's sermons arrives at

mistakenly characterizes Hooker as a Christian civilist who believes that reason will quell factionalism and who is also pious. Hooker's Ciceronianism is more accurately described as an appropriation of classical reason for the purpose of negotiating the split in a ceremonial discourse between the wise, mute governor and his inspirational devotion to truth.

While Sidney avoids the declaration that the poet-leader will use images to manipulate the populace, Hooker comes right to the point. To persuade the multitude, a priest-magistrate will make full use of a rhetoric of visual symbols: "[B]eing object to the eye, the liveliest and the most apprehensive sense of all other, [visible signs] have in that respect seemed the fittest to make a deepe and a strong impression" (4.1.3), keeping "even secret thoughtes under awe" (5.65.6). Bishops are the visible signs of authority, encouraging a sense of honor appropriate to various degrees (7.17–19). Even if the clergy neglect "many ways their duty unto God and men, [they] do notwithstanding by their Authority great good, in that they keep others at the leastwise in some aw under them" (7.18.6). The Commonwealth depends most on "one external thing . . . the Publique Marks and Tokens, whereby the estimation that Governors are in, is made manifest to the eyes of men" (7.19.1). The "impression" of a pageant of "Publique Marks and Tokens" is the quality Hooker strives to transfer to a prose that, lacking the visual conveniences of romance characters or the allegorical figures of Elizabeth's pageants, must rely on aural appeals.

The aural debt is to ceremonialism. It is customary to attribute Hooker's characteristically long sentences to a Renaissance imitation of Cicero. But there is an important difference between Hooker's long complex sentences and Cicero's. Cicero strives for *vis*—force, energy. In comparison to Cicero, Hooker rarely shifts higher than second gear. The source of this subdued emphasis in sentences that float at

---

a similar picture of a style massively controlled and confidently at ease ("The Authority of Hooker's Style," *Studies in Philology* 67 [1970]: 328–38). Daniel C. Boughner's view lies in the same tradition ("Notes on Hooker's Prose," *Review of English Studies* 15 [1939]: 194–200). The difficulties with a theory of style postulating a neat reflection of syntactical forms and subtleties of meaning have been aptly criticized by Alvin Vos: Hooker's elaborate parallelism may not in fact be used to make the argument that the universe is orderly but rather to contribute a general air of grandeur ("Models and Methodologies in Renaissance Prose Stylistics," *Studies in the Literary Imagination* 10 [1977]: 1–15).

great length is probably not Ciceronianism but the law.[29] Again, Hooker is candid: the multitudes must be persuaded, and to state things as if they were law is a very persuasive technique, for the simple think the law "doth speake with al indifferencie . . . as it were an oracle proceeded from wisedome and understanding" (1.10.7). "Indifferencie" is crucial here. The ceremonial oracle, which is the law of the universe, is indeed indifferent to the claims of the particular. There can be eternal grieving but no temporal grievances.[30]

Hooker's "ceremonial Ciceronianism" is most prominent in the first five books of the *Laws*. There, human life is embraced in a Boethian universe, one whose "unloosable connection of causes" is both lovely and reliable. But it has something that Philosophia's universe lacks:

29. In the following proclamation are the two most noticeable features of Hookerian prose: enormously long sentences and a massive wheeling on "notwithstanding" and on the concluding "therefore," the latter enforcing the incontrovertibility of the decree: "The new decrees of the Star-Chamber for orders in printing, vicesimo tertio die Junii, A.D. 1586. Whereas sundry decrees and ordinances have upon grave advice and deliberation been heretofore made and published for the repressing of such great enormities and abuses as of late more than in time past have been commonly used and practised by divers contentious and disorderly persons professing the art or mystery of printing or selling books, and *yet notwithstanding* the said abuses and enormities are nothing abated, but, as it is found by experience, do rather daily more and more increase to the wilful and manifest breach and contempt of the said ordinances and decrees, to the great displeasure and offence of the Queen's most excellent Majesty, by reason whereof sundry intolerable offences, troubles and disturbances have happened as well in the church as in the civil government of the state and commonwealth of this realm, which seem to have grown because the pains and penalties contained and set down in the said ordinances and decrees have been too light and small for the correction and punishment of so grievous and heinous offenses, and so the offenders and malefactors in that behalf have not been so severely punished as the quality of their offences have deserved. Her Majesty *therefore*, of her most godly and gracious disposition . . . " (emphasis mine; *Select Statutes and Other Constitutional Documents Illustrative of the Reigns of Elizabeth and James I*, ed. G. W. Prothero, 4th ed. [Oxford: Clarendon Press, 1913], 169). Edelen's "syntactical distance" might also come from the monotone completeness of the law (Edelen, "Hooker's Style," 275–76). On Cranmer's notes, see W. Speed Hill, "Hooker's *Polity*: The Problem of the 'Three Last Books,'" *Huntington Library Quarterly* 34 (1971): 317–36. For examples of Cranmer's and Sandys's complaints about Hooker's long sentences, see *Laws*, 4: 107, 108, 113. On the difficulty of Hooker's words and the ellipsis of his expression, see the remarks on "Chiefety of regiment" (117) and "Epicures opinion" (112).

30. Edelen compares the Senecan and the Ciceronian styles to illustrate Hooker's chanting imperturbability and his consequent diminution of the importance of any single member in a sentence—a metaphor, a startling item of diction, a felicitous *cursus* ("Hooker's Style," in *Studies in Richard Hooker*, ed. W. Speed Hill, 275–76). I would place the historical sources of "syntactical distance" in a ceremonial mode, not in Ciceronianism.

an enormous sociability. The law of nature embraces angels, beasts, and human beings in a beautifully arranged fellowship. It is both descriptive and prescriptive, passive and active: the beasts "keepe the law of their kind unwittingly," yet, since the creation, "heaven and earth have hearkned unto [God's] voice, and their labour hath bene to do his wil" (1.3.2). The angels are "unsatiable in their longing," and having received the inspiration of God, they bestow it on the rest of the universe by doing "by all meanes all maner good unto all the creatures of God, but especially unto the children of men" (1.4.1). Creatures look up in adoration and down in solicitude.

The most oft-quoted sentence in the whole of the eight books of the *Laws* amply expresses the joy of belonging to this corporate universe:

> Now if nature should intermit her course, and leave altogether, though it were but for a while, the observation of her own lawes: if those principall and mother elements of the world, wherof all things in this lower world are made, should loose the qualities which now they have, if the frame of that heavenly arch erected over our heads should loosen and dissolve it selfe: if celestiall spheres should forget their wonted motions and by irregular volubilitie, turne themselves any way as it might happen: if the prince of the lightes of heaven which now as a Giant doth runne his unwearied course, should as it were through a languishing faintnes begin to stand and to rest himselfe: if the Moone should wander from her beaten way, the times and seasons of the yeare blend themselves by disordered and confused mixture, the winds breath out their last gaspe, the cloudes yeeld no rayne, the earth be defeated of heavenly influence, the fruites of the earth pine away as children at the withered breasts of their mother no longer able to yeeld them reliefe, what would become of man himselfe, whom these things now do all serve? (1.3.2)

Rising to a plateau on parallel "if's" and evoking an unthinkable disaster, this sentence celebrates a truth existing apart from the struggles and confusions of human language. Doubling and restating, incantatory rhythm, and logically superfluous adjective clauses deck out the visual splendor of the universe. Praise of a point of stability is paralleled by images of senescence, wandering, falling apart. Protectors ward off dissolution: like a good knight, nature is absorbed in "the observation of her own lawes"; the "frame of that heavenly arch erected over our heads" shields human beings from chaos; the "prince of the lightes of heaven which now as a Giant doth runne his unwearied course" uncomplainingly performs his duties. Deep within this sentence of laud and thanksgiving are the old metaphors of familial comfort, nourishment, and safety.[31]

As in Sidney's *Defense*, the dependent relationship of this family is reinforced by femininity: nature, the church, and faith itself. In the pageant-of-nature sentence from book 1, nature provides the "principall and mother elements of the world"; if the mother should withdraw her sustenance, the "fruites of the earth [would] pine away as children at the withered breasts of their mother." Later in book 1, Nature is a feminine superintendent of order, whose works "are no lesse exact, then if she did both behold and studie how to expresse some absolute shape or mirror alwayes present before her" (1.3.4). In arguing for the primacy of belief independent of knowledge, Hooker invokes the feminine wisdom of Proverbs (5.63.1). Elsewhere, wisdom is "as Quene or Soveraigne commandresse over other vertues" (5.8.1; see also 5.52.3). Faith too is female (5.63.2), as is the Church, who is "that verie mother of our new birth, in whose bowels we are all bredd" (5.50.1). The church is "by office a mother unto such as crave at her handes the sacred mysterie of theire nue birth" (5.60.7), and her ministers are "nurces" (5.62.16). The "seate" of the law

> is the bosome of God, her voyce the harmony of the world, all thinges in heaven and earth doe her homage, the very least as feeling her care, and the greatest as not exempted from her power, but Angels and men and creatures of what condition so

31. In book 5's justification of feast days as reminders of God's perfect rest, there is the same split between the natural and supernatural: "the verie heathens them selves . . . have therefore taught that above the highest moveable sphere there is nothing which feeleth alteration motion or change, but all thinges immutable, unsubject to passion, blest with eternall continuance in a life of the highest perfection and of that complete abundant sufficiencie within it selfe, which no possibilitie of want maime or defect can touch" (5.70.4). In the architecture of book 1, chap. 2, Hooker moves from rational defense to ceremonial celebration, starting with a dry clarity—magisterially Baconian—and ending with parallel chanting ("that law . . . that law . . . that law") and apocalyptic finality: "This law therefore we may name eternall, being that order which God before all ages hath set down with himselfe, for himselfe to do all things by," with its chiastic finality of "before all ages . . . with himself, for himself . . . all things." For the significance of the repetitions of "all" at the end of this book, see the observations of James A. Devereux, S.J., on the "maximizing" tendencies in Cranmer's translations of the Catholic *orationes* in *The Book of Common Prayer* ("The Collects of the First *Book of Common Prayer* as Works of Translation," *Studies in Philology* 66 [1969]: 719–38).

ever, though ech in different sort and maner, yet all with uniforme consent, admiring her as the mother of their peace and joy. (1.16.8)

Hooker's debt to the political thinking of Thomas Aquinas should be accompanied by a recognition of a parallel debt to a medieval ceremonialism.[32]

The ceremonial heritage profoundly affects two central aspects of Hooker's argument. The first is a rhetorical coloration of "human reason" as borrowed from Aquinas. Although human beings are distinct from the beasts in following the law of nature wittingly, human choice is still bound up in intuitive responses. Human reason is "naturall reason" (1.6.3); its coming to maturity in the adult human being is as much a part of the "endevors of nature" (1.6.2) as are the capacities of fish and beasts. Although reason must be trained and although it can be deluded by appearances and hardened by vicious habits, it is not set in opposition to *desire*, which is also natural and which longs "to seeke the highest, and to covet more or lesse the participation of God himselfe" (1.5.1–2). Aquinas offered the philosophical ground of this position. Hooker's rhetoric justifies the "passion" to bask in the beauties of creation made expressly for human beings.

Then too the ceremonial split between a supernatural perfection and earthly imperfection affects Hooker's notion of history. It is commonly held that in contrast to the ahistorical biblicism of the Puritans, Hooker appreciates the historical circumstances under which laws were first instituted and the reasons for their desuetude. While Aquinas views society in terms of stability and order, Hooker sees society as "moving forces."[33] Because positive laws do not affect the invisible church, the laws of the ecclesiastical polity can change with historical circumstances. "[F]or as much as the whole body of the Church, hath power to alter with general consent and upon necessary occasions, even the positive laws of the Apostles, if there be no commandment to the contrary, and it manifestly appears to her, that change of times have clearly taken away the very reason of Gods first

32. Alexander Passerin D'Entrèves, *The Medieval Contribution to Political Thought: Thomas Aquinas, Marsilius of Padua, Richard Hooker* (1939; repr. New York: The Humanities Press, 1959).

33. Arthur B. Ferguson, *Clio Unbound: Perception of the Social and Cultural Past in Renaissance England*, Duke Monographs in Medieval and Renaissance Studies no. 2 (Durham: Duke University Press, 1979), 207–22, esp. 221.

institution" (7.5.8). In this argument, Hooker is said to show a "modern" sense of "purposeful change."[34]

But in fact the organization of experience in a ceremonial mode alters Hooker's putatively modern understanding of historical forces. If "history" is "custom," and custom adapts without struggle, then "purposefulness" belongs as much to a mysteriously knowing force that "figures out" how institutions have to change to fit new circumstances as it does to the judgments of human beings. Institutions that arise from wise custom's "purposefulness" are admittedly various. The variety does not indicate, however, that some men have judged well and others badly but rather (custom being very wise) that God's house has many mansions and his truth tolerates many different polities: "A more dutifull and religious way for us were to admire the wisedom of God, which shineth in the bewtifull varietie of all things, but most in the manifold and yet harmonious dissimilitude of those wayes, whereby his Church upon earth is guided from age to age, throughout all generations of men" (3.11.8). Indeed, the ceremonies of different churches, Hooker maintains, are no more than the liveries of different clans, "that as one familie is not abridged of libertie to be clothed in fryers gray, for that another doth weare clay-colour; so neither are all Churches bound to the selfe same indifferent Ceremonies which it liketh sundry to use" (4.13.6). The stability of customs and traditions, articulated in positive law, is the "consent" of a stable polity.[35] In unself-consciously following custom and by implication positive laws, a nation is following God's teleological intentions for the entire universe (8.4.6). The double focus on history as part of God's unfolding plan and as an arena constantly disordered by subjects' complaints about their governors enables Hooker to regard the English episcopacy as a natural outgrowth of smoothly changing institutions necessarily adapting to time and place, and *also* to regard the Puritan demand for change as an eruption in the law of nature, or a foreign organism invading the body politic.

34. Ibid., 217.

35. The "consent" given "the articles of compact" made between a king and those he has conquered are "by silent allowance famously notified through custome reaching beyonde the memorie of man" (8.3.3). See Lawrence Manley's useful discussion of Hooker's notion of consent and custom, especially Hooker's adjustments between the continuity of truth and the variety of conventional laws, in *Convention: 1500–1750* (Cambridge: Harvard University Press, 1980), 90–106. This adjustment is easily made when "custom" is able to carry both the authority of reason and the authority of nature.

The status of Hooker's priest-magistrate is much like his custom, historically located but having a special connection to ahistorical truth. Like Philosophia, the priest-magistrate must be quiet and steady; earthly contingencies merely distract him from the contemplation of the perfect patterns of nature's law: "But we must note, that it is in this case, as in a ship, he that sitteth at the stern is quiet, he moveth not, he seemeth in a manner to do little or Nothing" (7.18.4). Like nature, he makes no show of concern for human affairs (7.18.4). Knowing that quarrels are usually nothing but the product of "affection or fancie," with "litle appearance of reason," the "wisest" are "contented not to call to mind how errors" are often blown out of proportion (5.Ded.5).

The decorum of the opening paragraph of book 1 accommodates the contradiction between the silent authority of nature and the occasional need for human purposefulness. The audience of this paragraph is on the one hand Hooker's fellows in the sodality of the wise (which includes Athanasius and St. Basil [5.41.2–11]), who know that human nature is always given to complaints and that the current cry for purification of the church is no different. On the other hand his audience are the complainers themselves, who must be met head-on:

> He that goeth about to perswade a multitude, that they are not so well governed as they ought to be, shall never want attentive and favourable hearers; because they know the manifold defects whereunto every kind of regiment is subject, but the secret lets and difficulties, which is publike proceedings are innumerable and inevitable, they have not ordinarily the judgement to consider. And because such as openly reprove supposed disorders of state are taken for principall friends to the common benefite of all, and for men that carry singular freedome of mind; under this faire and plausible coulour whatsoever they utter passeth for good and currant. That which wanteth in the waight of their speech, is supplyed by the aptnes of mens minds to accept and believe it. Whereas on the other side, if we maintaine thinges that are established, we have not onely to strive with a number of heavie prejudices deeply rooted in the hearts of men, who thinke that herein we serve the time, and speake in favour of the present state, because therby we eyther holde or seeke preferment; but also to beare such exceptions as minds so averted before hand

usually take against that which they are loath should be powred into them. (1.1.1)

The possible justice of the Puritan argument is dismissed in an air of grand indifference to the predictable complaints of earthly "particulars," yet the articulateness of the paragraph also scolds and disciplines the complainers. The adjustments of this rhetoric between indifference and disgust can be felt by comparison with the translators' preface to the King James Version of the Bible, in which a similar "long view" does not see as far or as much.

The preface too shows the pressure of a decorum that disdains excitement and yet combats historically located foes. Although Calvin's name is introduced in the title of the second chapter of the preface ("The first establishment of new discipline by M. Calvins industry in the Church of Geneva"), in the actual beginning of the text, he is reduced to an anticipated type as "a founder," his proper name held off for another twenty-six lines. And after relating the history of Calvin's departure from Geneva and his eventual invitation back, Hooker describes him as returning "as it had beene another Tully" to his old city (Pref.2.3). Motivations do not change; great men have returned to their base of support before with as unreliable a political foundation as had Cicero.[36]

When Hooker comes to the end of his rehearsal of Calvin's relationship with the town of Geneva, it is with contempt for the pastors and learned guides who have published their inefficiency (Pref.2.7). What sounds to us like an outrageous charge—that Calvin's discipline was determined merely by expedience—hardly bothers Hooker. To the magistrate who understands the waverings of the multitude as a "law" of human nature, such strictness of discipline is warranted. "He ripely considered how grosse a thing it were for men of his qualitie, wise and grave men, to live with such a multitude, and to be tenants at will under them, as their ministers,

36. The same hauteur occurs in the description of the eagerness of the continental Protestant churches "to bee certaine degrees more removed from conformitie with the Church of Rome, then the rest before had bene" (Pref. 2.2). W. D. J. Cargill Thompson accuses Hooker of polemical bias in his treatment of Calvin ("The Philosopher of the 'Politic Society,'" in *Studies in Richard Hooker*, ed. W. Speed Hill, 3–76, esp. 15). P. D. L. Avis counters this argument in "Richard Hooker and John Calvin," *Journal of Ecclesiastical History* 32 (1981): 19–33. Richard Bauckham offers a moderate position, arguing that Hooker does not want so much to demolish Calvin as to cut the English controversy off from continental authorities, of whom Calvin was the chief ("Richard Hooker and John Calvin: A Comment," *Journal of Ecclesiastical History* 32 [1981]: 29–33).

both himselfe and others, had bene" (Pref.2.4). Calvin correctly "saw how needfull these bridles were to be put in the jawes of that Citie" (Pref.2.7). What Hooker condemns is the subsequent self-delusion of Calvin in calling the political expedience of the moment the word of Scripture. But that political leaders who are not obeying the truth should delude themselves is to be expected from human nature.

Sometimes the contest with historical particulars brings out the back of the hand. Subjects who act like horses ("champ upon the bit" [Pref. 2.2]) are rightly treated like horses. After all, "when *stomacke doth strive with wit*, the match is not equall" (Pref.2.6). The Genevans are contemptuously described as having decided to "play their parts on a stage" (Pref.2.6) and being given to fantastic claims of spiritual insight: "so that scarcely was there found any one of them, *the forge of whose brayne* was not possest with some speciall mysterie" (Pref.8.7; emphasis mine throughout). In his *History of Henry VII*, Bacon also uses this proverbial language of the body.[37] But unlike Hooker, Bacon identifies with the exasperations and satisfactions of politicians.[38] Ruling is meeting cunning with superior cunning. For Hooker, the natural law's distance from the particular *casus* diminishes the duel. To be persuasive with a body politic full of jabberers and outwitters, authority should present reasons but deny their contestability. Or, for the sake of the victims of heresies, the accusations of reformers should be confronted in all their exaggeration:

37. In describing Henry's reaction to the uprising of the Staffords in Worcestershire, Bacon shares Henry's aplomb: "The King, as a prince of great and profound judgment, was not much moved with it; for that he thought it was but a rag or remnant of Bosworth Field" (Francis Bacon, *The History of the Reign of King Henry the Seventh*, ed. F. J. Levy [New York: Bobbs-Merrill, 1972], 80. "But their snow-ball did not gather as it went" (93); "[s]o this rebellion proved but a blast, and the King having by this journey purged a little the dregs and leaven of the northern people" (81). For similarities to Bacon's curt style in Hooker, see Vickers, "Hooker's Prose Style," intro. to *Richard Hooker: Of the Laws of Ecclesiastical Polity*, ed. A. S. McGrade and Brian Vickers [New York: St. Martin's, 1975]), 48, and Edelen, "Hooker's Style," in *Studies in Richard Hooker*, ed. W. Speed Hill, 249–50.

38. "And as his [Henry VII's] manner was *to send his pardons rather before the sword than after* . . . "(81); "*All was inned at last into the King's barn;* but it was after a storm" (117); "But for the extirpating of the roots and causes of the like commotions in time to come, the King began *to find where his shoe did wring him;* and that it was his depressing of the house of York that did *rankle and fester* the affections of his people" (96); "[Y]et was she [Elizabeth Woodville] . . . precipitated and banished the world into a nunnery. . . . For this act the King sustained great obloquy, which nevertheless (besides the reason of state) *was somewhat sweetened to him* by a great confiscation" (88; emphasis mine throughout).

> Which thinge [the evils of heresy] they very well know and
> I doubt not will easilie confesse, who live to theire greate both
> toile and griefe where the blasphemies of Arrians, Samosate-
> nians, Tritheites, Eutychians and Macedonians are renued;
> renued by them who to hatch theire heresie have chosen those
> Churches as fittest nestes where *Athanasius Creed* is not heard; by
> them I say renued, who followinge the course of extreame
> reformation, were woont in the pride of theire own proceedinges
> to glorie that whereas Luther did but blowe away the roofe, and
> Zwinglius batter but the walls of popish superstition, the last and
> hardest worke of all remained, which was to race up the verie
> ground and foundation of poperie. (5.42.13)

Hooker's low diction and sarcasm have been admired for their
"energy,"[39] praise that can be easily directed to Bacon's prose as well.
But "energy" all by itself is a romantic valorization of strong feeling in
an individual subject. Hooker's "energy" should be historicized as the
right of natural law to define bestiality; transferred to a political realm,
it is "lordly severity."

   "Hooker" as we know him in the *Laws*, then, is best heard as a
prose version of the dramatic figures in many other works of
Renaissance literature. Like Nature at the end of Spenser's "Two
Cantos of Mutabilitie," who can answer the elaborate arguments of
Mutability in just two stanzas, Hooker's magistrate knows the
"doom" of things, the *secreta secretorum*. As this aspect of ceremony,
he has no human audience at all. But in relationship to subjects, he is
the lord of romance, who, merely by the sound of his voice and
presence of his body, brings order to disorderly wits, in the same
manner as Shakespeare's various dukes, also distanced from the
turmoil of the childish predicaments of their subjects: Theseus in *A
Midsummer Night's Dream*, the Duke in *The Merchant of Venice*, Prince
Escalus in *Romeo and Juliet*, Duke Vincentio of Vienna in *Measure for
Measure*, and, insofar as he has a story and is dramatized as giving up
spiritual contemplation in order to take up the burden of ruling, most
of all like Prospero in *The Tempest*. Assessing the rhetoric of gravity in
both Hooker and Shakespeare must confront the arguments (1) that
there are in the world truly wise leaders, pseudowise leaders, and an
easily persuadable multitude and (2) that the wise leaders fulfill their
duties when they keep their eye on the stability of the polity and the

---

39. Vickers "Hooker's Prose Style," in *Richard Hooker*, ed. A. S. McGrade and Brian
Vickers, 46.

goal of spiritual wisdom for all subjects to the extent that each is capable of it.

The Gravity of Prayer in Hooker's *Laws*

Besides scolding erring Christian leaders, Hooker has another compelling intention: to remind Christians of their creaturely dependence on God's law. For this purpose, he is not an articulate thinker about ecclesiastical polity but rather a representative of all weak human beings, magistrate-bishops and Puritan divines among them. As sinners in an imperfect world, Hooker and his audience are children in the protection of a mother. Members of the church are "her Children" (8.6.1; also 3.1.7), who see in each other their "own imbecillitie" (5.77.4). The simple word of Scripture is precious because "our children may of them selves by readinge understand" and so be converted (5.22.14, 4). From the double purpose of arguing to the intelligent and speaking to their childish Christian souls arises the profound disjunction in the *Laws* between reverence for an innocent story and its sophisticated protection.

Reverence is best when it is quiet. "[O]ur safest eloquence concerning him [God] is our silence" (1.2.2).[40] Hooker is clear: "[W]ee neither argue nor dispute about" the "principles whereupon wee do build our soules." Instead, "wee give unto them that assent which the oracles of God require" (5.63.1). The Puritans err in their willfulness (3.8.9), boldness (5.2.3), irreverence (5.47.4), profanity and derision (4.1.3), and "turbulent" and "wanton superfluitie of witt" (1.7.1; 5.2.2). The debates between Puritans and Anglicans are "a mutuall exchange of unseemely and unjust disgraces offered by men whose tongues and passions are out of rule" (5.Ded.7). "Curious and intricate speculations doe hinder, they abate, they quench such inflamed motions of delight and joy as divine graces use to raise when extraordinarily they are present" (5.67.3). Men should "more give them selves to meditate with silence what wee have by the sacrament, and lesse to dispute of the manner how" (5.67.3). Even human sermons are a "corrupt fountaine" that infects the "peculiar

---

40. At the end of the preface, quoting Gregory Nazianzen, Hooker withdraws dramatically into "some corner out of sight, where [he] may scape from this cloudie tempest of malitiousnes" (Pref.9.3).

glorie of the worde of God" with the "witt of man" (5.22.10; also 3.8.10).

For Englishmen specifically, the best kind of meditation is that embodied in the Anglican *Book of Common Prayer*, whose importance to the *Laws* extends beyond the defense of its ritual in book 5 to actual echoes of Cranmer's collects.[41] These collects are more or less epigrammatic versions of a ceremonial plot—unease with the journey one is called upon to perform and reassurances that there will be an end. In a single sentence, they can move from the helplessness at the beginning of the *Consolation* to the perfect safety of the end:

> Almighty God, which dost make the minds of all faithful men to be of one will: Grant unto thy people, that they may love the thing which thou commandest, and desire that which thou dost promise; that among the sundry and manifold changes of the world, our hearts may surely there be fixed, where as true joys are to be found; through Jesus

41. The opening chapter echoes the collects of *The Book of Common Prayer*. The long participial phrase "hartely beseeching Almightie God, whome wee desire to serve according to his owne will, that both we and others (all kinde of partiall affection being cleane laide aside) may have eyes to see, and harts to embrace the things that in his sight are most acceptable" (1.1.3) echoes both the collects' characteristic turn on "beseeching" or "we beseech thee" and also the prayer from Psalm 19, "let the words of my mouth and the meditation of my heart be always acceptable in thy sight." The turn on "beseech" is common in the prayers of the Anglican service, as in the prayers after Holy Communion: "And here we offer and present unto thee, O Lord, ourselves, our souls and bodies, to be a reasonable, holy, and lively sacrifice unto thee, humbly beseeching thee, that all we which be partakers of this Holy Communion, may be fulfilled with thy grace, and heavenly benediction" (*The Book of Common Prayer, 1559: The Elizabethan Prayer Book*, ed. John E. Booty [Charlottesville: University Press of Virginia for the Folger Shakespeare Library, 1976], 264. All quotations from the *Common Prayer* will be from this edition); or, "We now must humbly beseech thee, O heavenly Father" (265). The prayer, "let the words of my mouth" is from Psalm 19, which although not part of the regular service, would have been heard at least once a month because Cranmer so arranged the reading of the psalms that they would have been read through in their entirety in one month. This verse from Psalm 19 was used as an introit in the Mass. J. S. Marshall has argued that Hooker's book 5 is organized as a point-by-point defense of *The Book of Common Prayer* in *Hooker's Theology of Common Prayer, the Fifth Book of the Polity Paraphrased and Expanded into A Commentary on the Prayer Book* (Sewanee, Tenn.: University of the South, 1956). Collections of prayers and translations of liturgical texts in books of private devotions were common in England at least since the late fourteenth century. When they were incorporated into the official Anglican service, Cranmer's translations of the collects (called *orationes* in the Catholic mass) became the best known (James A. Devereux, S.J., "The Primers and the Prayer Book Collects," *Huntington Library Quarterly* 32 [1968–69]: 29–44).

Christ our Lord. (Collect for the Fourth Sunday After Easter)

The formulaic structure of these collects (address, phrase or relative clause, petition, concluding formula[42]) gives them a processional evenness:

> God, which knowest us to be set in the midst of so many and great dangers, that for man's frailness we cannot always stand uprightly: Grant to us the health of body and soul, that all those things which we suffer for sin, by thy help we may well pass and overcome; through Christ our Lord. (Collect for the Fourth Sunday after Epiphany)

The regularity of the pivot on the imperative verb, which turns the prayer from address to supplication, restrains both grief and joy. Expressing either purpose ("do this in order that we may serve you") or result ("doing this will result in our serving you"),[43] the final "that" clauses change a bargain into a statement of fact. If Cranmer's collects resound with echoes that description of their diction and syntax hardly touch upon, this is not because he is simply devotional or even because he is devotional in a specifically Protestant vein.[44] It is because he has an ease with Latin that permits him to transfer the Latin *cursus* to English, as Croll argued;[45] because he has an ear for a kind of ceremonial language that permitted him to combine a Malory-like simplicity of diction with occasional Latinate grandeur; but mostly because the superficial artifice of syntax and diction is drawing on a discourse of praise that had existed in many genres for centuries.

---

42. The collects fall into two regular patterns. The first kind of collect is a simple *oratio*, which is an address and a petition. The second is an amplified *oratio*, which is an address, followed by a phrase or relative clause, then a petition, and finally a concluding formula (James A. Devereux, S.J., "The Collects of the First *Book of Common Prayer* as Works of Translation," 721).

43. Mueller, *Native Tongue*, 240. This ambiguity exists in the *ut* clauses of the original *orationes* of the Sarum Missal, indicating either purpose or result.

44. Mueller's description of the "radically subjective and personal character" (*Native Tongue*, 238) of the collects is not wholly accurate. The association with the devotional writers of the fourteenth century (Love and Hilton) is too narrow.

45. For Cranmer's ability to reproduce the effect of the Latin rhythms in English see Morris W. Croll, "The Cadence of English Oratorical Prose," *Studies in Philology* 16 (1919): 1–55; for Cranmer's ability to hold to the simplicity of English but to maintain the impersonality of liturgy, see James A. Devereux, S.J., "The Collects of the First *Book of Common Prayer* as Works of Translation."

The Book of Common Prayer was useful to Hooker's argument because it too participates in a rhetoric of "silly sooth," the kind of songs that the Duke Orsino prefers to the airs of "these most brisk and giddy-paced times." Like the courtly poems of the miscellanies in the second half of the sixteenth century, the *Common Prayer*'s language is resolutely simple. As in Lydgate's Marian poems, Anglo-Saxon folkishness and Latinate aureation are both solemn: "partakers of thy resurrection" (118), "mercifully look upon our infirmities" (98), "all those things which we suffer for sin," "stand uprightly" (99), "leave us not comfortless" (167), "that we may always most thankfully receive that his inestimable benefit" (160), "make us to have a perpetual fear" (178). The simplicity of this diction was considered conservative even in 1549.[46] Grammatical forms too are slightly out-of-date; by the 1590s, many of the *Common Prayer*'s constructions and those of the *Great Bible*, from which the *Common Prayer* took its Psalter, were archaic.[47] Thus, like Puttenham's poetic standard, which is "pure" and opposed to the language of scholars, merchants, and the sort not "better brought up,"[48] and like Spenser's diction in *The Faerie Queene*, which E.K. finds simple and yet resonant with authority, *The Book of Common Prayer* is at the end of the sixteenth century participating in an idiom that is aristocratic, spiritual, and old.

Hooker's *Laws* capitalizes on this rhetoric of "silly sooth." It can make complex matters sound simple. Even scholarly Latinisms are brought into the communal fold.[49] Its calm allays the sharpness of the

46. Stella Brook traces its sources to various examples of Middle English, which show a similarly simple vocabulary, "easy movement between homely imagery and terms of abstract praise" (70), and "tranquil dignity" (71) (*The Language of The Book of Common Prayer* [New York: Oxford University Press, 1965], 68–76).

47. Brook notes that *The Book of Common Prayer* along with the King James Version of the Bible "helped to establish a standardised 'religious' usage . . . kept alive by tradition in the face of changing linguistic habits" (107). Both share archaic forms for the past tense of strong verbs and the *-en* ending on past participles (107–8).

48. *The Arte of English Poesie*, ed. Gladys Doidge Willcock and Alice Walker (1936; repr. Cambridge: Cambridge University Press, 1969), 144–45.

49. The preface opens with vatic simplicity: "Though for no other cause, yet for this; that posteritie may know we have not loosely through silence permitted things to passe away as in a dreame," "for that worke sake which we covet to performe," "it could not settle in my head," "what good is must be held." For Hooker's scholarly vocabulary, see "efficiencie" in 1.3.4 (according to the *OED*, first recorded in Hooker's *Laws*); "exulceration" in 2.5.7 (first recorded in 1594); "ministeriall imployment" in 1.4.2; "oral manducation" in 5.67.9; "publique coaction" in 5.68.10; "spectacle of commiseration" in 5.1.2; "faithfull sedulitie of freindship" in 5.3.1; "circuitions of discorse" in 5.9.2; and

Puritan conscience, for which sin was especially painful and redemp-
tion especially precarious.[50] In drawing the sinner into the *Common
Prayer*'s silly and old truth, Hooker is constituting him as a small part
of a great ill, for which he need not blame himself so much as lament
the weakness of human nature.

The rhetoric of silly sooth can maintain a dignity virtually silent.
When religious controversial literature picked up the idiom of the
literary entrepreneur, Hooker had a stroke of luck. The "Satyricall
immodestie of Martinisme" provided a readily available contrast to
his own notions of dignified reverence:

> [T]he first published schedules whereof [Marprelate's tracts]
> being brought to the hands of a grave and a very honourable
> Knight, with signification given that the Booke woulde refresh
> his spirits, hee tooke it, saw what the title was, red over an
> unsaverie sentence or two, and delivered backe the Libell with
> this answere, *I am sorie you are of the mind to be solaced with these
> sports, and sorier you have herein thought mine affection to bee like to
> your owne.* (5.Ded.7)

This is Sidney's priest-and-knight, only in Hooker, he is no longer a
youth. In "this present age full of tongue and weake of braine"
(1.8.2), those who do not know the aristocratic decorum of reverence
are full of "scorne and petulancie"; those who are truly spiritual know
the language of "patience and silence" (5.30.4). They also know that
fear is a necessary check on a *"familiaritie* with God" that too often
ends in "irreverend confidence wherewith true humilitie can never
stand" (5.47.4). To attackers like Marprelate, the decorous answer is
not to deign to speak: "Our answer therefore to theire reasons is *No;*
to theire scoffes nothinge" (5.30.4).

In book 5's treatment of the sacrament of the body and blood of
Christ, Hooker offers a prosopopoeia of how the "vertuouslie disposed
minde" would "resolve with it selfe" the disagreements between the
Puritans and Anglicans. It will observe that the discourses of Hooker's
opponents are full of "suttletie of witt" and "boisterous courage" and

---

"session at the right hand of God" in 5.55.8). Allied to this gravity of diction is a
restraint in grave circumlocutions: "St. Jerome whose custome is not to pardon over
easilie his adversaries" (5.29.2); "It was but a little overflowing of witt in Thomas
Aquinas to so play upon the wordes of Moses in the old, and of Peter in the new
Testament" (8.3.6).

50. W. Speed Hill, "Doctrine and Polity in Hooker's *Laws*," *English Literary Renaissance*
2 (1972): 189.

that their arguments are "hungrie and unpleasant, full of tedious and irksome labour." In contrast, the ceremonies of the Anglicans are "sweete as the honie comb, theire tounges melodiouslie tuned instrumentes, theire sentences meere consolation and joy." Hooker then moves away from argument toward the simple biblical word:

> "[A]re wee not hereby almost even with voice from heaven admonished which wee may safeliest cleave unto? Hee which hath said of the one sacrament *Wash and be cleane*, hath said concerninge the other likewise *Eat and live*. If therefore without any such particular and solemne warrant as this is, that poore distressed woman comminge unto Christ for health could so constantlie resolve hir selfe, *May I but touch the skirt of his garment I shalbe whole*, what moveth us to argue of the maner how life should come by bread, our dutie beinge here but to take what is offered, and most assuredly to rest perswaded of this, that can wee but eate wee are safe?" (5.67.12)

"Life . . . bread . . . duty . . . rest . . . eat . . . safe"—these are all the talismans of a ceremonial discourse.

Hooker again moves from necessary but unseemly justifications to ceremonial community in the distinction between the mystical and visible body of the church. The unified, mystical body cannot be discerned by any human being because its parts are either in heaven or, if on earth, spiritual and hence not visible. Nevertheless, it is apprehensible to "intellectual concept." From this mystical body derives Scripture's promise of love and mercy. After all this definition and distinction, the biblical quotation cuts through: "Concerning this flocke it is that our Lord and Saviour hath promised, *I give unto them eternall life, and they shall never perish, neither shall any plucke them out of my handes*" (3.1.2). The text gives way to the old longing for security that is the premise of the entire lawfully ordered universe of book 1.[51]

Shakespeare's plays show the same disjunction between articulate,

---

51. See also the cup of cold water from Matthew (2.8.4) and the description of Christ on the Mount of Olives (5.48). Georges Edelen is right when he remarks that Hooker, like Spenser, needs to be read in long sections, but not, as Edelen argues, because only then can one experience Hooker's majesty but because only then can the refusal of argument be felt (Edelen, "Hooker's Style," in *Studies in Richard Hooker*, ed. W. Speed Hill, 276). When Cranmer objected to Hooker's long sentences in preference for a plain, more straightforward argument, he failed to see how necessary these long sentences are to the move from rhetoric to ceremony. See *Laws*, IV: 107–8.

prudent rulers and the innocence they protect. In *A Midsummer Night's Dream*, Theseus is jovially confident that the lunatic, the lover, and the poet all live in a world of fantasy, but he also protects the memory of the nymph from whom he deflected the arrow of sexuality and who thereby remained "in maiden meditation, fancy-free" (2.1.164). In *Measure for Measure*, the sagacious Duke of Vienna watches Isabella argue with her fallen brother and plead for Angelo's life; although he eventually asks her "Give me your hand and say you will be mine" (5.1.488), we do not see him woo her. In *The Tempest*, Prospero presents a tableau of Miranda and Ferdinand playing chess, but when he finally renounces Miranda, the loss is underlined as giving up "a third of [his] own life" (4.1.3). It is a mark of how fully a ceremonial corporate language has dismembered that the promises of a Sidneian "discursive song" now must be authoritatively protected.

The Political Responsibilities of the Priest-Magistrate

In *All's Well That Ends Well*, Shakespeare feels as uneasy about the world's "modernness" as does Hooker. But being sick or weak, his elder guardians can do nothing about it. Lafew remarks wearily, "They say miracles are past, and we have our philosophical persons, to make modern and familiar, things supernatural and causeless. Hence is it that we make trifles of terrors, ensconcing ourselves into seeming knowledge when we should submit ourselves to an unknown fear" (2.3.1–6). When with Agrippa and the Goth, Sidney stumbles upon the coercive guarantors of his Mistress Poetry's "charm," he sings away their harshness. Hooker is neither so helpless as Lafew nor so insouciant as Sidney. In his view, the rigor of authority is especially necessary in "the present age full of tongue and weake of braine."[52] For him and for Shakespeare (at least in *All's Well*), the community is more likely to flourish with the traditions it has than with reckless novelties.

Because the truth is threatened, one of the responsibilities of those in authority is to understand just how ignorant and recalcitrant the multitude is. Hooker writes his defense of the names of churches "to

52. 1.8.2; see also 1.10.3; 5.2.2.

satisfie the mindes of the simpler sorte of men" (5.13.4); the reading
of Scripture is for the "verie *simplest* and *rudest* sorte" (5.22.2); "the
wits of the multitude are such, that many things they cannot lay hold
on at once" (5.Ded.8); "with grosse and popular capacities nothinge
doth more prevaile then unlimited generalities, because of theire
playnenes at the first sight" (5.9.2). Moreover, "poore people," who
are the charge of the clergy, "are alwaies querulous and apt to thinke
them selves lesse respected then they should be" (5.78.5). Those who
know the truth, on the other hand, are (Hooker here follows
Aristotelian distinctions) not-children, not-madmen, not-idiots
(1.7.4); instead, they show "maturitie of judgement" (1.6.3) and know
"how dull, how heavie and almost how without sense the greatest
part of the common multitude everie where is" (5.68.2). The decisions
of "wise, grave, and learned judgements" are not to be pitted against
those who can "scarce . . . utter five wordes in a sensible maner"
(2.7.6). Hooker reproves the Puritans because they have failed to
make these distinctions, accepting leaders who have authority with
the "ignorant and vulgar sort," drawing their allies from those "verie
neere the dregs" (Pref.4.6) and from women, who show "least
habilitie of judgement" and a characteristic "eagernesse of . . .
affection" and "naturall inclination unto pittie" (Pref.3.13). In many
places of the *Laws*, the Hookerian magistrate is called upon to resist
the folkishness, womanness, childishness, and emotionalism that are
so integral to the vitality of the ceremonial discourse he is defending.

However, although some children of the church are obviously less
intelligent than others, they must not be regarded as irrelevant to the
decisions of the polity. It is the magistrate's duty to see that the weak
are cared for. The "indifferency" of Hooker's *Laws* derives not only
from the language of the law but also from the echoes of a *consolatio*
for those who can hear but cannot understand (see 5.64.3). If one takes
away from the ordinary man his confidence in his understanding of
Scripture, "what shall the scripture be but a snare and a torment to
weake consciences, filling them with infinite perplexities, scrupulos-
ities, doubts insoluble, and extreme despaires?" (2.8.6). If those who
have "lived in schisme" return to the church, "God forbid wee should
thinke that the Church doth sinne in permittinge the woundes of
such to be suppled with that oile which this gracious sacrament [holy
communion] doth yeeld, and theire brused mindes not onlie neede
but begg" (5.68.11). Human beings need "comfort" and "consolation"
at the hour of death, and at that time the "Law of God doth exact at
our handes all the helpes that Christian lenitie and indulgence can
afforde" (5.68.12). Prayers for "thinges earthlie" are necessary "to

help the weaker sorte," who must be generally taught to pray not for temporal goods but for spiritual salvation.[53]

It is true that Hooker sometimes argues for the authority of natural reason in all men; it is "an infallible knowledge imprinted in the mindes of all the children of men" (2.8.6). Still, the magistrate having a superior intelligence, it behooves him to pretend to most men that they can understand even when he suspects—indeed, knows—they cannot: "We hold it safer a great deale and better to give them [those of weak understanding] incouragement; to put them in minde that it is not the deepnes of theire knowledge, but the singlenes of theire beliefe which God accepteth" (5.22.17). In the ceremonial body, innocents have a special status (see 5.61.4; 62.16; 64.2). Hooker is loyal to his obligations: "it behoveth that we vigilantly note and prevent by al meanes those evils whereby the harts of men are lost" (5.Ded.9). "[T]he summe of our whole labour in this kind is to honor God and to save men" (5.76.1). "Gravity" is absorbed as a full and proper understanding of the priest's responsibilities and is associated with gravity's etymological relative "grieving." Fulfilling the injunction of Paul that the ruler should be foremost in care (*praeest in sollicitudine* [Romans 12.8]), authority is distinguished from the multitude not only by its superior powers but by its "condescend[ing] unto common imbecillitie" (5.65.10).

Deep in Hooker's defense of the authority of the Anglican church is a defense of feudal obligations: the obligation of deference that the weak owe to their superiors and the obligation of care that the governors owe to their inferiors. The ardor of a ceremonial mode is now being watched by a consciousness that half adores the hieratic beauty of the universe and half realizes that that hieratic beauty cannot be its own justification to those who are unmoved by it. The same ambiguity appears in *The Tempest*, where Prospero, the magistrate-lord, can speak the civil rhetoric of Antonio and Sebastian, in which wit, allusiveness, sarcasm, and irony enforce a collusion of modern men who have learned how to act for themselves; no longer "ebbing," they have learned how to "flow" (1.2.220, 216). But in other parts of the play, it is the innocence of youth that is the center, and Prospero's dreaming analogue—the counselor Gonzalo—imagines a utopia where there is no work, no sovereignty, no magistrates, but also, significantly, no sophistication with language: "Letters should not be known" (2.1.146). Like Sidney's *Defense*, Hooker's *Laws* and

53. 5.35.2; see also 5.4.2, 5.21.2.

Shakespeare's *Tempest* are defenses of a ceremonial discourse *against* some of the incursions of humanism.

Recent readers of Hooker's *Laws* have emphasized that this work is a polemic, and when we remember that Hooker wanted to silence a noisy Puritan opposition, many of his arguments seem the tactics of obfuscation. In contrast to the Puritans, who argue by quoting passages from their adversaries' works and then rebutting them in a constant seesaw of "he says . . . but I say," Hooker writes as if his opponents had no identity. Thomas Cartwright, Hooker's chief antagonist, appears in the text only in chapter headings and marginal citations to "T.C."[54] Except for the dedication to book 5, Hooker does not mention Whitgift or his own collaborators Edwin Sandys and George Cranmer or other beleaguered Anglican clergy.

Not only does Hooker float above the particulars that prompted the *Laws* in the first place, he floats over all of contemporary history. Reading his work, one would have no inkling of the controversial literature that was pouring out of English and foreign presses at this time, baffling and exasperating government pursuivants: Catholic presses at Hart Street in London, at Smithfield, at Wales, at East Ham, abroad in Louvain, Paris, Rheims, and Flanders; and Puritan presses at the pseudonymous "Wandsworth" and in the traveling shop of Robert Waldegrave and at Middleburg, Dort, Amsterdam, and Leiden on the continent.[55] There is no mention of John Field's and Thomas Wilcox's *An Admonition to Parliament* of 1572 nor of Cartwright's *Second Admonition to Parliament* of 1574 nor of Whitgift's answer nor of Strowd's

54. One of the few direct references to Cartwright in the body of the text occurs in the eighth book (8.8.8). Particular human speakers do not matter. Hooker refers to individual opponents as "one of them" (Thomas Cartwright), and "[a]nother" (Dudley Fenner) and "[a] third" (8.3.3). According to Keble, Fenner is this third author; he wrote "An Humble Motion." Peter Milward however assigns the tract to a group of anonymous petitions to Parliament (*Religious Controversies of the Elizabethan Age: A Survey Of Printed Sources* [London: Scolar Press: 1978], 83–84]). Individualized speakers, like Richard Hooker and Thomas Cartwright, are absorbed in a language that does not use the first person and declines to distinguish between subject and object, speaker and audience. W. Speed Hill notes that Cranmer constantly urged Hooker to meet Cartwright head-on by explaining in the margin of his text what text in Cartwright he was answering (W. Speed Hill, "Hooker's *Polity*: The Problem of the 'Three Last Books,'" 334–35). Hooker's reluctance to do so may be interpreted as an effort to make the text rise ceremonially above particular arguers.

55. On the underground press, see Leona Rostenberg, *The Minority Press & The English Crown: A Study in Repression, 1558–1625* (Nieuwkoop, The Netherlands: B. De Graaf, 1971), 161–98.

translation of Walter Travers's *A Full and Plain Declaration of Ecclesiastical Discipline*.

Hooker might argue that his disdain for the historical here-and-now is precisely his value for the polity; his job is to remind the earth-creepers that there is a higher home. But Coleridge's remark that Hooker was always flying "off to the *General*, in which he is unassailable" is, from the opposition's point of view, right on target.[56] The philosophizing deflects the argument from specific charges by claiming that to change one plank will bring down the whole house. To characterize the Puritans as "turbulent wits," who think "the very disturbance of things established an hyre sufficient to set them on worke" (1.7.1), is to dismiss opposing arguments as mere opportunism. The characterization of the leader as a lonely figure (cf. Hal's "O polished perturbation! Golden care!" [*2 Henry IV*, 4.4] and before Agincourt, "And what art thou, thou idol Ceremony" [*Henry V*, 4.1]) sounds like a justification of authority by sentimentalizing it. Hooker's voice as silent governor and loving priest may have its liabilities too. If "Elizabeth Tudor" was in part the constitution of an erotic-pastoral-religious discourse adored by her subjects and in part the constitution of the political maneuvering of her councillors—Knollys, Walsingham, and especially Cecil—Hooker may have spoken "good Elizabethan" all too powerfully.

The philosophizing also masks Hooker's connections with established authority. Coleridge wrote in the margin where Hooker sarcastically dismisses the Puritan claims to the efficacy of preaching: "Doubtless Hooker was a theological Talus with a Club of Iron against opponents with paste-board Helmets and armed only with Crab-sticks!"[57] The comparison with book 5 of *The Faerie Queene* is appropriate. At the time Hooker was writing, the crown had the power to hang authors and printers of books it regarded as seditious. Indeed, for some, the argument that a ceremonial polity is necessary because it alone is capable of bending the strong to their obligations must be recognized as an ideal rather than a fact. As an ideal, it risks being a fantasy that works in the interest of some people more than others.

For Hooker, however, a political theory was an ideal. It should not be based on what human nature is but on what it ought to be according to the word of God as written in the Bible and in the Book of Nature, of which human reason is a part. If there is a gap between

56. *Coleridge on the Seventeenth Century*, ed. Roberta Florence Brinkley (Durham: Duke University Press, 1955), 149.
57. Ibid., 148.

what human nature is capable of and what it should aspire to (according to a loving God), the remedy should not be to lower the ideal. Such a move will produce two pernicious consequences. First, people will be fooled into thinking that fulfillment of their desires is the same thing as happiness. Second, they will not find pleasure in (they will not *know* how to find pleasure in) devotion to a superior kind of happiness. There are, of course, arguments on both sides. As More suggests in book 1 of *Utopia*, insisting on a superior spiritual happiness that most human beings cannot achieve often discourages analysis of the institutional pressures that incline people to be bad. Moreover, good may be good and evil evil, but too exaggerated an ideal gives rise to a monster that is easily projected onto aliens.

Once we know an argument is being put forward in order to defeat another position, anything can start to look suspicious. No doubt, the readers who find Hooker most satisfying are those who believe that answers to religious questions can be more or less rational and that questions about a specifically Christian polity or the place of religion in a polity are worth asking. With Sidney, it is possible to grant the religious premise and still find the *Defense* enchanting because the religious premise is kept under control by decorum: admittedly, the Bible is the best poetry, but who would want to get rid of the other means for lifting up the heart? With Hooker, the religious premise is harder, because the paternalism that follows is not just condescending but threatening: the Christian tradition must and will be protected against thoughtless marauders.

The argument can be refocused, however, by translating it into more secular terms, a recasting that Hooker himself invites when at the beginning of book 5 he maintains that citizens of a commonwealth are more likely to be virtuous if the commonwealth has a religious tradition. Insofar as all religions are said to have *some* truth in them, "religion" here seems to be understood as "the life of the spirit," opposed to an "atheistic" material pleasure (5.1–2). This "spirit" however is not the virtue of the great-souled man in an Aristotelian version of classical rhetoric. Hooker's constant emphasis on peace and order circumscribes the great-souled man's aggressive individuality by the other Aristotelian virtue of habit rightly disposed to temperance or restraint, Christianized as habit rightly disposed to love. For Hooker, love is a combination of devotion, self-abasement, and the vitality of belonging to the truth. His "life of the spirit" is an acceptance of the human condition as the best God could arrange for fallen human creatures. Acceptance is not "fulfillment" (as if it were achieved after many laborious steps) nor exhilaration (as if it took the breath away) but more like rest. It is brought into being in the moment of recognizing one's dependence on the family of nature. Its expression in the visible world is willing service. A tradition that combines philosophy (for those who wish to pursue it) and a simple story is the most useful for teaching this spirit; the philosophy explains the story, and yet only the story is comprehensible to most of the members of the polity.

Love is hard to talk about. It leads quickly to the propriety of Sunday school religion or to the pieties of a bourgeois marriage. Joyce hardly uses the word in the Cyclops chapter of *Ulysses* before he is parodying it: "Love loves to love love. Nurse loves the new chemist. Constable 14A loves Mary Kelly. . . . Jumbo, the elephant, loves Alice the elephant. . . . His Majesty the King loves Her Majesty the Queen. . . . You love a certain person. And this person loves that other person because everybody loves somebody but God loves everybody."[58] Critics of literature used to talk about love by ventriloquizing: they let Spenser do the talking and suffer the embarrassment—or Shakespeare, or Dickens, or whoever. But coming to terms with Hooker requires not only an analysis of how he uses love as a sweet suasion to a conservative politics but also understanding what he thought he was talking about. Hooker is sure that love is a part of truth. What part of truth it is can only be known the way Aristotle says we know a good deed. That is, a good dead is a deed done by a person we know is good, and good in an Aristotelian sort of way. Love in the way Hooker means it is something believed in by a person we know is good, and good in a Christian sort of way, a goodness that is deepened with experience and reflection. Besides self-abasement and devotion, love's vitality is grounded in a happiness that is best defined as "serenity." The erotic-pastoral-spiritual discourse that underlies so much literature of the Middle Ages and Renaissance holds that happiness and truth are not opposed, and it holds this position with a cheerfulness that is not fighting somberness or ignoring it but embracing it.

Even in the secularized version of Hooker's "life of the spirit," however, the disjunction between sagacious leaders and "believing children" raises a serious and perhaps unsolvable problem in communal tradition. Supposedly all members of the community believe in the tradition; this shared belief defines them as a people. But if priests-philosophers-governors fulfill their mission by "protecting"

58. James Joyce, *Ulysses* (New York: Modern Library, 1961), 333.

tradition (politically and philosophically), they cannot be said to "believe" it in the same way that their "children" believe it. In fact, Hooker sometimes talks as if the laws made by wise and learned men to "govern" tradition are formalities whose function is primarily to stabilize public order, not to encourage religious worship. Laws, Hooker maintains, can command outward compliance but not religious commitment: "[A]s opinions do cleave to the understanding and are in hart assented unto it is not in the power of any humane lawe to command them, because to prescribe what men shall think belongeth only unto God" (8.6.4). Of those taking communion, "[w]hat theire hartes are God doth knowe" (5.68.8). Because forms of worship are things indifferent, then purity of worship does not affect membership in the church (3.1.7); children baptized by heretics are still properly baptized. The Machiavellianism that Hooker edges toward at the beginning of book 5 is here a negotiation between public responsibilities and private religious ardor. Hooker's famed "judiciousness" runs the risk of destroying religion as a communal custom by separating religious devotion from a decorum necessary for public order, a decorum enforced by civil magistrates who have foremost on their minds a defense of the kingdom and who understand the dangers of emotionalism to political compromise.

Hooker argues by demonstration as much as does Sidney: "Are you moved when I evoke the prayers you are familiar with? Do you agree that argument only succeeds in fracturing the unself-conscious worship of a story we all love?—I rest my case." Love of the story—a love so strong it is bewildered by the need for defenses—must be the motivating force of the apologia. Without it, the philosophizing is reduced to logic and the fellowship sapped of its vitality. But the assimilation of rhetorical agon to the ceremonial story risks redefining unself-conscious belief as "childish" or "naive" and therefore irrelevant. Some people simply do not have the maturity to understand a religious polity as a problem in political philosophy. If they are "relevant" only in the sense that they are the ones whom the sophisticated must care for, surely they are being shunted aside. Of course, philosophizing inevitably raises difficulties because it so deliberately insists that belief should be based on intellectual choice, not tradition. Even Shakespeare, who also seemed to understand the contradiction between a leader's prudence and his power to inspire, stopped short of the philosophizing that would have brought the contradictions into the open. Rather than calling Hooker's effort a project so riddled with contradictions that it could never have been successful, however, we should appreciate his awareness of the complex adjustments, both philosophical and rhetorical, necessary to keep the parts together. After him, political theory could offer sharper, less ambiguous and less paradoxical formulations but only by limiting the definition of civil society.

4

Ceremony in a Seventeenth-Century Civil Mode: Thomas Browne's Religious Liberalism

Seventeenth-Century Discursivity and Generic Differentiation

For the twentieth-century reader, the foreignness of the sixteenth century is almost an advantage. Once the glass paperweight of "historical otherness" is set down over the period, its peculiarities are granted rather easily. This was a culture that believed in God and was eager to believe in a king. Henry VIII was able to put More to death in 1534 without large protest from his people because he still enjoyed a considerable popularity. With the seventeenth century, we are closer to home, and the peculiarities are for that reason harder to grant. Inevitably, we are looking at part of ourselves. Hence, the seventeenth century is a battleground for contemporary positions: the triumphant emergence of rationalism or the dismaying emergence of rationalism, or the dismaying emergence of individualism and private affectivity, or the triumphant first sign of a salvational "decentering." The familiar intellectual and social atmosphere of the seventeenth century is in part created by the radical change from Foucault's "language of resemblance" to a "language of representation." Accompanying this change are generic limitations we take for granted: political theory that is cut off from religion, history that investigates sources without mythologizing rulers, science that has dethroned Aristotle, a writer who conceives of himself as an independent intellectual, a public world of politics and economics distinguished from a private world of the domestic hearth, and the creation of individuals with distinct inner worlds and personalities. The new mode of scientific rationalism has the familiar ingredients of individualism, urbanity, and intellectual aggression. In its resistance to dissolution into the body of various authorities—God, king, *auctores*—it is altogether more comprehensible to the modern.

The rhetorical move of attacking the credulity of a former age is also familiar, as are the means of doing so: clear definitions, the coolness of irony, and the explicit separation between rational procedures and emotional fervor, both of love and the "thunder and denunciation of curses and anathemas," as Bacon characterized religious controversy (*Advancement*, 481). Seventeenth-century prose is constantly pushing off or holding to the background a ceremonial mode's visionary epistemology. This "pushing off" creates an arhythmic, dispassionate civil prose—"aculeate" [pointed], in Bacon's word.[1] Modern critics tend to find the pointedness more literarily interesting, as if it were a formal matter of compound sentences and aphoristic wit; in fact, what they are attracted to is the modern freedom to "parse" the world according to one's own grammar. It was never hard to accept Croll's argument that Senecan prose is interesting because it brings on stage the idiosyncrasies of individualized consciousness.[2] It is harder to see that the individualized consciousness is a product not only of rich metaphors and broken syntax but also of argumentative procedures not usually thought of as literary at all (generalization, definition, and differentiation).

A seventeenth-century pointed style sharpened the contradictions in a classical rhetoric nurtured at court. To create a full-fledged and up-to-date royal seat, the Tudors gathered around them articulate men who could represent the "amiable display" of royalty. But in gathering witty men of letters, the court created the very conditions that would encourage them to "talk of princes" *to one another* and not

---

1. The Latin translation of *The Advancement of Learning* of 1623, trans. Gilbert Wats Oxford, 1640, 29; quoted in Trimpi, *Ben Jonson's Poems*, 52.

2. "Attic Prose: Lipsius, Montaigne, Bacon," in *Style, Rhetoric, and Rhythm*, ed. J. Max Patrick et al., 195–99.

in a tone of reverence. Under Elizabeth, this contradiction was obscured but not erased. After the great triumph of 1588, the obvious stuff for a national myth were stories of happy communities and erotic quests. Still, the group of young men that the enchanting Tudor queen gathered around her were not always content with the role of Petrarchan servant to Belphoebe or Diana; they were passionate for other things—the honors of war and the spoils of office. At the end of Elizabeth's reign, restiveness under an older generation unwilling to cede its power (not obviously without justification), and an intellectual fashion for Tacitus, Bodin, and Machiavelli motivated young aristocrats to dispense with a discourse that funneled the vision toward authority legitimized by a connection with the supernatural.[3] Ceremony's fragmented forms (pastorals, sonnets, sestinas, elegies, love songs), which told a communal story and also advertised the wit of individual courtly "makers," could no longer sustain the contradiction between the suppression of individualism and the courtier's personal ambitions. In the early part of the next century, the old images of authority—the church and the crown—dramatically lost ground. Attacks on the liturgy of the established church, on the corruption of ecclesiastical patronage, on the frivolousness of James's court (and a king who wasted entirely too much money and too much time hunting), and on the crown's interpretation of its prerogatives rubbed down the velvet of a discourse that robed the monarch in everything that was old, natural, and blessed by God.[4]

To be sure, some of the splintering of a ceremonial discourse was caused by Protestant resistance to a state church. In rendering individual conscience in interpretation of Scripture the sole authority of truth, morality was interiorized and intensified. It was also cut off from the civil polity, which, according to Protestants and eventually Puritans, should be denied authority in church doctrine. Customary church ritual, once so happily assumed to be a part of God's plenitude, was now subjected to the scrutiny of individual conscience, and, needless to say, often found wanting. Anglicans hoped that the stability of the ecclesiastical body could be saved by the

3. On the political context in which Bacon's style was forged and its connection with the Essex affair, see F. J. Levy, "Francis Bacon and the Style of Politics," *ELR* 16 (1986): 101–22. In his letter book, Gabriel Harvey noted that students were reading Machiavelli and Bodin as early as the 1570s (*The Letter-Book of Gabriel Harvey, A.D. 1573–1580*, ed. E. J. L. Scott, Camden Society, n.s. 33 [1884]: 79–80).

4. On the decline of the aristocracy generally from the mid-sixteenth to the mid-seventeenth century, see Lawrence Stone, *The Crisis of the Aristocracy 1558–1641* (Oxford: Clarendon Press, 1965).

doctrine of adiaphorism, that is, making liturgical forms "indifferent." God is not scrupulous about forms of worship; Christians can still be Christians by adhering to the basics of the creed and regarding more or less disinterestedly the details of the liturgy. The separation between public liturgy and private belief, an ecclesiastical solution hinted at in Hooker, is expanded in the various generic experiments of the seventeenth century. These experiments have dual motivations: to acknowledge the advantage of rationality in matters of public concern and to preserve an inner spirituality.

The religious solution of adiaphorism, which was also a social solution, reinforced the newly sharpened line between reason and theology. This line had been drawn earlier by Duns Scotus, who argued that theology should be separated from reason, and by Ockham, who argued that the natural world should be separated from theology. The goal of these thinkers, however, was still religious: to give greater glory to God. When Bacon separated reason from theology, his motivation was quite different: to create a science "such as shall be operative to the endowment and benefit of man's life" (*Advancement*, 333). He acknowledged the secularity of this project when he defined his opposition as the belief that study of secondary causes detracted from the worship of God (*Advancement*, 4). Bacon's intellectual solution was not unlike the religious solution of adiaphorism: to rope off areas where God-questions are irrelevant or at least less pressing. Bacon's "roping off" is achieved by elaborate differentiation of the "parts of human learning": "History is natural, civil, ecclesiastical, and literary. . . . History of Nature is of three sorts . . . history of Creatures, history of Marvels, and history of Arts" (330); "For Civil History, it is of three kinds" (333); "The division of poesy . . . is into Poesy Narrative, Representative, and Allusive" (344)—and so on all the way to a science "to teach men how to raise and make their fortune" (456). Bacon was not the first to sever reason from religion; but unlike earlier thinkers he aggressively defined the discourses left to reason alone. In a ceremonial discourse, everything is connected to everything else, logically or allegorically; touch the universe in its tiniest part and soon the whole structure is vibrating. In Baconian compartmentalized learning, the very limitation of the field permits the answers to be much more detailed. The winds of morality and God are not suddenly going to swoop into a discussion and render irrelevant a studied look at particulars.

The pointed style's fundamental separation of secular (and useful) thinking from religious belief in turn gives a sharper edge to "individualism." It has been maintained that the inwardness of the Puritan experience is the heart of seventeenth-century individualism. But this argument is exaggerated. Although the Puritan revival of Augustinian religious intensity drives experience inward, it does not individualize it. The community of the elect still subsumes the particular believer in an Everyman story. Much more powerfully do the abstract definitions of rationalism differentiate human lives, first by distinguishing human goals but second, and more important, by constituting different goals as "rational" and hence justified. These goals are deployed in genres that stabilize both the human being as a secular, autonomous creature and the secular, masterable world in which he lives. The essay, chorography, familiar epistle, satire, Theophrastan character, the resolve, diary, biography, autobiography, and eventually the novel situate human beings in a historical scene as medieval romance did not. Now people are who they are because they are measured by a discourse that processes secularized manners, society, and politics. The personal bonds between dependent creature (or servant) and a savior (religious or aristocratic) has been replaced by rationalized formality.

The key words of a ceremonial discourse are reaccented. "Reason" is cut off from "right reason" and reduced to Hobbes's "reckoning of consequences." "Passion" is not storied as a fallen inclination redeemable by another passionate story of rescuing grace. Instead, it is a human inclination with effects that can be controlled by adjusting social mechanisms. For this argument, Machiavelli is a helpful thinker, not a monster.[5] Secularized "manners" are no longer collusions with a deceptive world of appearances but accommodations necessary to a society with a multitude of believers who must all somehow get along with each other. Political order is justified on practical grounds, grounds that either expand the sovereign's authority (Hobbes) or limit it (Locke). The hugeness of Milton—of his determination, of his denunciation, of his belief in the mission of poetry to teach the highest truths, and of his misery—is a protest against this generic differentiation; why else do the ways of God to men have to be "justified" at such length and with such mythic efforts? Why else does the superiority of the poet's craft to "verbal curiosities" and the superiority of his mission to that of the "riming parasite" and

5. Felix Raab, *The English Face of Machiavelli: A Changing Interpretation 1500–1700* (London: Routledge and Kegan Paul, 1965), 77–184.

"libidinous and ignorant Poetasters" have to be urged with such intensity?[6]

A fundamental tension exists at the heart of the new tool of rational discursiveness. For a Baconian, it makes the world masterable, obedient to human needs. Socially, however, for those who want to raise their status, it makes the world fluid. Erasmus's farmer singing verses behind his plow did not threaten a culture of obedience; after all, the farmer is singing about Christianity, not his plans for a future career. But linguistic power could advance secular business. Colet's educational program to make schoolboys into "gret clarkes"[7] had the effect of socializing schoolboys to *want* the rewards of "gret clarkes"; articulateness exacerbated the social fluidity the Tudors had already introduced with the spoils of patronage.

The tension in articulateness comes to a head at the end of the century, when it is as much of a social commodity as aristocratic grace.[8] In the hard word dictionaries of the early seventeenth century, the alliance of language, money, and social-climbing is explicit. Robert Cawdrey offers *A Table Alphabeticall* (1604) to teach "the true writing" and "hard usuall English wordes" borrowed from foreign languages to "Ladies, Gentlewomen, or any other unskilfull persons" both for understanding books but also for their own use.[9] Henry Cockeram intends *The English Dictionarie* (1623) for "Ladies and Gentlewomen, Clarkes, Merchants, young Schollers, Strangers, [and] Travellers." He assures his reader that his method is "plaine and easie . . . by which the capacity of the meanest may soone be inlightened" and offers a second book of "vulgar words" with their more "refined and elegant" equivalents.[10] In *An English Expositor* (1616), John Bullokar defends his explanation of hard words on the grounds that the language now contains "divers termes of art, proper to the learned in Logicke, Philosophy, Law, Physicke, Astronomie"

---

6. John Milton, "The Reason of Church Government," in *The Complete Prose Works of John Milton*, ed. Don M. Wolfe, 1:811, 820, 818.

7. Quoted in Mackie, *The Earlier Tudors*, 245.

8. On literacy in the early seventeenth century as a means for rising in the world, see David Cressy, *Literacy and the Social Order: Reading and Writing in Tudor and Stuart England* (Cambridge: Cambridge University Press, 1980), 9–10.

9. Robert Cawdrey, *A Table Alphabeticall of Hard Usual English Words (1604)*, facsim. ed., ed. Robert A. Peters (Gainesville, Fla.: Scholars' Facsimiles and Reprints, 1966), title page.

10. Henry Cockeram, "A Premonition from the Author to the Reader," *The English Dictionarie of 1623*, ed. Chauncey Brewster Tinker (New York: Huntington, 1930), xv–xvi.

("To the Courteous Reader"). But he is nervous about opening learning to anyone who can purchase his book: "And herein I hope such learned will deeme no wrong offered to themselves or dishonour to Learning, in that I open the signification of such words, to the capacitie of the ignorant, whereby they may conceive and use them as well as those which have bestowed long study in the languages."[11] These dictionary-makers see a market in purveying to women and shopkeepers the powers of articulation that used to belong to the aristocracy, yet they are uneasy about scattering this information too liberally.

Tom Nashe shows none of the schoolmaster's nervousness. Rhet-oricians may be troubled by selling articulateness and regulating it, but he is quite happy to consume a classicized English. In his flyting with Harvey, Nashe flaunts the neologisms by which he wittily triumphs over class origins: "Had I a Ropemaker to my father, and somebody had cast it in my teeth, I would foorthwith have writ in praise of Ropemakers, and prov'd it by sound sillogistry to be one of the 7. liberal sciences."[12] By his own self-created "syllogistry," Nashe would have given himself a pedigree. In the preface to the second issue of *Christs Teares Over Jerusalem* (1594), Nashe defends his coinages against detractors:

> For the compounding of my wordes, therein I imitate rich men who, having gathered store of white single money together, convert a number of those small little scutes into great peeces of gold, such as double Pistols and Portugues. Our English tongue of all languages most swarmeth with the single money of monasillables, which are the onely scandall of it. Bookes written in them and no other seeme like Shop-keepers boxes, that contain nothing else save halfe-pence, three-farthings, and two-pences. Therefore what did me I, but having a huge heape of those worthlesse shreds of small English in my *Pia maters* purse, to make the royaller shew with them to mens eyes, had them to the compounders immediately, and ex-changed them foure into one. (*Works*, 2:184)

As always, Nashe is streetwise in a fluid society, where titles can be bought and a "royaller shew" put on with just a little available cash.

11. John Bullokar, *An English Expositor: Teaching the Interpretation of the hardest words used in our Language with Sundry Explications, Descriptions, and Discourses* (London: John Legatt, 1621).

12. Nashe, *Strange Newes*, in *The Works of Thomas Nashe*, ed. R. B. McKerrow, 3 vols. (1904–10; repr. ed., ed. F. P. Wilson [Oxford: Basil Blackwell, 1958]), 1:270.

The same metaphors of coining words and usurious self-aggrandizement are used by other writers. In the preface to his translation of Homer, Chapman boasts of the riches he has brought to English: "For my varietie of new wordes, I have none Inckepot I am sure you know, but such as I give pasport with such authoritie, so significant and not ill sounding, that if my countrey language were an usurer, or a man of this age speaking it, hee would thanke mee for enriching him."[13] A royal show of invented words will bring new blood into worn-out aristocratic stock. In 1609, Robert Armin rejoices in the power of language to raise the low: "Onely I wander with it now [his pen] in a strange time of taxation, wherein every Pen & inck-horne Boy, will throw up his Cap at the hornes of the Moone in censure, although his wit hang there, not returning, unlesse monthly in the wane: such is our ticklish age, & the itching braine of aboundance."[14] Armin apparently condemns the availability of rhetoric to "every Pen & inck-horne Boy," but he confesses that he is wandering around with his own pen himself. John Earle's character sketches in *Microcosmography* similarly exult in the availability of language; Paul's Walk is "the great exchange of all discourse."[15] The "skill with tongues" that Hooker so despised is loosening the levels of a highly stratified society.

The weakening of aristocratic grace as a normative force is reflected in the swing to the universities as a standard of diction. For Puttenham, a linguistic standard is a courtly one, its conservatism maintained against both the universities and commercialism.[16] In Sidney's *Defense*, the natural and pure art of the courtier-poet is superior to the labored art of the professor of learning. In the seventeenth century, the norms for proper diction are established not by courtiers but by scholars. For Alexander Gill in *Logonomia Anglica* (1619) a linguistic standard is based "in sermone consuetudo docto-

---

13. "To the Understander," *Achilles Shield, Translated as the other seven Bookes of Homer out of his eighteenth booke of Iliades (1598)*, in *Elizabethan Critical Essays*, ed. G. Gregory Smith, 2 vols. (Oxford: Oxford University Press, 1904), 2:305.

14. Robert Armin, *The Italian Taylor, and his Boy* (1609), in *The Works of Robert Armin*, ed. Alexander B. Grosart (Blackburn, England: printed for the subscribers by Charles Simms, 1880), 143.

15. John Earle, "Paul's Walk," in *Microcosmography: Or, A Piece of the World Discover'd in Essays and Characters* (London: E. Say, 1732), 131.

16. Puttenham, *Arte of English Poesie*, 144. Ever since *Tottel's Miscellany* in the middle of the century, simple purity in verse was the standard (Veré L. Rubel, *Poetic Diction in the English Renaissance From Skelton through Spenser* [New York: Modern Language Association of America, 1941], 95).

rum," and specifically not on the speech of children, women, and porters. In *English Grammar* (1633), Charles Butler bases the standard on the speech "of the Universities and Citties." In *Grammatica Linguae Anglicanae* (1653), John Wallis rejects the speech of the vulgar and of the courtiers. His epigone Owen Price says he has followed the speech "of London and our Universities."[17] The movement of "standard English" from a spoken, courtly idiom to a prosaic, printed standard appears in the sixteenth-century fuss over spelling and in the programs for a proper grammar.[18] With Ben Jonson, an author with a considerable stake in his personal "works" appearing in print, the concern with rules, print, and civil manners flow together. Gill's phrase "consuetudo doctorum" (which echoes Quintilian's *Institutes* 1.6.45) occurs in Jonson's *Discoveries*: "*Custome* is the most certaine Mistresse of Language. . . . Yet when I name Custome, I understand not the vulgar Custome: For that were a precept no lesse dangerous to Language, then life, if wee should speake or live after the manners of the vulgar: But that I call Custome of speech, which is the consent of the Learned."[19]

When printed articulateness unleashes self-made "masters" there is all the more need for linguistic arbiters. To the sixteenth-century Ascham, careless language is impious; it leads to Anabaptism and Catholicism. To the seventeenth-century Jonson, careless language is uncivilized; it leads to a "publicke riot."[20] The world is spawning linguistic entrepreneurs, and it is the business of Jonsonian critics to limit the amount of money-words in the marketplace.[21] Into his borrowing from Quintilian ("*Custome* is the most certain Mistresse of Language, as the publicke stampe makes the current money"), Jonson interpolates conservative restrictions: "But wee must not be

17. Dobson, "Early Modern Standard English," in *Approaches to English Historical Linguistics*, ed. Roger Lass, 421.

18. Richard Foster Jones, *The Triumph of the English Language: A Survey of Opinions Concerning the Vernacular from the Introduction of Printing to the Restoration* (Stanford: Stanford University Press, 1953), 142–67 and 281–84.

19. Ben Jonson, *Discoveries*, in *Ben Jonson*, ed. C. H. Herford and Percy Simpson, 11 vols. (1925–52; repr. Oxford: Clarendon Press, 1954), 8:622. Jonson is following Quintilian, *Institutes* 1.6.3 and 43–45 (editors' note, 11:267). All further references to Jonson's *Discoveries* will be to this edition.

20. Jonson, *Discoveries*, 8:622 and 593.

21. Don E. Wayne analyzes Jonson's "To Penshurst" as a justification of the Sidneys against other Tudor *arrivistes* who wrongly build houses that inspire envy and also as justification of Jonson himself as deserving of aristocratic patronage, in *Penshurst: The Semiotics of Place and the Poetics of History* (Madison: University of Wisconsin Press, 1984).

too frequent with the mint, every day coyning."[22] Language should not be in the power of the *"Tamerlanes, and Tamer-Chams* of the late Age," whose verbal individualism in "furious vociferation" turns an audience into "ignorant gapers."[23] Samuel Daniel too wants lawful procedures for those who borrow "without a Parliament" and who "without any consent or allowance" establish new words as "Free-denizens in our language"; writers should not be allowed the "presumption" to decide these things "of themselves."[24] When custom or God or doctrine or the king's pursuivants cannot control the "itching braine of aboundance," then arbiters of taste have to step in.

These judges derive their authority from clear thought, which distinguishes between poetry and prose or between poetic prose and prosaic prose. Poetry, says Bacon, is like "inspiration" because it "doth raise and erect the mind, by submitting the shows of things to the desires of the mind; whereas reason doth buckle and bow the mind into the nature of things" (*Advancement*, 343–44). In the essay "Of Fame," Bacon assaults the language of poets, who only distract with their elegance and portentousness: "The poets make fame a monster. They describe her in part finely and elegantly; and in part gravely and sententiously. They say, look how many feathers she hath, so many eyes she hath underneath; so many tongues; so many voices; she pricks up so many ears" ("Of Fame," 195). Bacon dismisses these metaphors as a "flourish" followed by "excellent parables." He then cuts his parody short, differentiating between prose and poetry: "But we are infected with the stile of the poets. To speak now in a sad and serious manner. . . ." Prosaic reason is the *"lumen siccum"* that the "watery and soft natures" of most men cannot tolerate (*Advancement*, 383). For Jonson, poetry itself should be prosaic. If it is not, it is effeminate. "Womens-*Poets*" write in a songlike style, with merely "a kind of tuneing, and riming fall."[25]

Instead of drifting allegorically, associatively, musically, prosaic prose sticks to the point. Bacon's repeated announcement of his logical organization in the *Essays* is something new: "To pass from theological and philosophical truth to the truth of civil business ("Of Truth," 48); "But let us pass from this part of predictions [of

22. Jonson, *Discoveries*, 8:622, following *Inst.* 4.6.3.

23. Ibid., 8:587.

24. Samuel Daniel, *A Defence of Rhyme* (1603?), in *Elizabethan Critical Essays*, ed. G. Gregory Smith, 2:384.

25. Jonson, *Discoveries*, 8:585.

rebellion] . . . and let us speak first of the Materials of seditions; then of the Motives of them; and thirdly of the Remedies" ("Of Seditions and Troubles," 81); "The parts of a judge in hearing are four: to direct evidence; to moderate length, repetition, or impertinency of speech; to recapitulate, select, and collate the material points of that which hath been said; and to give the rule or sentence" ("Of Judicature," 185–86). Prosaic sobriety eschews emotional appeals. Although Bacon's *Essays* are often vividly metaphorical, they do not slide into sermons or anecdotally concrete stories. When sermon matter is introduced, it is only a brief allusion: "But above all, believe it, the sweetest canticle is, *Nunc Dimittis*" ("Of Death," 50). Urbane readers know the iceberg that lies beneath that allusive tip. To spell it out would be to lapse into the old rhetorical relationship between schoolmaster and pupil, and Bacon speaks to adults.

Abstractions facilitate procedural tightening. By defining an argument, they prevent it from drifting into a story of God's providence. In Bacon's *Essays*, an item of knowledge is first discriminated and then attached to other items of knowledge: "The personal fruition in any man cannot reach to feel great riches; there is a custody of them, or a power of dole and donative of them, or a fame of them, but no solid use to the owner" ("Of Riches," 147). "I like a plantation in a pure soil; that is, where people are not displanted to the end to plant in others. For else it is rather an extirpation than a plantation" ("Of Plantations," 134); "Ambition is like choler, which is an humour that maketh men active, earnest, full of alacrity, and stirring, if it be not stopped" ("Of Ambition," 143); "The wisest princes need not think it any diminution to their greatness or derogation to their sufficiency to rely upon counsel" ("Of Counsel," 97). The skill lies in marshaling and organizing details, a keener challenge than retelling the oft-told story of good and evil. In prosaic prose, intellectual difficulty is itself a pleasure.

Prosaic prose also requires stipulative definitions. "Goodness" is now a quality that Bacon is free to "take" in any sense he pleases, to assign it a definition for his own purposes: "I take Goodness in this sense, the affecting of the weal of men, which is that the Grecians call *Philanthropia;* and the word *humanity* (as it is used) is a little too light to express it" ("Of Goodness and Goodness Of Nature," 75). "My judgment is that they [prophecies] ought all to be despised, and ought to serve but for winter talk by the fireside. Though when I say *despised*, I mean it as for belief, for otherwise, the spreading or publishing of them is in no sort to be despised" ("Of Prophecies," 142). In the *Essays*, Bacon uses many unusual words for precision:

"And let them not come in multitudes or in a *tribunitious* manner" ("Of Counsel," 101); "Some there are who, though they lead a single life, yet their thoughts do end with themselves, and account future times *impertinences*" ("Of Marriage and Single Life," 62); "Neither doth this weakness appear to others only, and not to the party loved, but to the loved most of all, except the love be *reciproque*" ("Of Love," 69); "A good continued speech, without a good speech of *interlocution,* shows slowness" ("Of Discourse," 133; emphasis mine throughout). From the resulting compression, Bacon gains intellectual authority. In *The Advancement of Learning*, the final dismissal of the scholastics is peremptory: "vain imaginations, vain altercations, and vain affectations" (282). The most important characteristic of the new discourse is linguistic discrimination, defining and refining at the same time.

The encoded distinction between precise and imprecise, mature and immature, rational and emotional enables a useful tool for the cultural regulator: irony. For John Hoskins, the great value of irony is all that does not have to be said; those who need it to be said belong to the class of the "to-be-governed." As an example of "intimation," the fourth way of amplifying, which "leaves the collection of greatness to our understanding, by expressing some mark of it," Hoskins offers this sentence: "that a man is grown gross, *he is grown from a body to a corporation.*" The value of this figure is its subtlety: "It exceedeth speech in silence, and makes our meaning more palpable by a touch than by a direct handling."[26] Here the wit depends on the "greatness," as Hoskins puts it, of the Latinate polysyllable ("corporation") being played against the native English disyllable ("body") and forcing the sense of the Latin derivative, conventionally used as an abstraction for a collection of men, back into the Latin root *corpus*, an individual man's body. As Hoskins remarks, this figure "savors something of hyperbole": "corporation" is a disproportionately hyperbolic expression for the human body. Another kind of "intimation" is *"ironia,* or denial," a figure in which the "denial" is suggested by a negative (26). Hoskins's example is, "He was no notorious malefactor, but he had been twice on the pillory and once burnt in the hand for trifling oversights." When the Latinate assessment ("no notorious malefactor") is held up to the concrete English data, its caution becomes a joke. Despite Ben Jonson's protestations against the inkhorning of the day, he too exploits the potential of macaronic

26. John Hoskins, *Directions for Speech and Style*, ed. Hoyt H. Hudson (Princeton: Princeton University Press, 1935), 25.

English-Latin for irony: "*And some,* by a cunning protestation against all reading, and false venditation of their owne *naturals,* thinke to divert the *sagacity* of their Readers from themselves, and coole the sent of their owne *fox-like* thefts."[27] "[P]rotestation," "venditation," and "sagacity" chafe against "fox" and "scent," the language for coarse people. Latinisms enable the "slight touch" against loud-mouthers: "*Indeed,* the multitude commend Writers, as they doe Fencers, or Wrastlers; who if they come in robustiously, and put for it, with a deale of violence, are received for the *braver-fellowes:* when many times their owne rudenesse is a cause of their disgrace; and a slight touch of their Adversary, gives all that boisterous force the foyle."[28] Mature readers can hear the evaluation of intellectual positions in the play among levels of diction.

Rational analysis and ridicule are closely connected; in both, a great deal is assumed. Bacon's history of sixteenth-century prose styles in *The Advancement of Learning* ends with the pun on the last two syllables of *Cicerone* (in Greek, "ass").[29] In the *Essays,* Bacon constantly deploys the inflections of assessment and scorn: "It is a trivial grammar-school text, but yet worthy a wise man's consideration" ("Of Boldness," 74); "The speech of Themistocles the Athenian, which was haughty and arrogant in taking so much to himself, had been a grave and wise observation and censure, applied at large to others" ("Of the True Greatness of Kingdoms and Estates," 120); "It was a high speech of Seneca (after the manner of the Stoics). . . . It is yet a higher speech of his than the other (much too high for a heathen)" ("Of Adversity," 56–57); "But this last were fitter for a satire than for a serious observation" ("Of Boldness," 75); "Many have made witty invectives against Usury. They say that it is a pity the devil should have God's part, which is the tithe" ("Of Usury," 151). In a tone that shifts rapidly from sardonic to serious to dismissive to thoughtful, Bacon invites his reader to join a sophisticated vanguard. The imitation of classical rhetoric has taken a final step toward a "language with a smack of the city in its words, accent and idiom, [that] further suggests a certain tincture of learning derived from associating with well-educated men" (Quintilian, *Inst.* 6.3.17). After a good dose of sixteenth-century prose, an encounter with Bacon's

27. Jonson, *Discoveries,* 8:586.
28. Ibid., 8:583.
29. "Then did Erasmus take occasion to make the scoffing echo; *Decem annos consumpsi in legendo Cicerone,* and the echo answered in Greek, *one, Asine*" (Bacon, *Advancement,* in *Works,* 3:284).

produces a rush of confidence in a mind that can sift the implications of a question without once losing control of the main event, like a commander surveying a future battle site. Such intelligence has the right to dismiss cant with a peremptory gesture of contempt, as if it were the gabble of so many superannuated officers.

To writers who wish to justify themselves as the guardians of a secular morality, the new pointed style is especially advantageous. Its difficult language, density of argument, careful logic, and irony sharpen the distinction in early humanism between the mature and immature. Wyatt's reinterpretation of the Petrarchan lover's adoration, Ascham's and Jonson's attacks on romance,[30] and Bacon's surmise that posterity will judge him not as a man who did great things but as one who "simply made less account of things that were accounted great"[31] legitimize those who are willing to endure the strain of fewer appeals to revelation. But the new seventeenth-century proser intensifies the distinction by announcing not only his maturity but his modernity. Pointedly sententious courtiers have put away the "rudeness" (Hoskins's word) of the past.[32] Harvey upbraids Nashe's refusal to square his periods as a dereliction of duty to the classical world; but Nashe ridicules Harvey's Chaucerian diction because it is pompously old-fashioned. Jonson too scorns old-fashioned tastes: in the induction to *Bartholomew Fair* he says a "virtuous and staid ignorance" is one that "hath stood still these five and twenty or thirty years" and that still admires *The Spanish Tragedy* and *Titus Andronicus*.[33] In rehearsing the history of Ciceronianism, Bacon implies that Carr of Cambridge and Ascham exulted in their new-found maturity when they helped "the learning of the schoolmen to be utterly despised as barbarous"; but Bacon then advertises his even more advanced maturity when he accuses Carr and Ascham of unwarranted self-satisfaction in "allur[ing] all young men that were studious unto that delicate and polished kind of learning" (*Advancement*, 284). In the Latin translation of *The Advancement of Learning*,

30. For the humanist rejection of romance, see Robert P. Adams, *The Better Part of Valor; More, Erasmus, Colet, and Vives, on Humanism, War, and Peace, 1496–1535* (Seattle: University of Washington Press, 1962).

31. Bacon, *The New Organon*, book 1, Aphorism XCVII, in *Works*, 4:94.

32. "It is true that we study according to the predominancy of courtly inclinations: whilst mathematics were in request, all our similitudes came from lines, circles, and angles; whilst moral philosophy is now a while spoken of, it is rudeness not to be sententious" (Hoskins, *Directions*, 39).

33. Ben Jonson, *Bartholomew Fair*, in *Drama of the English Renaissance*, ed. Russell A. Fraser and Norman Rabkin, 2 vols. (New York: Macmillan, 1976), 2:195.

Bacon dismisses even Senecanism as a fashion: "this kind of expression hath found such acceptance with meaner capacit[i]es, as to be a dignity and ornament to Learning; neverthelesse, by the more exact judgements, it hath bin deservedly dispised, and may be set down *as a distemper of Learning*, seeing it is nothing else but a hunting after words, and fine placing of them." For Bacon, sound judgments are "exact," and exactitude depends upon a modern rhetoric of the prosaic—precise, subtle, difficult.

The Social Deployment of the Pointed Style in Satire, Character, and Epistle

Although Croll acknowledged that the new aculeate style was an intellectual tool in the sciences, he focused his attention almost exclusively on its advantages for the man of letters musing about life's ambiguities in essays and letters. Had Croll's view been less influenced by Romanticism, he might have turned his attention to other kinds of literary experience besides musing and to other literary forms besides essays. Indeed, along with reflection in the curt style or the libertine style, the new prose brings to the fore a keen social competitiveness. Writers of the end of the sixteenth and beginning of the seventeenth century fairly writhe with frustrated ambition. John Marston's address to the reader in a prefatory poem to *The Scourge of Villanie* (1599) is pugnaciously entitled "To those that seeme judiciall perusers."[34] In the prefatory matter to *Achilles Shield* of 1598, Chapman defends his dedicatory epistle and his coinages with a nervous bravado.[35] When Jonson announces in the preface to *The Alchemist* that it would be futile to ask an audience to vote on the value of his work and that of other playwrights, we know that he would like to name names, as he was more than willing to do with Drummond.[36] The witty seeker of patronage competes with the same "perusers" whose approval he seeks in order to gain distinction. Marston, Jonson, Chapman, Hoskins, and Bacon enjoy their freedom from the

34. John Marston, *The Scourge of Villanie*, in *The Poems of John Marston*, ed. Arnold Davenport (Liverpool: Liverpool University Press, 1961), 100 and 101.
35. "To the Understander," *Achilles Shield*, in *Elizabethan Critical Essays*, ed. G. Gregory Smith, 2:306.
36. *The Alchemist*, in *Drama of the English Renaissance*, ed. Fraser and Rabkin, 2:144.

didacticism of an earlier generation. At the same time, however, they are vexed by the very self-consciousness that gives them this freedom in the first place.

Self-consciousness and aggression are deployed socially in the minor, prosaic genres that allow the new wit to trounce the aristocrat. Nashe, who felt keenly the difficulties of getting a place, could not revenge himself on would-be patrons because he had only an anecdotal prose of terrors and monsters and manic ridicule to fall back on. For the new concise proser, however, the secular genres of the Theophrastan character, satire, and verse epistle create a stage (a secular city and marketplace) for a social duel.[37] We are accustomed to thinking of the literary glories of the seventeenth century as the lyric, drama, epic, and finally the novel—the major genres. But before the novel is born, its discourse of intellectual detachment, social know-ingness, and individual ambition is worked out in the smaller prose forms.

In the prosaic genres, the city is a liberal education. John Earle regards Paul's Walk as a thrilling marketplace:

> It is more than this, the whole world's map, which you may here discern in its perfectest motion, justling and turning. It is a heap of stones and men, with a vast confusion of languages; and were the steeple not sanctified, nothing liker *Bable*.
>
> The noise in it is like that of bees, a strange humming or buzz mix'd with walking tongues and feet. . . . and no business whatsoever but is here stirring and a-foot. (131)

In "St. Paul's Church," Donald Lupton similarly exults in the mixing of social classes at the cathedral:

> The middle aisle is much frequented at noon with a company of Hungarians, not walking so much for recreation, as need;

---

37. The Theophrastan character became extremely popular in England after the publication of Casaubon's edition of Theophrastus in 1592 and again in 1599. This volume was followed by Joseph Hall's *Characters of Vertues and Vices* (1608), which was reprinted more than ten times, *The Overburian Characters* (1614, 1615, 1622), John Stephens's *Satyrical Essayes Characters and Others. Or accurate and quick Descriptions, fitted to the Life of their Subjects* (1615), John Earle's *Microcosmography* (1628). Other character books followed, by Francis Lenton (1629), Richard Brathwaite (1631), and Wye Salstonstall (1631) (Benjamin Boyce, *The Theophrastan Character in England to 1642* [1947; repr. London: Frank Cass, 1967], 122–51, 220–86).

and if any of these meet with a yonker, that hath his pockets well lined with silver, they will relate to him the meaning of Tycho Brashe [sic], or the north star: and never leave flattering him in his own words and stick as close to him, as a burr upon a traveller's cloak; and never leave him till he and they have saluted the Green Dragon, or the Swan behind the Shambles, where I leave them.[38]

For Earle, London will bring a man to a proper (that is, modern and urban) degree of sophistication. When he says of "A down right Scholar" that he "names this word Colledge too often, and his discourse beats too much on the University" and "[h]e cannot speak to a dog in his own dialect, and understands Greek better than the language of a Falconer" (71–72), he implies that a good dunking in London would save this student from parochialism: "But practise him a little in men, and brush him over with good company, and he shall outballance those glisterers, as far as a solid substance do's a feather, or gold gold-lace" (72). The city itself is a schoolroom for the world's polish.

It is especially "practise . . . in men" that the city gives the educated greenhorn. From the practice eventually will come victory. In the free market of London, the wit has an advantage that he loses in the claustrophobic atmosphere of court. Brandishing the secular equipment of worldly experience and language whetted with abstractions and irony, he sallies forth to meet his rivals.[39] In Donne's "Satire 2," which is a Theophrastan character in verse, Coscus's "insolence" is defeated by Donne's own contempt for one whom only "Time . . . Hath made a Lawyer" and who has all the complacency of "new benefic'd ministers" (lines 41–45). Donne's "Satire 4" is a similar contest between a linguistic swordsman and a linguistic mountebank, whose "tongue" is nothing but courtly "compliment" (line 44).

The obvious intellectual superiority of the linguistic swordsmen gives them the right to set standards. They deploy in the social arena the intellectual contempt of Bacon:

A FINE GENTLEMAN is the cinnamon tree, whose bark is more worth than his body. He hath read the book of good

38. Donald Lupton, *London and the Country Carbonadoed into Several Characters*, in *A Book of "Characters,"* trans. and ed. Richard Aldington (London: George Routledge and Sons, 1924), 357.
39. Boyce, *The Theophrastan Character in England*, 141, 236.

manners, and by this time each of his limbs may read it. He
alloweth of no judge but the eye; painting, bolstering, and
bombasting are his orators; by these also he proves his
industry: for he hath purchased legs, hair, beauty, and
straightness, more than nature left him. He unlocks maiden-
heads with his language, and speaks Euphues, not so grace-
fully as heartily. His discourse makes not his behavior, but he
buys it at court, as countrymen their clothes in Birchin Lane.[40]

"Behavior" should be governed by an independently fashioned
"discourse," not by the stock types at court.

In the character, the man of wit erects the "true" hierarchy of
modern intelligence over gentlemen mannequins and modern taste
over passé enthusiasms: only the "vulgar man" thinks "all *Spaniards*
and *Jesuits* very villains, and is still cursing the Pope and
Spinola . . . cries, *Chaucer* for his money above all our *English*
poets . . . is foremost still to kiss the king's hand, and cries God
bless his majesty loudest" (Earle, "A vulgar-spirited Man," 125). For
the character writer, those with a "stately kind of behaviour" foolishly
imagine they can escape. But insofar as "[t]hey are men whose
preferment does us a great deal of wrong," then "when they are
down, we may laugh at them without a breach of good nature" (Earle,
"An Insolent Man," 44–45).

The epistle is another arena for social competition, but here the
victory is won by withdrawal. Jonson's line "Rare poemes aske rare
friends" ("To Lucy, Countesse of Bedford, with Mr. Donnes
Satyres"[41]) tells a rich story: the proser's demonstration of his rarity
requires a circle in which he can have that rarity corroborated without
the effort required in public. He imagines a subtle audience, and
then, because that audience admires him, he can rest assured of his
superiority. The new Senecanism generally reinforces a rhetoric of
fine moderation and Stoic independence from worldly power, but the
rhetoric of sincerity in the epistle intensifies the distinctions between
urban and provincial, public and private. The formal letter, says
Hoskins, requires rhetorical cajoling; but the familiar letter can be
more forthright and direct.[42] It can omit the prefatory compliments of

---

40. *The Overburian Characters (1616),* in *Seventeenth-Century Prose and Poetry,* ed.
Alexander M. Witherspoon and Frank J. Warnke, 2d ed. (New York: Harcourt, Brace
Jovanovich, 1957), 199.

41. Jonson, *Discoveries,* 8:60.

42. For the old-fashioned Ciceronian epistle, based on the classical oration, see Angel

the ordinary office seeker and can neglect scrupulous organization.[43] Its sincerity, Lipsius implies, is written into the speaker's occasional lapses into thinking out loud: "[N]ec ad Epistolam scribendam veniatur nisi argumento concepto, et mente (ut ita dicam) tumente" (Nor should one set about writing a letter unless the argument is already conceived and one's mind is, as it were, boiling).[44] Although Lipsius agrees that the familiar letter should be clear, he gives great latitude to implication and to what Hoskins calls "diligent negligence" (7). As a result, the rhetoric of the Senecan familiar letter's dense and witty style looks in two directions: while explicitly speaking to the understandings shared by the writer and his friend, it is implicitly aware of the large, faceless crowd of those deliberately excluded from this conversation.[45] Montaigne's stated purpose—to bare himself to the reader—is, according to the rhetorical tradition since Demetrius, the province of the letter, in which a man speaks his soul to an absent friend. Montaigne says he would have preferred to write his essays in the form of letters.[46]

In an epistolary friendship, fortunately, one does not have to abandon the thrill of the marketplace. One brings it to the Stoic garden in a sparkling articulateness, which lightly snaps and sneers in the midst of its musings. The composure of the sixteenth-century singing aristocrat, so light in his *sprezzatura*, is reappropriated and reauthorized by the independence of Stoic "honesty." With their lively, idiosyncratic styles, Montaigne and Browne embrace the

---

Day, *The English Secretary, or Methode of Writing of Epistles and Letters (1599)*, facsim. reprod. by Robert O. Evans (Gainesville, Fla.: Scholars' Facsimiles and Reprints, 1967). On Lipsian epistolary style, see E. Catherine Dunn, "Lipsius and the Art of Letter-Writing," *Studies in the Renaissance* 3 (1956): 145–56.

43. Lipsius, *Institutio Epistolica*, in *Opera Omnia*, 2 vols. (Vesaliae: 1675), 2:1073; Hoskins, *Directions*, 6.

44. Lipsius, 2:1073. See also Hoskins, *Directions*, 6–7. See Dunn for a useful analysis of Lipsius's treatment of conversation as the basis of the style of the familiar letter.

45. Allusions, wit, and simplified syntax, whether curt or libertine, are generally anti-Ciceronian and belong to the essay style as well as to the epistolary. Still, the anti-Ciceronian essay itself derives from Seneca's epistles, as Bacon notes in arguing that the distinction between the two genres is not firm. See his dedication to Prince Henry, intended for, though omitted from the 1612 edition of the *Essays*, in *The Prose of the English Renaissance*, ed. J. William Hebel and Hoyt H. Hudson et al. (New York: Appleton, 1952), 615–16.

46. See Montaigne, "To the Reader," *The Complete Essays of Montaigne*, trans. Donald M. Frame (Stanford: Stanford University Press, 1948), 2, and Demetrius, *On Style: The Greek Text of Demetrius "De Elocutione" Edited after the Paris Manuscript*, trans. W. Rhys Roberts (Cambridge: Cambridge University Press, 1902), 175.

reader in a private confidence and then claim that this private confidence is more interesting, more sophisticated, more alive than the florid rhetoric demanded by a hierarchical society. Letter-writing, says Montaigne, brings out the best in him: it leaves him "more attentive and confident" ("A Consideration Upon Cicero," 185–86). In writing letters, he has a friend "to lead me on, sustain me and raise me up." The verse epistle allows seekers of office to talk to each other about their frustrations—as Donne says to Sir Henry Wotton, *"At Court*; though *From Court*, were the better stile" ("To Sir Henry Wotton," line 27). The quiet ironies of the epistle celebrate the subtle inflections of those who know what it is to be a civilizer in an uncivilized world.

Ceremony in a New Key

The sophistication of prosaic rationalism that legitimizes an aristocracy of the intelligent against an aristocracy of family line sets the old ceremonial songs to new melodies. Old ceremonialism came easily, we are inclined to say naively. Its childishness remained unmarked. The solicitude and dismay of Spenser's Cuddie and Piers and Colin Clout are part of their proper sense of dependence on a transcendent order. Now, in the seventeenth century, that dependence has to be defended against a more mature understanding. Seventeenth-century poets are emotional, but not "rudely" passionate. Singing many of the old themes, they protect themselves from condescension with ironies that ricochet against a strict meter. Thus, in the generic containments of the newly "prosed" world, ceremonial gestures flourish in miniature. If Herbert and Herrick often strike a posture that seems markedly childish to us, it is precisely because their childishness *is* marked—by their experiments with stanzas, length of verse line, and conversational idiom as well as by their acknowledgment that the religious calling provides no easy road for a man who has enjoyed the "great exchange of discourse" in London.[47] In Herbert's "The Collar," the speaker's initial desires for independence stand justified as "mature" almost to the end. Only the

47. Cf. Leah Sinanoglou Marcus, *Childhood and Cultural Despair: A Theme and Variations in Seventeenth-Century Literature* (Pittsburgh: University of Pittsburgh Press, 1978).

final two lines ("Me thought I heard one calling, *Child:* / And I reply'd, *My Lord*"[48]) indict the expostulations as a false notion of adulthood.

Similarly, ceremony's agricultural laborers were unmarked. Spenser's months in "Two Cantos of Mutabilitie," carrying a spade, a scythe, and a seed bag, are Nature's mythic representatives. But in Herrick, agricultural labor is specifically nonurban, "country festivity." It belongs in a rural setting, which, measured against an urban capital ("dull Devonshire"), becomes "quaint" and "refreshing" and "recreative." Even in *Paradise Lost*, where Milton sternly justifies hierarchical ceremonialism among his heavenly dwellers, Eve's reverential sonnet-evensong in book 4 and Adam's epithalamion in book 8 have a nostalgic cast for a family of creation that no longer exists. It is not just knowledge that destroys Paradise but a knowledge filled with the knowingness of secularized language.

Friendship too is marked. The song of the Sidneian courtier, both affable and plangent, is now fractured by irony, and the emphasis in friendship falls as much onto a collaboration against unsophistication as knightly comradeship.[49] "Honest" friends mutually understand that political factionalism is an unwise idea. Herrick's wishes that a "golden Age wo'd come again, / And *Charles* here rule, as he before did Raign; / If smooth and unperplext the Seasons were, / As when the *"Sweet Maria* lived here." But the political gesture is diffused with ironic self-depreciation: "And once more yet (ere I am laid out dead)," he could, even though he is not Horace, *"Knock at a Starre with my exalted Head."*[50] In "Upon Appleton House," Marvell, the Puritan with cavalier tastes, invokes an ideal reader who agrees that "'Tis not, what once it was, the *World;* / But a rude heap together hurl'd." The only "decent Order" lies in the enclosed world of Fairfax's estate.[51]

Most important, the new pointed rationalism creates "the religious experience." With so many religious assumptions in the poetry of the sixteenth century, this sounds like a strange claim. But the creation of secular manners and attitudes reinflects religion as an experience of a

48. *The English Poems of George Herbert*, ed. C. A. Patrides (London: J. M. Dent, 1974), 162.

49. On Horatian friendship in cavalier poetry, see Earl Miner, *The Cavalier Mode from Jonson to Cotton* (Princeton: Princeton University Press, 1971).

50. Robert Herrick, "The bad season makes the Poet sad," in *The Poems of Robert Herrick*, ed. L. C. Martin (London: Oxford University Press, 1965), 214.

51. Andrew Marvell, "Upon Appleton House, to my Lord Fairfax," in *The Poems and Letters of Andrew Marvell*, ed. H. M. Margoliouth, rev. Pierre Legouis and E. E. Duncan-Jones, 2 vols. (Oxford: Clarendon Press, 1971), 1:86.

special kind. The effect of both Catholic and Puritan manuals of meditation is to differentiate the "meditation" as a personal and private genre.[52] Whatever the differences between the Catholic deliberate meditation and the Protestant occasional meditation, they share a lyricism that is always undoing the norms of rational articulateness. Joseph Hall calls the meditation a "whispering self-conference"; the title of one of Hall's books of meditations is *Susurrium cum Deo. Soliloquies; or, Holy Self-Conferences of the Devout Soul.*[53] Richard Baker calls the meditation a "sighing": "Heare then, O Thou which hearest where no sound is, the sound of our soules sighing."[54] The lyricism of the meditation is now more intense for being measured against both the chatty amiability and procedural straitjacketing of secular discourse. Like the epistle, the meditation is the generic arena of "true and devout feeling." "Devout" does not make much sense when applied to Spenser; it does when applied to Traherne, Crashaw, and Vaughan.

The new rationalism also creates "the baroque," a discourse in which ceremonial features now stand in significant relationship to public genres and discourses that existed weakly if at all in the Middle Ages and sixteenth century.[55] Baroque's ardors are put forward in a context in which artist and audience share the understanding that art is constituted by the generic differentiations that make it discussable. That is, the baroque belongs to an age when secular "feeling" has come into existence. When poetry's passion does not have the protection of wit, the protection instead derives from the assumed generic differentiations of discursiveness, which shields poetry's "indecorum" and heightens its emotional "effects." With a refined language of emotion, the private life too comes into existence, a realm

---

52. On Catholic meditation, see Louis L. Martz, *The Poetry of Meditation: A Study in English Religious Literature of the Seventeenth Century*, rev. ed. (New Haven: Yale University Press, 1962), 25–70. On Protestant meditation, see Barbara K. Lewalski, *Donne's Anniversaries and the Poetry of Praise: The Creation of a Symbolic Mode* (Princeton: Princeton University Press, 1973), 73–107.

53. Harold Fisch, "Bishop Hall's Meditations," *Review of English Studies* 25 (1949): 210–21.

54. *Meditations and Disquisitions upon the Lord's Prayer* (London: Anne Griffin, 1636), 4.

55. Baroque seeks to turn "away from the world of appearances to seek for truth within the inner life"; it is "obsessed with the absoluteness of [its] subject"; it is "phantasmagoric"; it is often playful; it unites the finite and infinite; it expresses the "gaping impossibility" of the desire to meet God on his own terms; it has a passive hero; and it is concerned with the mysteries of love and of God (Frank J. Warnke, *Versions of Baroque: European Literature in the Seventeenth Century* [New Haven: Yale University Press, 1972], 22, 31, 54–55, 90–129, 131, 187–204, and passim).

where all the gestures and symbols of ceremonialism are available for the creation of personal lives and personal philosophies.

Meditational inwardness is the ground of these true personal philosophies. It is a sign of a profound change in the beginning of the seventeenth century that in *Basilikon Doron*, James feels called upon to defend his religious "sinceritie" against detractors, a defense Elizabeth would never have made.[56] Perhaps seventeenth-century religious poetry has been attractive to modern readers because it confronts the argument that moderns want to hear: that religious belief, to be strong and mature, must meet the claims of secularity. Greville's "I know the world and believe in God"[57] (or pastoralism or simplicity or childish obedience) marks traditional belief as a personal choice made in the face of sophisticated skepticism. Similarly, in "The Pearl," Herbert "know[s] the wayes" of the secular wit's life in London—learning, the press, the court, ambition, personal glory, flirtations—and he is confident he could have them if he wanted ("All these stand open, or I have the keyes"). The refrain's return to obedience ("Yet I love thee") stands as a purely personal choice. The "right" to such a personal philosophy is "argued" by the acknowledgment of the rational claims of a secular world, which cannot be exorcised out of existence and in which, besides, others with their own personal philosophies seem to flourish quite happily. One can have all the emotions and religion one likes, as long as they are confessed to be part of a private realm.

Character, Epistle, and Meditation in the *Religio Medici*

At this point, I would like to turn to a text that, for an earlier generation, was the testing ground for the vigorous critic. Seventeenth-century poetry was the *pater* of modern lyric toughness, but Browne's *Religio Medici*, whose prose has all the surface features of a tough style, was unacceptable. When we judge the *Religio*, as critics have been remarkably eager to do, we are measuring not this

56. James I, *Basilikon Doron*, in *The Political Works of James I (1616)*, ed. Charles Howard McIlwain (1918; repr. New York: Russell and Russell, 1965), 7.

57. Letter to John Coke, quoted in Ronald A. Rebholz, *The Life of Fulke Greville, First Lord Brooke* (Oxford: Clarendon Press, 1971), 232.

particular work but a sensitive paradox in liberalism: the best arguments are justified by reason and reason demonstrates the necessity for separating civil order from private belief, but belief confined to the private space is justified by sincerity, however mistaken its tenets.

Browne's *Religio* is one of the various seventeenth-century reclamations of a ceremonial discourse in the private realm. In his diary, Samuel Pepys recounts a visit to a coffeehouse in January 1664, during which he heard the remarks of Sir William Petty, "one of the most rational men that ever I heard speak with a tongue, having all his notions the most distinct and clear." According to Petty, the *Religio*, along with Osborne's *Advice to a Son* and Butler's *Hudibras*, was one of three books most "cried up for wit in the world."[58] With the ostentatious maturity of the new pointed style, Petty informs his listeners that this popular admiration is shallow, for the wit of these three works lies merely in "pretty sayings, which are generally like paradoxes, by some argument smartly and pleasantly urged—which takes with people who do not trouble themselfs to examine the force of an argument which pleases them in the delivery, upon a subject which they like." Philosophically unsophisticated people admire the works of Browne, Osborne, and Butler, but Petty knows that in "downright disputation" their smart and pleasant arguments "would not bear weight." Nevertheless, his remarks corroborate the popularity that the *Religio*'s eight English editions in Browne's lifetime suggest. Apparently, this was a work of amateurish philosophy that many readers "cried up." The popularity may have had something to do with Browne's renegotiating a place for a medieval ceremonial mode's communal story within a new secular discourse.

At the beginning of the *Religio*, Browne announces the work not as a meditation but as a mixture of secular genres: essay, character, and epistle. An epistolary intention is implied in the protestation that he intended the work as a private memorial to himself that he then communicated to a friend. Indeed, the opening, with its abrupt entrance into a discussion of Browne's own religion and its generally ruminative air, strikes the note of the epistle's ease in conversation with another man of the world:

> For my Religion, though there be severall circumstances that
> might perswade the world I have none at all, as the generall
> scandall of my profession, the naturall course of my studies,

58. *The Diary of Samuel Pepys*, ed. Robert Latham and William Matthews, 11 vols. (Berkeley and Los Angeles: University of California Press, 1971), 27 January 1664, 5:27.

the indifferency of my behaviour, and discourse in matters of Religion, neither violently defending one, nor with that common ardour and contention opposing another; yet in despight hereof I dare, without usurpation, assume the honorable stile of a Christian.[59]

The intimacy, the delicate points of stress, and the dispelling of mere "common" ardor build the walls of privacy among friends who understand the world according to the new prose. They know that faith and reason "have a due time and place, according to the restraint and limit of circumstance" (1.19); they rely on this basic generic differentiation to explore the subtleties of various questions; and they prefer not to have everything spelled out with earnest didacticism.

The opening bears the banner of a Theophrastan character as well. The "religion of a doctor" is as susceptible to caricature as the activities of a university student, of a flatterer, or of a shopkeeper.[60] The character's typical "he believes," "he holds," "he says" become, merely by a change in pronoun, Browne's "I believe," "I hold," "I say."[61] Like the speaker in the character, Browne claims authority

59. *Religio Medici*, 1.1, in *The Prose of Sir Thomas Browne*, ed. Norman Endicott (New York: New York University Press, 1968), 7. All further references to the *Religio* will be to this edition.

60. Denonain has pointed out that Browne struck "Religio Medici" from the title page of the pirated 1642 edition and has argued from this evidence that the title may have been the work of a transcriber, not of Browne (Jean Jacques Denonain, ed., intro. to *Religio Medici: A New Edition with Biographical and Critical Introduction* [Cambridge: Cambridge University Press, 1955], xi). Browne did allow the title to remain on the first page of text, however. A more plausible interpretation of these facts is that the title made no sense in the middle of Marshall's woodcut showing a hand reaching out of the heavens to rescue a man falling off a cliff into the sea; indeed, that it made sense only when placed in obvious conjunction with the ironically extravagant disclaimers of the opening lines. On the other hand, if the title was indeed the work of a transcriber, his giving the work a title that sounded so much like a character is an indication of the way contemporary readers fitted the work into available literary categories.

On Browne's style, see Austin Warren, "The Style of Sir Thomas Browne," *Kenyon Review* 13 (1951): 674–87; Frank Livingstone Huntley, *Sir Thomas Browne: A Biographical and Critical Study* (Ann Arbor: University of Michigan Press, 1962), 117–34; Morris Croll, "The Baroque Style in Prose," in *Style, Rhetoric, and Rhythm*, ed. J. May Patrick et al. 207–33. On the *Religio* as personal essay, see Norman Endicott, "Some Aspects of Self-Revelation and Self-Portraiture in *Religio Medici*," in *Essays in English Literature from the Renaissance to the Victorian Age Presented to A. S. P. Woodhouse*, ed. Millar MacLure and F. W. Watt (Toronto: University of Toronto Press, 1964), 85–102; and Joan Webber, *The Eloquent "I": Style and Self in Seventeenth-Century Prose* (Madison: University of Wisconsin Press, 1968), 149–83.

61. This shift is not a violation of the character's outlines. Although the Theophrastan

from his cosmopolitanism. He knows six languages; he has traveled in several foreign countries and "beheld the nature of their climes, the Chorography of their Provinces, Topography of their Cities, [and] understood their severall Lawes, Customes and Policies" (2.8). He has the character-writer's enthusiasm for the details of the great busy world: the doctor in Italy who was not convinced of the immortality of the soul and the priest in France who was disturbed by three lines in Seneca (1.21), the rituals of the Catholics (1.3), the souls of Browne's own patients (2.6), and the "catalogue" of his friends he includes in his prayers (2.6). The enthusiasm carries over to science and theology: whether the snake slid along the ground only after the fall (1.10), the wisdom of insects in building communities (1.15), whether anything in nature can be ugly (1.16), whether the winds that hit the Spanish Armada in 1588 was Providence or good luck (1.17), the pigeon who was left on the ark without a mate (1.21), the properties of naphtha and of the fire in Purgatory (1.19, 50). Earle's great marketplace of discourse at St. Paul's is for Browne the treasure-house of the classics—Aristotle, Plato, Philo, Plutarch, Herodotus, Augustine, Paracelsus, Porphyry, Cicero, Pliny, Galen—a tradition that can be dismantled and reassembled by a self-confessed amateur.

The dependence of the *Religio* on the character focuses Browne's relationship with an urban world regulated by manners. Browne disapproves of behavior that does not show an awareness of the rules for social intercourse; even the pope is owed "the duty of good language" (1.5). Unlike others, he is not troubled by differences in religion: "I could never perceive any rationall consequence from those many texts which prohibite the children of Israel to pollute themselves with the Temple of the Heathens. . . . Holy water and [the] Crucifix (dangerous to the common people) deceive not my judgement, nor abuse my devotion at all" (1.3). Browne's rational judgment enforces restraint for the sake of social harmony. Formalities in religion are things indifferent. Regarding them with skeptical condescension, he seeks the central wisdom that will be the "leaven

---

character seems so resolutely impersonal in its ridicule of the types in the urban scene, it is nevertheless as fluid as many of the essayistic and satiric genres of the period and hence allows many quite "personal" elements. Richard Brathwaite's character entitled "The Authors Opinion of Marriage: Delivered in a Satisfying Character to His Friend," in *Essaies upon the Five Senses* (London: E. Griffin for R. Whittaker, 1620) suggests the Theophrastan character's exploration of an authorial self, an exploration usually ascribed exclusively to the essay.

and . . . ferment of all, not onely Civill, but Religious actions"
(1.26).

Browne justifies his personal religion on the grounds that it is
reasonable and private (1.5). For this purpose, the epistle's and
character's pointed definitions are extremely useful, for they enable
him to defend a cause "not . . . patron'd by a passion." Most
important, they enable him to "difference [him]self neerer" (1.5), to
establish his individuality. The articulateness of the new pointed
prose constructs this individuality; it is only by way of the rationalized descriptions of the public world that he can define his distinc-
tiveness. The "libertie of [his] reason" is measured against the
strictures of some of the "assertions and common tenents [sic] drawn
from Scripture" (1.22); he has a "common and authentick Philosophy" that he learned at school "whereby [he] discourse[s] and
satisfie[s] the reason of other men"; but he also has "another more
reserved and drawne from experience, whereby [he] content[s his]
owne" (2.8).[62] No one, Browne insists, can see him; his friends know
his inner self so little that they "behold [him] but in a cloud" (2.4). His
devotions are invisible (1.9). He has a "private method which others
observe not" (2.13). "Men that look upon my outside, perusing onely
my condition, and fortunes, do erre in my altitude" (2.11). The most
human beings can know of each other is their social selves: "No man
can justly censure or condemne another, because indeed no man
truely knowes another. . . . Further, no man can judge another,
because no man knowes himselfe; for we censure others but as they
disagree from that humour which wee fancy laudable in our selves,
and commend others but for that wherein they seeme to quadrate and
consent with us" (2.4).

Irony too is enlisted to protect Browne's "difference" as an individual. In the title's invitation to his reader to interpret his tone as the
character's aloof ease, Browne suggests that what follows may be
taken by some as a straightforward apology (an explanation of how a
doctor can be a Christian); the knowing, however, will take it as an
ironic hit at those who demand "apologies," who crudely think that
the religion of all doctors is atheism, and who regard the profession
of a doctor as a "generall scandall" (1.1). Irony is itself a "Synod" that

62. The angels in the "Scale of creatures" passage guarantee the individual his
identity, for they have "knowledge not onely of the specificall [of the species], but [of
the] numericall formes of individualls, and understand[ing] by what reserved difference each single *Hypostasis* (besides the relation to its species) becomes its numericall
selfe" (1.33).

can rid the world of nonsense, "those swarms and millions of *Rhapsodies*, begotten onely to distract and abuse the weaker judgements of Scholars, and to maintaine the Trade and Mystery of Typographers" (1.24). Irony also deflects the doctrinaire opinions of those with too keen a conscience: "The Councell of *Constance* condemnes *John Husse* for an Heretick, the Stories of his owne party stile him a Martyr: He must needs offend the Divinity of both, that sayes hee was neither the one nor the other" (1.26). Browne disdains popular tastes (the "multitude" is "one great beast," and social climbers have nothing but money [2.67]). His irony performs socially the function of philosophical skepticism, clearing out delusions in order to find the core belief of mannerly Christians. Browne shares with other prosers the exultation in the power of speech to define the world, to individualize the speaker, and to free him from ceremony's old dissolution of the individual into a communal body.

The basic impulse of the *Religio Medici*, however, is not a display of civil wit but rather meditative reflection. It is the meditation that generates the familiar outlines of the anxious journey that ends in absorption in a higher truth. Browne would gladly give up his individuality to be part of the oldest and greatest story: "[A]nd thus was I dead before I was alive; though my grave be *England*, my dying place was Paradise, and Eve miscarried of mee before she conceiv'd of *Cain*" (1.59). He likes music because "it unties the ligaments of my frame, takes me to pieces, dilates me out of my self, and by degrees, me thinkes, resolves me into Heaven" (2.9). He imagines how after death the "consumable" parts of human bodies shall be "refined" and "lye immortall in the arms of fire" (1.50). Heaven is the soul's happiness and the termination of longing: "Briefely therefore, where the soule hath the full measure and complement of happinesse, where the boundlesse appetite of that spirit remaines compleately satisfied, that it can neither desire addition nor alteration; that I thinke is truely Heaven: and this can onely be in the enjoyment of that essence, whose infinite goodnesse is able to terminate the desires of it selfe, and the insatiable wishes of ours" (1.49). Having jettisoned the old ceremonial narratives, the new proser maintains some of their heat in diction and rhythm. But it makes a difference that he is presenting his feelings discursively instead of narrating a story.

Like the meditation, the *Religio* performs a ceremonial initiation: the removal of fear in order that the soul's hymn of praise may be free of earthly trouble.[63] Exaltation to the level of perfect faith is often signaled by a striking image, phrase, or paradox. Passages added to the edition of 1643 show Browne trying to give a final flourish to his paragraphs as a way of bringing them to closure. Two of his most famous paradoxes are added endings: "*Omneity* informed *Nullity* into an essence" (1.35) and "though my grave be *England*, my dying place was Paradise, and *Eve* miscarried of mee before she conceiv'd of *Cain*" (1.59). Apparently following Protestant manuals of meditation, which concentrated on the psalms for meditational inspiration,[64] Browne marks the end of a section with Hebraic synonymy: "This onely [the Bible] is a Worke too hard for the teeth of time, and cannot perish but in the generall flames, when all things shall confesse their ashes" (1.23); "for in his yeares there is no Climacter; his duration is eternity, and farre more venerable then antiquitie" (1.28). True to the meditative structure of "given this problem in the human condition, then this is the Christian answer," whole sections will swing from the secular world to the religious on a "therefore" or a "thus" (see 1.36, 43, 44, 47, 53). Toward the end of one section, Browne moves into the repetitions, parallel synonymies, and cursus of the meditation, one thought tacked onto another in radically paratactic fashion, as the voice dissolves into ceremonial chanting: "[F]or that indeed which I admire is farre before antiquity, that is, Eternity, and that is God himselfe; who though hee be stiled the Antient of dayes, cannot receive the adjunct of antiquity, who was before the world, and shall be after it, yet is not older then it" (1.28).[65] Speech gives way to communal ritual, and the Latinisms that in an epistolary style function as precise definitions or as the labels for procedures become a ceremonial mode's stylized argument, a defense from worldly mutability: "*Omneity* informed *Nullity* into an essence" and "for in his yeares there is no Climacter; his duration is eternity, and farre more venerable then antiquitie" (1.35 and 53).

63. Helen C. White, *English Devotional Literature (Prose) 1600–1640*, University of Wisconsin Studies in Language and Literature, no. 29 (Madison: University of Wisconsin Press, 1931), 153–54.

64. Frank Livingstone Huntley, ed., intro. to *Bishop Joseph Hall and Protestant Meditation in Seventeenth-Century England: A Study with the texts of The Art of Divine Meditation (1606) and Occasional Meditations (1633)* (Binghamton, N.Y.: Center for Medieval & Early Renaissance Studies, 1981), 10.

65. Those who discuss Browne's use of the cursus usually concentrate on *Urn Burial*, infrequently on the *Religio Medici*; but see Michael F. Maloney, "Metre and *Cursus* in Sir Thomas Browne's Prose," *Journal of English and Germanic Philology* 58 (1959): 60–67. For the influence of the Old Testament, see William Whallon, "Hebraic Synonymy in Sir Thomas Browne," *ELH* 28 (1961): 335–52.

But the most important aspect of the meditational journey in this work is the shift from articulate proser's mastery of the world to incomprehension before a higher power.[66] In this shift, Browne pushes prosaic discursiveness toward prayer: "There is therfore some other hand that twines the thread of life than that of nature; wee are not onely ignorant in Antipathies and occult qualities, our ends are as obscure as our beginnings; the line of our dayes is drawne by night, and the various effects therein by a pencill that is invisible; wherein though wee confesse our ignorance, I am sure wee doe not erre, if wee say, it is the hand of God" (1.43). The movement of the individual sections, moreover, is the pattern for the *Religio* as a whole. Epistolary urbanity is strongest at the beginning, serene passivity strongest at the end. The sense of backing away from the immediacy of a public audience and viewing life *sub specie aeternitatis* is especially pronounced in the concluding sections of part 2. Section 8 ends with a rejection of human knowledge: "There is yet another conceit that hath sometimes made me shut my bookes; which tels mee it is a vanity to waste our dayes in the blind pursuit of knowledge; it is but attending a little longer, and wee shall enjoy that by instinct and infusion which we endeavour at here by labour and inquisition" (2.8). Sections 9, 10, 11, and 12 all look to the next life. In section 11, Browne adopts a divine language: "For then [at the hour of death] the soule begins to bee freed from the ligaments of the body, begins to reason like her selfe, and to discourse in a straine above mortality" (2.11). In sections 13 and 14, the speaker confesses the futility of trying to perfect life: section 13 ends with the reminder that Christ said the poor would always be with us, section 14 with the observation that there is nothing reliable in the affections of men. The last section begins, "I conclude therefore," as if the whole section itself were a conclusion to a meditation. The prayer to God at the end, the first time the divine is addressed in the second person, brings the feeling fully into the isolated, relational self of a ceremonial discourse: "These are O Lord the humble desires of my most reasonable ambition and all I dare call happinesse on earth: wherein I set no rule or limit to thy hand or providence. Dispose of me according to the wisedome of thy pleasure. Thy will bee done, though in my owne undoing." The hope for a civil, religious polity is to take a ceremonially long view. Heresies come and go like the river

66. The rise from the created world of the many to the spiritual world of the One, which is characteristic of the movement of Browne's sentences (Huntley, *Sir Thomas Browne*, 122), is fundamental to the entire work.

Arethusa. It is the spirit of wisdom in a struggling humanity that maintains charity in the commonwealth (1.6, 24, 32).

Ceremonial Devotion in a Civil Mode

As others have pointed out, in the effort to distinguish between public formalities and private belief, Browne shares the impulses of the Anglican latitudinarians, for whom the solution of the sectarianism of the seventeenth century was to reduce the articles of Christian belief to a few basic principles.[67] These were the two commandments of Christ: to love God and to love one's neighbor. From the Anglican point of view, the Puritans insisted all too ferociously on the first; from the Puritan point of view, the Anglicans insisted all too genially on the second.

"Public" and "private" are the poles of the latitudinarian argument, which pits rational (and difficult) struggle against blind (and easy) obedience and uses rational clarity (that all must, in good logic, assent to) to protect religious conviction (that is legitimate, even when irrational). For Lucius Cary, Viscount Falkland, religious conviction is based on the individual, private reason; if it is enforced by a superior authority claiming infallibility (the pope), then it is no longer belief. Still, even if the conviction is not rational, the effort of spiritual questioning is pious and therefore good.[68] William Chillingworth follows Falkland's emphasis on individual experience. As long as the soul is growing spiritually, God approves even the mistakes of reason. Indeed, sincerity may be superior to rational justifications: "Some experience makes mee fear, that the faith of considering and discoursing men, is like to be crack't with too much straining."[69] Devotion should be easy and natural; it should not be tangled in self-justification.

67. Leonard Nathanson, *The Strategy of Truth: A Study of Sir Thomas Browne* (Chicago: University of Chicago Press), 111–41, and Raymond B. Waddington, "The Two Tables in *Religio Medici*," in *Approaches to Sir Thomas Browne: The Ann Arbor Tercentenary Lectures and Essays*, ed. C. A. Patrides (Columbia: University of Missouri Press, 1982), 81–99.

68. W. K. Jordan, *The Development of Religious Toleration in England From the Accession of James I to the Convention of the Long Parliament (1603–1640)* (Cambridge: Harvard University Press, 1936), 373–74.

69. William Chillingworth, *The Religion of Protestants: A Safe Way to Salvation* (London: Leonard Lichfield, 1638), 37.

Like Falkland, Chillingworth holds that the articles of the Protestant faith are as true as "very common Principles of Geometry and Metaphysicks." But it is not true that Christian belief demands "a knowledge of them, and an adherence to them, as certain as that of sense or science" (325). Here, open and reliable reason defining a core Christianity is pitted against a belief acquired by some more flexible process. For John Hales, this polarity reappears as truth and forgiveable error. Granted, God asks for "inward and private Devotion" as well as public praise, but the first is far more important than the second.[70] In fact, public devotion can be a mere formality. Hence, the historical accretions to the celebration of the Lord's Supper are not heresies but minor mistakes.[71] They do not carry enough truth value to warrant outrage: "[T]o load our publick Forms with the private Fancies upon which we differ, is the most soveraign way to perpetuate *Schism* unto the Worlds end" ("Of Schism and Schismaticks," 216). The ecstasies of inspiration should be left instead to the inward soul: the Holy Spirit "is confined to those happy Souls in whom it is, and cannot extend itself to the Church in publicke" ("The Sacrament of the Lord's Supper," 76). Jeremy Taylor draws out the corollaries of this argument by reducing the practical consequences of religious belief. The doctrine of purgatory is offensive to Protestants, but it cannot be a heresy because it is "not *practically* impious"; "it neither proceeds from the will, nor hath any immediate or direct influence upon choice and manners" (emphasis mine).[72] If public formalities cannot lead to heresy, then there is no point in the zealous persecution of those who do not observe them. "[I]neffective contemplation" should "be left to the judgment of God" (115). Men should not worry over heresies to the extent of disturbing "public charity, or the private confidence" (115).

The first consequence of this argument is to undermine religion as a social and political force. If the individual can and must exercise his individual reason in defining the heart of Christian belief, then the church's claim to correct doctrine can have little status except as rhetorical persuasion. The individual believer is free to choose among the tenets of official doctrine. The second consequence is the stratifi-

---

70. John Hales, "Of Schism and Schismaticks," in *Several Tracts, By the ever memorable Mr. John Hales* (London: printed for John Blyth, 1677), 227.

71. John Hales, "A Tract Concerning the Sacrament of the Lord's Supper," in *Several Tracts*, 47–49.

72. Jeremy Taylor, "A Discourse of the Liberty of Prophesying," in *The Whole Works of the Right Rev. Jeremy Taylor*, ed. Reginald Heber, 15 vols. (London: Ogle, Duncan; and Richard Priestley, 1822), 8:114.

cation of believers into those who worship with mature reason and those who believe with mere sincerity. Mature reason examines carefully the various outward forms by which sacraments are celebrated and decides for itself which are worthy of inward assent. Belief founded on insufficiently examined outward forms may be "sincere," but it is also by implication childish and can be regarded with condescension. Still, as a mistake, not a heresy, it is harmless.

Browne's allegiances to the latitudinarian argument are obvious. Despite his constant differencing of himself, he claims that his true stance is cheerful "indifferency" (1.1) to religious divisions. The four sections added to the edition of 1643 show he is quite conscious of the arguments over heresy and sectarianism. Section 1.8 argues that it is futile to try to rid the world of heresies. Section 1.28 mocks the superstitious belief in the power of relics and offers a piece of antiquity that all sects may acknowledge: God's eternity. Section 1.43 argues that because human life is fragile and we are ignorant of God's intentions for us certain men cannot presume that they alone know the truth. And Section 1.56 ridicules the condemnations and countercondemnations among the various sects of Christianity. All of these added sections support Browne's position that zeal is "the unhappy method of angry devotions." In the preface, in which "private" and "public" echo again and again, rationality justifies his retreat to a private dilation of the joys of faith. Browne laments the violations of the commercial world on truth: through the "tyranny" of the press, he has seen "his Majesty defamed, the honour of Parliament depraved, the writings of both depravedly, anticipatively, counterfeitly imprinted." The private citizen is vulnerable to these attacks and has no hope to reform them: "complaints may seeme ridiculous in private persons, and men of my condition may be as incapable of affronts, as hopelesse of their reparations." Puritan "misguided zeale" vigorously condemns as "superstition" the doctrines to which Browne is "naturally inclined" (1.3). Zeal transforms flexible agreements that protect personal individuality into laws demanding strict conformity. The "articles, constitutions, and customes" of Anglicanism are to be preferred to other religious organizations because they most approximate a liberal polity.

Browne's instructions on how the *Religio* should be interpreted are an attempt to teach his audience how to "read privacy." Browne's own manuscript found its way, "imperfectly and surreptitiously," to a printer and was made public without permission. In the preface, he disclaims any intention to persuade; the work is a "private exercise directed to my selfe." Readers should understand that it is "rather a memoriall unto me then an example or rule unto any other" with "sundry particularities and personall expressions" to be taken in a "soft and flexible sense, and not to be called unto the rigid test of reason." What boldness there might be in the epistolary immediacy and irony of the first sentence is erased by the deference to public opinion, a deference that continues throughout the *Religio*: "It is not, I confesse, an unlawfull Prayer" (1.42), "I hope I shall not offend Divinity" (1.35), "Now if you demand my opinion" (1.33), "That Miracles are ceased, I can neither prove, nor absolutely deny," "I could wish it were true," "[t]hough indeed, to speake properly" (1.27), "[t]hese opinions I never maintained with pertinacity" (1.7). Although Browne is sure that there will be no "calling to the Barre" in heaven (1.45), he hopes that urbane manners will exempt the spiritualist from a calling to the bar in an earthly public. "[M]en of singular parts and humors have not beene free from singular opinions and conceits in all ages . . . which . . . a sober judgement may doe without offence or heresie" (1.8). The private spiritual quest must constantly deflect doctrinaire opinion without zealously pronouncing it wrong.

The reward is the free imagination of the "particular devotion" of the individual, which may wander quite far from the great wheel of the Anglican church. In the public world, Browne is nettled, cautious, hemmed in; in his own interior world, by contrast, the passions can be set free. There he enjoys the "solitary recreation" (1.9) of his interior fancies, transforming the world into [him]self and "turn[ing] it round sometime for [his] recreation" (2.11). Within this private world he can contemplate the individuality of his "particular genius" (2.9). In his dreams, Browne "can compose a whole Comedy, behold the action, apprehend the jests, and laugh my selfe awake at the conceits thereof" (2.11). "[H]appy in a dreame," he can find more than three hundred sixty degrees in his personal circle and define death according to his own "fancie" (2.11; see also 1.39). In this inner world, he can "expatiate," go outside the limits defined by publicly agreed upon doctrine (1.8). He can even interpret Scripture according to his own inclinations, dispensing with a "Judiciall proceeding" on the last day (1.45). In an old ceremonial discourse, the return home was sweet in comparison to the terror of being lost from the political body of God's nature; when seen from the right perspective, the world would fade away to harmless shadows. Here, in a ceremonial mode framed by articulateness, the return home—not to a castle or to a supernatural world but to one's own thoughts—is sweet in comparison to the elaborate self-justification before other selves in the public world. In the *Religio Medici*, spiritual serenity is always just below the surface of a civil mode's eagerness, either about manic humor figures (in the character) or about false arguments (in religious controversy). In transferring the protections of pluralism to the old corporation of ceremony, Browne frees the interior imagination.

The protections of pluralism reassure Browne's fellow spiritualists on two issues. First, Browne's epistolary prose promises that he is never going to get too serious about his religion. Second, his epistolary subtlety promises that he *has* a spiritual life without being perfervid about it. The confidence that others have a similar ceremonialized inner world unites a social body that would otherwise fracture into a myriad of private imaginations. One of the most repeated words of the *Religio* is "common." It is used in two senses. The first is the proser's disdain for what is ordinary, vulgar, popular; "This noble affection [of friendship] fals not on vulgar and common constitutions" (2.6); Browne can hold to his religion without "opposing another" with "common ardour and contention" (1.1); he is not troubled by "those common antipathies that I can discover in others" (2.1). The second is custom and universality: "[M]y common conversation I do acknowledge austere" (1.3); "there is between us one common name and appellation, one faith, and necessary body of principles common to us both" (1.3); "It is the common wonder of all men, how among so many millions of faces, there should be none alike" (2.2). The meditation's sense of the commonness of the spiritual goal returns to the social world as a silently shared bond: "At a solemne Procession I have wept abundantly, while my consorts, blinde with opposition and prejudice, have fallen into an accesse of scorne and laughter" (1.3). Browne feels more acutely than most the miseries of other people; he is easily moved by "counterfeit griefes" of stage plays (2.5). The goodwill that he extends to his friends in prayer is also extended to the faceless crowd that his Stoic rhetoric in other places condemns; even in the midst of "mirth" in a tavern, the tolling bell will elicit his prayers for the unknown dead. In church, "I cannot see one say his Prayers, but in stead of imitating him, I fall into a supplication for him, who perhaps is no more to mee than a common nature" (2.6). He cannot pass a begger without giving alms, for beneath all the "accidentall differences betweene us" there is a "common and untoucht part of us both" (2.13). The sensitivity of a ceremonial speaker in a civil world validates the social man: "It is an act within the power of charity, to translate a passion out of one breast into another, and to divide a sorrow almost out of it selfe" (2.5). Later in explaining his sociable temperament, he says, "For my conversation, it is like the Sunne's with all men, and with a friendly aspect of good and bad. . . . *Magnae virtutes nec minora vitia* is the poesie of the best natures" (2.10). Browne claims his fitness for a liberal, pluralistic society because he can tolerate doctrinal differences and hope for a common goal for all humanity. In his view, this should be the "social rhetoric" for all.

The *Religio Medici*, Generic Anomalies, and the Rhetoric of Communal Hope

One of the long-standing problems in English scholarship is accounting for the rise of the novel. Ian Watt argued that the novel met the demands of a middle class, that is, of a practical and realistic reading public. Refining this thesis, Michael McKeon has attributed the success of the novel to its mediation of a profound epistemological shift and of a redefinition of virtue from the inherited trait of family line to the acquired trait of virtue.[73] The scope of the novel's origins has been broadened by Nancy Armstrong, who focuses not on the canonical novel but on a rhetoric of middle-class domesticity and gender differentiation, a rhetoric deployed in courtesy books and then given generic shape in the novel's favorite plot of love and marriage. That the generic "novel" is a fiction of the nineteenth century is Armstrong's most powerful point. Instead of trying to locate the origins of a certain kind of narrative, she rearranges the pieces of the old puzzle—the dearth of novels in the early part of the seventeenth century—by characterizing "novelistic discourse" as a change in the processing of social information, the most important aspect of which is gender distinctions. Differences between worldly men and domestic women generate the glorification of the middle-class household, divorced from politics and economics. For Armstrong, courtesy books written for women are a crucial ingredient in the rise of the novel.

Courtesy books may perhaps be pertinent to the novel, but a "novelistic discourse" is surely one of many manifestations of prosa-icism's deployment of the opposition between experience that is

73. Ian Watt, *The Rise of the Novel* (Berkeley and Los Angeles: University of California Press, 1957).

rational, public, secular, rigorous, and masculine and experience that is emotional, private, frequently religious, flexible, and feminine. In the first half of the seventeenth century, the inflection of these two rhetorics is explored in many other genres besides the novel: the familiar epistle (a translation of Cicero's letters appeared in 1611), the Stoic resolve, the diary, the autobiography, the biography, and various anomalous genres that depend heavily on the personality of a speaking voice to hold together the bits and pieces of a fragmented tradition.[74] The creation of a "tough prose" in a context of highly charged religious controversy fosters the need for a "flexible prose." This flexible prose in turn creates a space for a rhetoric of private emotion that openly disclaims political intentions. It gives private affect a new freedom and individualizes emotion in a personal philosophy assembled from whatever philosophies are out there (for Browne, a religious and philosophical tradition). Lastly, and indeed most significant for defining the modern genre of "literary criticism," it justifies such personal philosophies as socially helpful. Although Browne's *Religio* is not the linchpin that suddenly brings this discourse into being, it is a rich representation of its compromises.

It is noteworthy that in the first part of the seventeenth century, prose writers have to fumble to describe what genres they are appealing to. Browne has an easier time declaring what the *Religio* is not than what it is. He is not writing a satire, which he associates with the "invectives of the Pulpit" (1.5), nor even an argument, for persuasion is the job of Lucifer. In the passage on the scale of creatures, Browne comes closer to placing the *Religio* generically: he declares that his opinion of the scale of creatures is "of a good and wholesome use in the course and actions of a mans life, and would serve as an *Hypothesis* to salve many doubts, whereof common Philosophy affordeth no solution" (1.33). The *Religio* as a whole is a personal "hypothesis" for the "course and actions of a mans life." It is not intended as a philosophical treatise and should not be read as a "round and uniform" (Bacon's phrase) treatise on divinity. It is a frankly amateurish, self-made belief.

In *The Anatomy of Melancholy*, Burton too mashes and molds traditional generic definitions in order to define a rhetoric of private

---

74. A prenovelistic "discourse of marriage" might be found in Fulke Greville's "Letter to an Honourable Lady," where advice on marriage mixes with Stoic obedience, or in the section on love melancholy at the end of Burton's *Anatomy*, or in Richard Brathwaite's "The Author's Opinion of Marriage: Delivered in a Satisfying Character to His Friend," in *Essaies upon the Five Senses*.

belief. He struggles to define the kind of satire he prefers and apparently the kind of "satire" he thought the *Anatomy* was:

> [*Comitas*] must not exceed, but be still accompanied with that *ablabeia* or innocency, *quae nemini nocet, omnem injuriae oblationem abhorrens,* [which] hurts no man, abhors all offer of injury. Though a man be liable to a jest or obloquy, have been overseen, or committeed a foul fact, yet it is no good manners or humanity to upbraid him, to hit him in the teeth with this offence, or to scoff at such a one. . . . [B]iting jests, *mordentes and aculeati,* they are poisoned jests, leave a sting behind them, and ought not to be used.

Significant here is a discomfort with "aculeate" satire and a wish for "good manners or humanity." Like Browne, Burton holds that the common bond of comradeship will free individuals to forge the personal philosophies that will most ease their souls. Like Browne, he rings the changes on public and private and the necessity for "charity":

> If these rules could be kept, we should have much more ease and quietness than we have, less melancholy: whereas on the contrary, we study to misuse each other, how to sting and gall, like two fighting boars, bending all our force and wit, friends, fortune to crucify one another's souls; by means of which there is little content and charity, much virulency, hatred, malice, and disquietness among us.[75]

Izaak Walton's *The Compleat Angler* is also about an interior self who processes social relations by the "rules" of good manners. The "whole discourse is, or rather was, a picture of [Walton's] own disposition,"[76] a discourse framed by the procedures of civility: Piscator says he is "not so unmannerly as to ingross all the discourse to my self" (179); Auceps says he will not "break the rules of Civility with you, by taking up more than the proportion of time allotted to me" (183).

The novel emerges from these generic experiments with a discourse that protects the right to a philosophy tailor-made to one's own personal needs and deferent to the tailor-made philosophies of

---

75. Robert Burton, *The Anatomy of Melancholy*, part I, sec 2. memb. 4, subs. 5, ed. Holbrook Jackson (1932; repr. New York: Random House, 1977), 343.

76. Izaak Walton, "To the Reader," *The Compleat Angler*, (1653–76), ed. Jonquil Bevan (Oxford: Clarendon Press, 1983), 170.

others. The coincidence of the assimilation of classical political thinking with the rise of scientific rationalism, the intensification of Puritan conscience, and the vestiges of a ceremonial mode creates a discourse that declares the superior maturity of pluralism regulated by good taste yet protects the space where a highly inflected rhetoric of emotion can thrive. Ceremony's emotional package of anxiety, entrapment, devotion, self-abasement, service, rescue, and exaltation is broken apart and reconstituted.

Browne has had the misfortune to be a virtual litmus paper for the contradictions of critical literary history as a discipline that mixes historical questions about what has been with philosophical judgments about what should be. Some of these contradictions appear in the "for better or worse" rhetoric of historical culture criticism. This rhetoric works better with some periods than with others. With the sixteenth century, for instance, it does not ring true to say, "For better or for worse, humanism introduced the discourse that demythologized the aristocracy," for no one is likely to maintain that an aristocracy should be reinstated. Nor does it ring true to say, "For better or for worse, humanism introduced the discourse that would put God into the background," for no one is likely to suggest that intellectual problems can be cleared up by bringing God to the foreground once again. In the seventeenth century, however, we see so much of ourselves that this portentous rhetoric does not sound quite so hollow. There is a point in saying, "For better or for worse, the novel domesticated desire and depoliticized the family," for whether such a development was better or worse is still a question. There is also a point in saying, "For better or for worse, modern notions of freedom were born during the period of religious controversy, with the result that public authority is a necessary but neutral apparatus for protecting freedom of belief," for whether the modern definition of freedom as "freedom from coercion" is better or worse is also still a serious question.

The better part of freedom as "freedom from coercion" is the protection both of speculative thought and of virgorous criticism of an existing regime; the worst part is the quietistic definition of citizenship and satisfaction with personal "hypotheses" as all the philosophizing a society needs, as if a society's vitality was merely the "Brownian movement" of independently self-sufficient particles. The difficulties of this liberal compromise ought to be the eye of the storm that swirls around Browne. But they are not. Instead, the issue is narrowly focused on Browne's complacency. For the majority of readers, the most famous attack on the *Religio Medici* is Stanley Fish's chapter in *Self-Consuming Artifacts*.[77] In comparison to Bacon, Herbert, Milton, and Burton, who, according to Fish, urge their readers to self-examination and further inquiry, Browne lacks moral pressure and a strenuous drive for truth.[78] There have been earlier attacks. Browne's sweetness was compared unfavorably with Donne's toughness by Gilbert Phelps in 1956.[79] James Winney found Browne's paradoxes too easily removed by a God who finds all nature beautiful.[80] And a book-length criticism of the *Religio Medici* by Dewey Ziegler appeared in 1943, with an attack on Browne far more devastating than that of Fish because it goes to the heart of literary study itself.[81]

For Ziegler, Browne is a former-day I. A. Richards. In his view, both authors separated emotional wonder from reason and justified the object of wonder on the grounds of good taste. Instead of arguing why Anglicanism is a rationally better religion, Browne treats religion as the individual's fancy, which can be despised but not prosecuted. Although Ziegler initially accuses Browne of viciously gutting religious commitments of their rational content, in the conclusion of the essay, when he lines up the Puritans against Browne and the Marxists against New Critics, his complaint seems to be that the Browne–Richards axis has viciously gutted *political* commitments of their rational content. Having made this move, it is odd that Ziegler does not offer a defense of Puritanism or of Marxism; in the omission, Puritans and Marxists are made to seem merely token true-believers. Like Fish, Ziegler wants strenuousness: it is good to have strong beliefs, whatever they are. But in this argument, "taste" has been replaced by aestheticized "commitment," which no one prosecutes either.

Browne's trouble was to make his religion not only irrational but happily irrational. The world in which public decisions are made is authoritative, social, and stern; the public man's notions are rationally distinct and clear, as Pepys sees them in William Petty. For Browne, a private, inner self is shy, idiosyncratic, unprofessional. In preserving the old ceremonial values—admiration, gentleness, generosity, patience,

77. Stanley E. Fish, *Self-Consuming Artifacts*, 353–73.

78. Ibid., 370–71.

79. Gilbert Phelps, "The Prose of Donne and Browne," in *The Pelican Guide to English Literature*, vol. 3, ed. Boris Ford (Harmondsworth, England: Penguin, 1956), 116–30.

80. *Religio Medici*, ed. James Winney (Cambridge: Cambridge University Press, 1963).

81. Dewey Kiper Ziegler, *In Divided and Distinguished Worlds: Religion and Rhetoric in the Writings of Sir Thomas Browne* (Cambridge: Harvard University Press, 1943).

submission, childishness—against the rationalistic procedures of those skilled in making distinctions, Browne conceded any claim to authority or leadership. He also conceded a claim to a religious, political, or tragic struggle. It is not religion that Fish objects to in Browne; after all, Fish grants Herbert, Milton, and Burton their belief in the final authority of God. Rather, he objects to a belief that is so embarrassingly amiable. In Fish's view (at least in *Self-Consuming Artifacts*), it is more humanly dignified to accept the strains of living in a world without clarity or to believe in a God who demands absolute loyalty. Fish grants the liberal premise that people can believe what they like, but if they are going to believe what they like, their creeds should not leave them too happy. Compensation for a loss of authority and the consequent loss of the struggle for truth lies in the imagination, in whose domain literature argues for the superiority of being troubled by life, of noble striving, and of tragic defiance. It seems that the liberal compromise that has made politics orderly and predictable has increased the demand for an uncomfortable conscience. It is not surprising therefore that Browne's happy and social religion does not stand up to comparison with Bacon's magisterial clarity, Herbert's self-abasement, Milton's strength, and Burton's restless despair.

Ziegler was right to draw a parallel between New Criticism and Browne's personal religion. For both Browne and the New Critic, rational justifications are necessary for responsible moral choice. Yet other important stories exist in an ontological realm in which human reasons are irrelevant because, as Hooker would say, that realm is "absorbed in the contemplation of [its] own laws." For Hooker, the "other realm" is the story of the Incarnation, Passion, and Crucifixion. Despite all the subtle articulateness of New Criticism, it too persuades by evocation of another order of being, gestured toward but never fully comprehended. For New Criticism as only "empty formalism," the "other order" is the self-sufficiency of beauty; for New Criticism interested in the human quest for truth (as in Fish), the "other order" is a struggle against personal despair or against the community's corruption. Because discursiveness promises that the world and despair are both fixable, or if not fixable then faceable, to plumb the darkness of the "other order"—*truly* to plumb it— demands the notes of the tragic (as in Milton) or a mournful lyricism (for those who find Milton's fervor *de trop*) or a rationalist's cool (for the really tough). Since the seventeenth century, despair has to be worked for, and the critic must carefully calibrate the amount of "inspiration" that should go with an urbanity that half disbelieves in both inspiration and despair from the first.

Browne's complacency may be annoying to heroic strugglers because in removing the gap between transcendent and discursive
language, he dispels the possibility of failure; for him, transcendence
is there to be embraced if you just turn around and look at it. Ziegler
argued that Browne "aestheticized" religion. It is more accurate to say
that he intermittently aestheticized discursiveness itself. Under the
eye of faith, the differences of the new prosaic prose become an even
richer *débat* than a ceremonial mode had known—richer and *kinder*,
because the debate is not foreclosed in a higher corporation guaranteed by the power to punish. For Ziegler as for Fish, this is all too
pleasant. Still, discursivity's reconstitution of *auctores* as "great thinkers" and its willingness to grant them some angle on the truth does
result in something like a "discursive *débat*." Browne is not a great
thinker, but his "viewing" of ideas, as if he were the organizer of a
film festival, may be necessary for the atmosphere in which great
thinkers are educated. Ideas do have to be given an audience—
treated politely, attentively, patiently—before they are dismissed, if
their implications, subtleties, blind alleys, evasions, and illuminations
are to be understood. Perhaps the political comforts of liberalism have
made desperation attractive for the intellectual hero. But there is a
place for something quieter and steadier and more filled with
gratitude, as long as large claims are not made for it and it is not used
to set off a stagy version of heroics.

There is also a place for something quieter and steadier and more
filled with fellowship. Browne wants to save the gracefulness of
ceremonial love in a demoted aristocratic "gentleness" that checks the
wit's hectic interest in disproving mere "pretty sayings" by "downright disputation." There may be times when even the clever person
may doubt that wit can cure all causes of sorrow. True, Browne
recovers the old ceremonial story of common suffering only by
conceding that it can never again be brought into the public space
with its full political implications and only by forgetting for a while a
political critique. But there is no getting around the fact that political
movements can fail (as Milton knew) and that for the survivors, it
does not hurt to have a rhetoric of communal hope to fall back on, a
rhetoric that should be preserved for the utopia which is, after all, the
goal of political struggle—Milton's "still time, when there shall be no
chiding."[82]

---

82. John Milton, "Apology for Smectymnuus," in *The Complete Prose Works of John Milton*, ed. Don M. Wolfe, 1:892.

Conclusion

The recovery of past authors for a modern audience sooner or later raises an awkward problem. These writers believed in things many modern readers regard as empty categories: God, transcendent truth, human nature. The old appearances need saving, and these authors are reclaimed for modernity in ways similar to those by which Ovid was rehabilitated for the Christian Middle Ages, by making them answer questions wholly different from the ones they had uppermost on their minds—linguistic theory in Chaucer or the Lacanian body in Spenser or dissemination in Donne or subversion in Renaissance drama. Recently, critics on a rescue mission have set themselves a very nice rhetorical task indeed: how to argue for the goal of debunked liberal humanism—freedom—without using any of the liberal shibboleths—human dignity and human responsibility.

Confronting the problem of the belief of past authors in transcendent truth might not be so much a dead end as is often assumed. It can, in fact, lead to a rich understanding of the consequences of rejecting the past. Take, for instance, the demanding morality of Boethius. For Boethius, happiness is freedom, and the way to freedom is to deny desire, especially desire for worldly status. In this position, Boethius is not so much offering a consolation of philosophy, as his title suggests, as demanding from the individual a complete moral overhaul that he alone can accomplish. Boethius nowhere reflects on the influence of institutions on human inclinations to good or evil. The sole way to freedom is through the spiritual quest. To us this position is utterly unrealistic. It is too uncompromising, too unworldly, and too . . . well, *medieval*.

When Burckhardt set up his "Renaissance" in opposition to this medieval view (a "consciousness . . . that lay dreaming or half awake beneath a common veil," a veil of "faith, illusion, and childish preposession"[1]), he could hardly fail to persuade. His warnings about Renaissance individualism were soon forgotten, and the preferred narrative became the "rightful" rebirth of human vitality in the early modern period. When the Burckhardtian picture of the Renaissance was adjusted to contractual theories of government, the package was complete: Renaissance exuberance had to be restrained only when it infringed the liberties of others. Having learned to accommodate differences, human beings could enjoy earthly life to the fullest and trust their own, various definitions of the good. Moreover, the formula justified the demise of the past. An unrealistic moral ideal was lowered to what is possible for most human beings to achieve; but then the expectations were higher for human beings in general. Although it may have looked as though the middle class chose a morality that permitted it to enjoy the materiality of life, in fact it was being hard on itself, relinquishing the childishness of faith for the greater strenuousness of autonomy and dispassionate analysis.

Now to the extent that the new political-historical criticism has made us aware that writers of the past had an argument and that that argument had a bearing on politics, it has indeed brought fresh air into the halls of critical declamation. It forces us to come to terms with the assumption of most Renaissance writers that there is a normative standard for proper human behavior. It also forces us to imagine a defense of such a standard against attackers that the Middle Ages and the Renaissance never dreamt of. Hence, to come to terms with

---

1. Jacob Burckhardt, *The Civilization of the Renaissance in Italy*, trans. S. G. C. Middlemore (1929; repr. New York: Harper Torchbooks, 1958), 1:143.

Boethius means neither turning the *Consolation* into an object of aesthetic pleasure nor into an object of derision. It means to face the heart of his argument and to define precisely wherein we disagree.

It might be good to imagine how Boethius might speak in his defense, acknowledging, of course, that he had no idea he might one day have to argue against died-in-the-wool secularists and relativists. Might he not have balked at the characterization of his moral ideal as inhuman? True, his highest moral life is difficult to achieve, and perhaps only the philosopher can fully achieve it. But Boethius is not maintaining that those who do not achieve it fully do not achieve it at all. Moreover, he might have wondered about the claim that equal material conditions will make human beings equally free. Finally, and most important, he would probably have questioned the wisdom of expecting people to come to the truth without their natural instinct to admire people they feel are superior to them. To understand the liberal democrat's freedom requires a high level of political philosophizing (liberal democracy at its best; liberal freedom can of course dispense with thought altogether). To understand Boethius's freedom requires only two things: a natural inclination to be happy in a fellowship that either is a family or functions like one and a natural inclination to love beauty. To tell human beings that the good has nothing to do with the beautiful—indeed, to make them distrust the beautiful—is more than most of them can understand.

Turning next to the modern rejection of normative standards, Boethius might say the following. First, to reject such standards is unrealistic; people do in fact hold to moral positions by which they measure other people, radical democrats as much as anybody. Second, the rejection is spirit-killing. If the right to autonomous choice means that any behavior is acceptable, what is to provide the human being with a ground for esteeming himself or others? Finally, the rejection leads to a loss of hierarchy. Choice should produce convictions, not just whims. For Boethius, conviction can come from love of a superior human being; analysis of ideas is not necessary. The liberal democrat rejects what he regards as the mindless subservience of this position and prefers a freedom won from the diligent study of the philosophies of others. But then this study will produce critical judgment and the elevation of one thinker over another. Love or thought, both lead to a hierarchy of intelligence and morality.

Perhaps as heirs of the Enlightenment but certainly as members of the post-Enlightenment we disagree profoundly with Boethius's unproblematic assumption of a moral hierarchy. We disagree with his unproblematic assumption that the human pleasure in aesthetic delight should not be distrusted but used. And we emphatically reject the condescension that flows from both positions, a condescension that only confirms the power of the priest or of the lord.

But having articulated all this, we have to face two problems prompted by the authors in this study. The first is a problem in political philosophy. How does an educated person who values prudential action and social analysis regard the people in his charge who do not have the intelligence for prudence or analysis and who hold to an ethic of simple goodwill? The second is a problem in ethics and philosophy. How does an educated person whose customary discourse is not parables and stories but reflective criticism regard a wisdom that is based almost entirely on parables and stories? Neither problem is new with the Renaissance. Both are exacerbated, however, by the rise of civil prose, which in acknowledging the influence of political institutions on human choices, not only accepts the necessity for prudence and social analysis but encourages them. And both are especially exacerbated by the modern version of civil prose, where prudential thinking turns away from action to the methodological concerns of the social sciences.

Insofar as much contemporary criticism authorizes itself on the moral argument that we in the academy need to think about those who cannot possibly understand our arguments, we might do well to sift the difficulties of this position by way of a treatise whose condescension to the uneducated would repel anyone. John Locke's *The Reasonableness of Christianity* is about as chilling a title as I can imagine, advertising as it does the power of Enlightenment reason to find a convenient place for the traditions that call into question the very ground of Enlightenment thinking.

To summarize Locke's position in this treatise is not easy, for Locke is apparently untroubled by what might seem a gross contradiction between pious belief and a utilitarian assessment of religion (the "reasonableness" of Christianity). He announces himself as a believer. He insists upon the truth of monotheism, the divinity of Christ, and the fact of the miracles. On at least one issue—the exposure of infants—Locke is confident that Christianity is superior to any ethical system the ancients had to offer.[2] But the whole thrust of the treatise is not the glory of God and the wisdom of Christ and the happiness of Christian fellowship, but rather the suitability of Christianity for teaching virtue to people who cannot reason. Aside

2. *The Reasonableness of Christianity As Delivered in the Scriptures*, ed. George W. Ewing (Chicago: Henry Regnery, n.d.), 176.

from the exposure of infants, Locke concedes that practically all the teachings of the Bible can be found in ancient doctrine.

Christianity is clearly superior to the ancients only in one respect, that it can more effectively persuade the simple. Realizing that human reason could not find truth and that all the wise men of the ancient world had not been able to lead men to virtue, God the loving Father robed truth in the authority of a savior, the evidence of the miracles, and the promise of an afterlife. These paraphernalia, which are not necessary to a reasonable man, are crucial in leading tradesmen and laborers, dairymaids and spinsters, to the restraint necessary for public order. Presumably, for Locke himself and other reasonable men like him, the wisdom of the ancients will suffice, for reasonable men are not perplexed by having to sift through the philosophers' various dicta. But the weak need the coherence and authority of revelation. "Divinity" then has a peculiar status for Locke. That Christ was divine is not an argument why Christ should be worshiped as superior to all other wise teachers but a good rhetorical strategy on God's part. Locke called his treatise *The Reasonableness of Christianity;* but he might well have called it *The Advantages of Christianity For Those Who Understand the Necessity of Public Order for Human Happiness, Which is the Pursuit of Material Comforts.* Indeed, in the latter part of the book, he switches from the "convenience" of Christianity to its "advantages." The political implications of the split between educated and uneducated, adumbrated in More and Hooker, are now clear.

Following Locke closely through this argument, one comes away baffled how he could have thought himself a believer. Here, the split between the educated and uneducated has taken a turn that sharply differentiates him from More and Hooker. The latter two would have argued that public order is necessary to lead men to worship, not to "virtue" defined as "restraint." For them worship of the truth is the way to spiritual freedom and hence happiness. In Locke, however, the rhetorical adjustment that Hooker handled so carefully between defending ritual and calling on its evocative power, is flattened to a reasonable assessment of ritual's usefulness. The old song of love has been discarded by the educated and left to the weak-minded, in whose loves the educated do not participate.

We are still afflicted by this split between a rational adjudication of the claims of an emotive text and the acknowledgment that the emotive text still moves some people. It ties contemporary critics in knots. Naive believers in religion or naive believers in the "content" of literature have vitality on their side; the theorists and critics have reason on theirs. The naive believer, so it is maintained by the

high-tech theorist, is cut off from power; the rational critic, so it is
maintained by the counterculturalist, is cut off from life. Articulate
reason is the way to freedom, and yet it is the great repressor, the
discourse of a middle class that contains life in the refinement of
civilization.[3] A commonly heard justification for studying noncanon-
ical works is the need to save the "voices" marginalized by the
dominant class. Yet the only way to redeem "voice" is by means of
highly articulate disciplines that announce from the first their skeptical distance from "voice" and its various quasi-religious assumptions: an integral self, the sanctity of the individual life, freedom of
will, and the dignity of human beings. The condescension that is so
easily spotted in aristocratic largesse is still there, but rational
principle has given it a new edge. Neutralizing the violence of a
ceremonial discourse's hate, contempt, and fear, rational principle
also neutralizes ceremony's love, which is reduced to (or, more
neutrally, "becomes") a hygienic recipe for the happy life, and, at the
level of the polity, to a managerial recipe for group harmony—the
"smoothly functioning group."

Locke's treatise thrusts forward the unpleasant question: Do aca-
demics also function like Lockean managers when they justify their
continuing to teach literary works that they themselves have demystified on the grounds that some people still need to "hear the old
stories"? If the true wisdom lies deeper than the metaphorical
paraphernalia of stories, why confuse the issue by trying to teach it
through stories in the first place? This is, to be sure, not a troublesome
question for everyone, only for those who do not find the old
melodies (the lyricism of what Lovejoy once called, in a wonderful
phrase, "metaphysical pathos"[4]) as tuneless as do the skeptics. But
even these would-be believers acknowledge the weight of the skeptical arguments. Otherwise, they would not use the *genus mixtum* of
"literary history" to do their counterskeptical ventriloquizing for
them: "I am making the (merely historical?) point that Milton thought
thus-'n-so (but as a matter of fact I think he was right)."

Actually, ventriloquizing is not a bad solution to the Enlightenment
dilemma. Milton can probably make a better case for a hierarchy of
morality and intelligence than any of us can, and with less banality,
less cowardice, fewer evasions. Still, the state of the art in literary
ventriloquizing requires subtleties undreamt of only twenty years
ago. The ventriloquist's dummy stands accused. He is not nearly so

3. Stallybrass and White, *The Politics and Poetics of Transgression*, 192.
4. Arthur O. Lovejoy, *The Great Chain of Being: A Study of the History of An Idea* (1936;
repr. New York: Harper Torchbooks, 1960), 11.

dumb as he once seemed; in fact, he is a virtuoso propagandist of Western values.[5] It seems that the generic differentiations of the Enlightenment had their dangers as well as their strengths. On the positive side, the severance of art from politics enabled the analysis of political institutions with a language of determinate meaning. On the negative side, however, the generic protection of "the aesthetic" from both logic and politics resulted in a sentimentalization of irrational vision. The ground was all too well prepared for the pooh-poohers, who now regard art as merely a secularist's vestigial paradise—Yeatsian "Gardens where a [prosaic] soul's at ease"—and who announce that we have a *duty* to regard it skeptically.

In the introduction to this book, I wondered if the only resolution to the Enlightenment dilemma is what Auden offers in "In Praise of Limestone," to throw in one's hand with modern skepticism and then admit, with no attempt at logical coherence, that the old loves are still there: the prosaic commitment and the shrug. In this poem, the "limestone landscape" is a metaphor for life untrammeled by modern defensiveness, restlessness, and purposefulness. It is not busy, not organized, not programmatically skeptical. It is affectionate (the poem is addressed to a "dear") and happy. At the beginning, the landscape is virtually a Garden of Adonis ("rounded slopes / With their surface fragrance of thyme"[6]), where the human male languishes under the eye of a Mother-Venus-Nature, confident of his power to charm. At the end, this landscape has become a wish, for the innocence of art (blessed statues that do not mind what angle they are regarded from) and for the furniture of the Christian promise (sins being forgiven, bodies rising from the dead).

The strength of the poem is Auden's self-conscious admission of the weaknesses of his position. He acknowledges the danger of sentimentalizing the pastoral ease of art and Christianity. He admits that in the limestone landscape, tenors go in for stagy effects, street-urchins hawk crummy souvenirs, and the religious are content with a god who is satisfied with "a clever line / Or a good lay." The charmed life, which is at the end associated with "the blessed" and "the life to come," can look like the life of an amoral child, which the

---

5. For a full-scale radical assault on western humanism as the deployment of repressive reason, see Paul A. Bové *Intellectuals in Power: A Geneology of Critical Humanism* (New York: Columbia University Press, 1986).

6. W. H. Auden, "In Praise of Limestone," in *W. H. Auden: Collected Poems*, ed. Edward Mendelson (New York: Random House, 1976), 414–15.

adult recaptures during vacations on an island off the coast of Italy. The weak stresses at the ends of the free verse lines and at caesuras loosen the lyricism with a prosaic distance that constantly defers to the charge that the limestone landscape is a childish fantasy. When Auden says his strongest allegiances lie with the world-improvers and the nihilists ("They were right, my dear, all of these voices were right / And still are"), his attraction to the limestone landscape is a puzzling recidivism.

Auden declines to justify his longings. He says that the limestone landscape "calls into question / All the Great Powers assume" and "disturbs our rights." But how it calls these powers into question and how it disturbs our rights are left unstated. In this evasion the poem is liable to the charge of wistfulness, the "homesickness" that the first line confesses. Auden tries to mute the leap to faith at the end by a secular argument: there is, even for the nonbelieving modern prosaicist, something deeply compelling in loving creation as it was given and in a happiness that does not feel the need to justify itself.

The particular inflection of Auden's solution can be measured by comparing it with Philip Larkin's "Church Going." Larkin too takes up the problem of religion, not ambiguously, as a longing for pastoralism, but explicitly, as the fate of churches in a nation of secularists: "I wonder who / Will be the last, the very last, to seek / This place for what it was."[7] Unlike Auden, Larkin pushes beyond competing claims of tradition and skepticism to a conclusion. The different plotline helps. While Auden moves from secular to specifically Christian freight, Larkin moves from specifically Christian freight (the accoutrements of churches) to a secular rephrasing of the problem. At the beginning of the poem, religion becomes an issue only because a church happens to be a stop on a weekend bicycle tour. Even then, it is just "Another church" with "some brass and stuff / Up at the holy end." The silence that in one breath is "unignorable" is in the next "Brewed God knows how long." The verses of the New Testament "snigger" in the echo. And at the end the aura of Christianity is dispelled by categorizing the church as a secular architectural genre: "A serious house on serious earth," a place where Larkin's double will have heard it was "proper to grow wise in." The parodic jauntiness of the beginning of the poem ("Ruin bibbers, randy for antique") is a useful rhetorical register; merely in

7. "Church Going," in *Philip Larkin: Collected Poems*, ed. Anthony Thwaite (London: Marvell Press and Faber and Faber, 1988), 97–98.

dropping it, Larkin can seem to renounce the characteristically modern inclination to protect oneself with reductiveness.

Larkin may challenge the self-protections of wit, but he can hardly be accused of making any grand gestures himself. The last line is a bit of a throwaway: the proximity of graveyards to churches is a lame reason for "gravitating" toward serious ground. And the other proffered justification for standing in a church's silence—the "hunger to be more serious"—is cautious, its longing felt only in comparison to the ostentatious breeziness of the earlier parts of the poem. Then too, Larkin skirts a considerable amount of trouble by failing to acknowledge the argument that the future age will be better precisely *because* it has discarded religion and its potential fanaticism. Instead, Larkin tries to get away with the truth of a descriptive "is": enlightened moderns do in fact have a hunger for seriousness in them, which they will always be driven to satisfy ("And that much never can be obsolete"). Faithful to the parody's promise not to do any grandstanding, Larkin avoids an outright sermon; but there is still at the end of this poem a large statement about what human nature really is.

To demand a sifting of this problem is to ask the poem to do too much. But it is finally the chief difficulty in "saving" a ceremonial discourse for a prosaic age. In the name of true human nature, the Enlightenment sought to take the aura from tradition; but in the name of true human nature Larkin wonders if tradition can be lightly cast aside. The "wondering" is historically telling, for certainly Renaissance writers—the Hooker of the *Laws*, the Shakespeare of *King Lear*—do not do anything so mild as to "wonder" about this question. Insofar as we hold that wondering about it, speculating about it, is better than fury, desperation, and tyranny, we risk the quiet invulnerability of Locke's reason, enough to drive one mad, as Shakespeare argued about Goneril's and Regan's rationality in *King Lear*. Indeed, we cut ourselves off from the "murmur of literature," as Foucault liked to call it and in which he prophesied (and hoped?) we would immerse ourselves again (although he too was caught in the Enlightenment dilemma, constituting his murmuring literature by means of a highly abstract argument). If one is not happy with the pronouncement that human nature will always have a hunger to grow wise (either too much sentiment in the claim or too much evidence against it), Auden's hesitations in "In Praise of Limestone" are probably more attractive. As moderns, we choose Enlightenment reflection, but in this choice, we hold at arm's length the comic plenitude of Spenser's Garden of Adonis and the bodily fury of Lear on the heath—and perhaps beauty itself.

Such a statement can easily slide into a lament for lost meaning-fulness or an indictment of reason or a call for tougher reason, all three accompanied by flamboyant rhetorical gestures. The choice for democratic pluralism necessarily alters a truth that once could be taught without worrying at what age children should hear the rejected alternatives. Browne chose a ceremony by which he could enthusiastically "recreate" himself in a private dream. It might be better, as Auden and Larkin do, to declare one's strongest allegiance to the disengagement of public discussion and to scale down accordingly the passion of one's loyalties and detestations.

Depending on the perspective, the compromises of this "scaling down" are either growing up or growing old. To the romantic, who wants vitality and freedom, it is growing old, the submission to a disciplinary society. To the political critic who *wants* discipline because it will destroy the last vestiges of old-world hierarchy, it is also growing old, a tired renunciation of struggle. On either side— iconoclastic vitality or iconoclastic toughness—the exaggeration comes easily. The need for a compromise between them is a consequence of democracy, and, as Auden's and Larkin's poems demonstrate, how to inflect this compromise is an extremely difficult question. Conscientious avoiders of the grand moral statements of Hooker's sort, Auden and Larkin can be accused of restricting conviction to what propriety will tolerate. On the other hand, if conviction is not restricted in some ways, if it is allowed the claim that private belief *is* political and that there is a right kind of belief, then Hooker has been revived.

The difficulty is to acknowledge that if human dignity and human responsibility are still the truths they were for a ceremonial discourse, they cannot so readily be endowed with beauty as they once were. But to say that beauty and truth are now not easily allied is not the same thing as saying the alliance must be abandoned altogether. Auden and Larkin think about the difficulty poetically, as a dilemma for modern human beings. At the end of Erich Auerbach's *Mimesis* the dilemma is recast as a rhetorical matter: what a Jewish author who has been forced to flee from Germany to Istanbul during World War II should say at a particular moment in history about a book whose argument is that careful discrimination among texts will enable a more accurate account of their moral arguments. The final few sentences of Auerbach's epilogue are virtually a ceremonial prayer. Auerbach hopes that his book will reach former friends and other readers, "[a]nd may it contribute to bringing together again those whose love for our western history has serenely persevered."[8] The restraint speaks more resonantly than in Auden and Larkin, "serenity" reverberating quietly against the pressure of the historical facts of the war. It hardly needs pointing out that the celebratory motive expressed here generates much of *Mimesis*. This muted prayer is its justification. While Auden restricts ceremony to an apologetic wish and Larkin restricts it to an apologetic wonder, Auerbach frankly admits the old motive of love and hope. Perhaps his historical circumstances served him well in one regard at least; few people are likely to accuse his conclusion of nostalgia, an accusation leveled rather freely elsewhere. Auerbach's rhetorical decorum teaches what Auden's and Larkin's poems cannot. Committed to prosaicism, we nevertheless have the task of carefully reinflecting the old ceremonial devotions and lamentations for times when they will be needed, for confronting the truth, embracing it, or enduring it.

8. Erich Auerbach, *Mimesis*, 557.

Index

Tacitus, 25, 62
Taylor, Jeremy, 180
Thucydides, 24, 56
Trimpi, Wesley, 23 n. 3, 30 n. 15, 35 n. 28
Tunstall, Cuthbert, 78, 80, 103
Tyndale, William, 7

Valla, Lorenzo, 60–61
Vergil, 31–32
Vergil, Polydore, 69, 70 n. 42, 71, 71 n. 46, 85

Voltaire, 54 n. 2

Wallis, John, 157
Walton, Izaak, 186
Watt, Ian, 184
Whitgift, John, 122, 122 n. 26
Wilson, Thomas, 107
Winney, James, 188

Ziegler, Dewey, 188–90